AA FORWOOD

E ...amovitch

Author
Eric Hamovitch
Contributor
Alexis Mantha

Publisher
Pascale Couture

Editor
Jacqueline Grekin

Copy Editing
Jacqueline Grekin
Cindy Garayt

Computer Graphics
Stéphanie Routhier

Page Layout
Typesetting
Jenny Jasper
Cindy Garayt
Anne Joyce

Final Layout
Jenny Jasper

Cartographers
André Duchesne
Patrick Thivierge
Yanik Landreville
Brad Fenton

Artistic Director
Patrick Farei (Atoll)

Illustrations
Sophie Czaplejewicz
Marie-Annick Viatour
Lorette Pierson
Jenny Jasper

Photography
Cover Page
T. Chinami/
The Image Bank

Inside Pages
Claude Hervé-Bazin
Vicente Murphy
John Haught

OFFICES
CANADA: Ulysses Travel Guides, 4176 Rue St-Denis, Montréal, Québec, H2W 2M5,
☎ (514) 843-9447 or 1-877-542-7247, ≠(514) 843-9448, info@ulysses.ca, www.ulyssesguides.com

EUROPE: Les Guides de Voyage Ulysse SARL, BP 159, 75523 Paris Cedex 11, France,
☎ 01 43 38 89 50, ≠01 43 38 89 52, voyage@ulysse.ca, www.ulyssesguides.com

U.S.A.: Ulysses Travel Guides, 305 Madison Avenue, Suite 1166, New York, NY 10165,
☎ 1-877-542-7247, info@ulysses.ca, www.ulyssesguides.com

DISTRIBUTORS
CANADA: Ulysses Books & Maps, 4176 Saint-Denis, Montréal, Québec, H2W 2M5,
☎ (514) 843-9882, ext.2232, 800-748-9171, Fax: 514-843-9448, info@ulysses.ca,
www.ulyssesguides.com

GREAT BRITAIN AND IRELAND: World Leisure Marketing, Unit 11, Newmarket Court, Newmarket
Drive, Derby DE24 8NW, ☎ 1 332 57 37 37, Fax: 1 332 57 33 99
office@wlmsales.co.uk

SCANDINAVIA: Scanvik, Esplanaden 8B, 1263 Copenhagen K, DK, ☎ (45) 33.12.77.66,
Fax: (45) 33.91.28.82

SPAIN: Altaïr, Balmes 69, E-08007 Barcelona, ☎ 454 29 66, Fax: 451 25 59,
altair@globalcom.es

SWITZERLAND: OLF, P.O. Box 1061, CH-1701 Fribourg, ☎ (026) 467.51.11,
Fax: (026) 467.54.66

U.S.A.: The Globe Pequot Press, 246 Goose Lane, Guilford, CT 06437 - 0480,
☎1-800-243-0495, Fax: 800-820-2329, sales@globe-pequot.com

Other countries, contact Ulysses Books & Maps, 4176 Rue Saint-Denis, Montréal, Québec, H2W
2M5, ☎ (514) 843-9882, ext.2232, 800-748-9171, Fax: 514-843-9448, info@ulysses.ca,
www.ulyssesguides.com

Canadian Cataloguing in Publication Data (see page 6)
© June 2000, Ulysses Travel Guides.
All rights reserved
Printed in Canada
ISBN 2-89464-132X

"Este país, que por su clima, su origen, su cielo y sus montañas está hablando constantemente a la fantasía et lenguage de la poesía y el arte, refleja sus influencias en las ardientes imaginaciones de sus hijos, que son poetas por sentimiento y artistas por naturaleza."

Tomás Mur
Founder in 1890 of the Academia
de Bellas Artes in Tegucigalpa

This country, whose climate, origins, skies and mountains speak constantly of fantasy in the language of poetry and art, reflects its influences in the spiritual imaginations of its progeny, who are poets by sentiment and artists by nature.

Table of Contents

Symbols

🚢	Ulysses's Favourite
☎	Telephone Number
⇄	Fax Number
≡	Air Conditioning
⊗	Fan
≈	Pool
ℜ	Restaurant
⊛	Whirlpool
ℝ	Refrigerator
K	Kitchenette
⌂	Sauna
⊝	Exercise Room
tv	Colour Television
pb	Private Bathroom
sb	Shared Bathroom
½ b	Half Board (Lodging + 2 Meals)
bkfst incl.	Breakfast Included
♯	Screen
ps	Private Shower
hw	Hot Water

ATTRACTION CLASSIFICATION

★	Interesting
★★	Worth a visit
★★★	Not to be missed

The prices listed in this guide are for the admission of one adult.

HOTEL CLASSIFICATION

The prices in this guide are for one room, double occupancy
in high season.

RESTAURANT CLASSIFICATION

$	$5 or less
$$	$5 to $10
$$$	$10 to $15
$$$$	$15 and more

The prices in the guide are for a meal for one
person, not including drinks or tip.

All prices in this guide are in U.S. dollars.

Write to Us

The information contained in this guide was correct at press time. However, mistakes can slip in, omissions are always possible, places can disappear, etc. The authors and publisher hereby disclaim any liability for loss or damage resulting from omissions or errors.

We value your comments, corrections and suggestions, as they allow us to keep each guide up to date. The best contributions will be rewarded with a free book from Ulysses Travel Guides. All you have to do is write us at the following address and indicate which title you would be interested in receiving (see the list at the end of guide).

Ulysses Travel Guides
4176 Rue Saint-Denis
Montréal, Québec
Canada H2W 2M5
www.ulyssesguides.com
E-mail: text@ulysses.ca

Many thanks to the staff of the Instituto Hondureño de Turismo for their help with information and photos. Thanks also to the many people, Hondurans and resident foreigners alike, who offered valuable suggestions. Last but not least, a word of thanks to the numerous hotel clerks, taxi drivers, restaurant staff and others whose constant cheerfulness helped make this worthwhile.

We acknowledge the financial support of the Government of Canada through the Book Publishing Industry Development Program (BPIDP) for our publishing activities.

We would also like to thank SODEC (Québec) for its financial support.

Cataloguing

Canadian Cataloguing in Publication Data

Hamovich, Eric

    Honduras

    2nd ed.
    (Ulysses travel guide)
    Includes index.

    ISBN 2-89464-132-X

    1. Honduras - Guidebooks. I. Title. II. Series

F1503.5.H35 1999   917.28304'53   C99-940869-0

List of Maps

Map Symbols

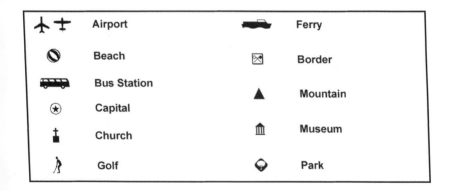

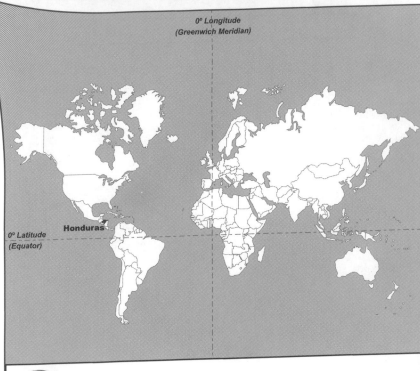

0° Longitude
(Greenwich Meridian)

Honduras

0° Latitude
(Equator)

Where is Honduras?

Honduras	
Capital:	Tegucigalpa
Language:	Spanish
Population:	6,147,000 inhab.
Currency:	Lempira
Area:	112,088 km²

Tegucigalpa
14 N 86 W

Caribbean
Sea

Pacific
Ocean

©ULYSSES

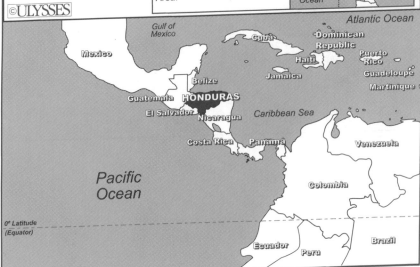

Atlantic Ocean

Gulf of
Mexico

Cuba

Dominican
Republic

Mexico

Haiti

Puerto
Rico

Guadeloupe

Belize

Jamaica

Martinique

Guatemala   HONDURAS

El Salvador   Nicaragua

Caribbean Sea

Costa Rica   Panama

Venezuela

Pacific
Ocean

Colombia

0° Latitude
(Equator)

Ecuador   Peru

Brazil

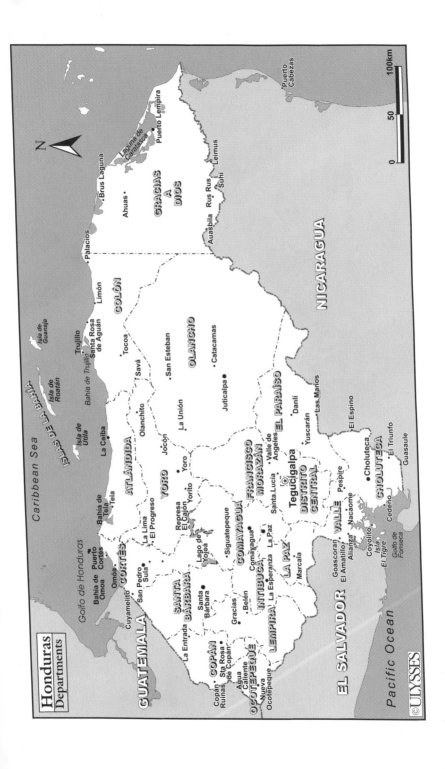

Honduras
Departments

When thoughts turn to the Caribbean, Honduras is not a place that comes readily to mind.

Here is a country with a sizeable land mass anchored firmly in the Central American isthmus, with cultures and traditions dominated by its Amerindian and Spanish past, and with problems and pleasures that bear much in common with those of its sometimes troubled Central American neighbours.

As a glance at any atlas will show, however, Honduras also has a long Caribbean coastline. Unlike its immediate neighbours, where the great majority of the population lives on the Pacific side of the continental divide, Honduras has millions of people living and working in places near the Caribbean shore. This, of course, adds a whole other cultural dimension. Most Hondurans do tend to see their country as a fundamentally Central American land that just happens to have some Caribbean geography, but for many visitors and residents alike, Honduras is a Caribbean country with an added Central American flavour. It is largely a matter of perception.

Honduras never burst into world consciousness the way each of its three neighbours did when they were engulfed by civil wars in the late 1970s and throughout the 1980s. As El Salvador, Guatemala and Nicaragua descended into chaos and bloodshed, Honduras stood largely aloof. Although Nicaraguan Contras opposed to Sandinista rule established base camps inside Honduras, and although the United States used Honduran territory for military exercises and for some limited training of Salvadoran troops, political life in Honduras remained mostly nonviolent throughout that tumultuous period.

The country's cultural roots extend far into the past, as the magnificent Mayan ruins of Copán can testify. Three centuries of Spanish domination have bestowed picturesque hillside villages and many fine examples of colonial architecture. But most of all, Honduras is a land of abundant nature, with majestic mountains, varied tropical forests, wild rivers and wild animals. It has sparkling, uncrowded beaches and enchanting islands lying next to coral reefs that will delight the most seasoned divers and snorkellers, and beginners too. Adding to the pleasures of a visit are the Honduran people, among the world's friendliest and most easy-going.

Honduras is a sleeping giant in the world of tourism. The key question is not whether it is worth visiting but why it has taken so long to be discovered. Until relatively recently, tourism development was concentrated on the island of Roatán, the biggest of the Islas de la Bahía and a favourite of di-

vers. But the giant has begun to awaken, and plans are hatching for development in several parts of the country. Transformations will occur, but not suddenly, for Honduras is a place where things move at a slower rhythm than people from more northerly climes may be accustomed to. This does have its advantages. In terms of tourism development, Honduras can draw upon unhappy lessons and will have the chance to avoid some of the errors that a gung-ho attitude has wreaked in other places.

Something that did bring Honduras briefly to the attention of the world's headline writers was Mitch, a hurricane of unusual ferocity and duration that struck in the final days of October 1998, inflicting huge damage and leaving parts of the country crippled for months afterwards. (Please see inset p 69) What was worse than Mitch, in the eyes of many hotel-keepers and other tourism operators in Honduras the period that followed the fury of the storm.

Visitors, frightened by accounts of the devastation, stayed away in droves. Some businesses that relied heavily on the tourist trade simply closed shop, others struggled to scrape by, and the development of the tourism industry as a whole was set back probably by years.

As the post-Mitch recovery proceeded (and it has been remarkably rapid by local standards), reasons for not visiting Honduras faded into the background. So much for the negatives. What, then, are some positive reasons for coming? Many places are better known, better travelled, better served by international airlines and hotel chains. The answer, simply put, is that Honduras has a little something for nearly everyone. It satisfies a wide variety of tastes.

What should a visitor look for? How much can be squeezed into a visit of, say, two weeks? It is hardly an accident that Roatán and the neighbouring islands of Utila and Guanaja have been among the most popular of destinations, for they are ideal spots for swimming, diving or simple relaxation in idyllic tropical surroundings. Guanaja is known for its simple luxury resorts, while Utila appeals more to budget travellers and Roatán has something for everyone. Prices on all three islands are higher than on the mainland but still modest by the standards of most Caribbean countries.

A long the Caribbean coast itself, Tela and Trujillo, set in tranquil bays, are both worthy of mention for the quality of their palm-shaded beaches, their Antillean charm and the nearby nature reserves. The Punta Sal reserve near Tela is quite special, with its abundant and varied vegetation and its fine beaches; the Lancetilla botanical gardens also merit a visit. Trujillo boasts historical attractions, including the remains of an old Spanish fort. La Ceiba, the country's third largest city, offers little of particular interest, but its outdoor restaurants are enjoyable for languorous evenings, and it is

a jumping-off point for nearby nature reserves and beaches as well as for the Islas de la Bahía. Puerto Cortés is a nondescript port city with good beaches nearby and an ancient fort at Omoa a short distance west.

C ertainly not to be missed are the splendid Mayan ruins of Copán in the west of Honduras. With their spectacularly carved stelae and majestic stairways, they evoke Central America's mysterious past in stunning fashion. The adjacent town of Copán Ruinas offers a special Central American flavour with its hilly, cobbled streets and tile-roofed buildings. This is the other side of Honduras, where the Caribbean seems quite far away. Tegucigalpa, the country's largest city and centre of government, has plenty of colonial and contemporary charms. Although it will never rank among the world's great capitals, Tegucigalpa, along with some of the nearby colonial towns, is well worth a couple of days.

O nce again, Honduras holds only a

small place in the international tourism industry, but this is bound to change as more people discover its pleasures and treasures. For now, and for several years to come, it is still possible to get in ahead of the crowds. Why resist the opportunity?

Geography

Honduras lies smack in the middle of the Central American isthmus, bordered to the west by Guatemala, to the southwest by El Salvador and to the southeast by Nicaragua. The northern limit of Honduras is formed by its 644km coastline along the Caribbean, and the country also reaches south to the Pacific Ocean with 124km of coast along the Gulf of Fonseca, a shallow bay shared with El Salvador and Nicaragua.

Unlike the three neighbouring countries, with their populations and economic activity heavily slanted toward the Pacific side of the isthmus, Honduras has seen considerable development along a large part of its Caribbean side as well. Although it has no land boundary with Belize, a country formerly known as British Honduras, the two lie a short distance apart by sea or by air. A small island group called the

Islas de la Bahía (*Islas de la Bahía* in Spanish) is popular with tourists and is situated just off the Caribbean coast. Roatán is the biggest of these islands.

With a surface area of 122,088km², Honduras is about half the size of Britain and just slightly smaller than Pennsylvania. Among the Central American countries, only Nicaragua is bigger. In 1999, the population of Honduras was estimated at 6.3 million, about equal to that of its much more densely populated neighbour, El Salvador. Slightly less than half the population lives in cities.

The most populous areas lie in the valleys in the southern part of the country as well as along the coastal plain in the northwest. Northeastern Honduras, a vast jungle area called Mosquitia which extends into Nicaragua, is very sparsely populated. About 63% of Honduran territory is mountainous, with an average altitude of about 1,000m. Only about one sixth of the land is arable, and slightly more than one quarter is forested.

A large area of highlands rises abruptly from the Salvadoran border, reaching elevations of more than 2,750m. A deep structural valley forms a 280km long trough from the basin of the

Río Ulúa in the north to the Gulf of Fonseca in the south, with a top elevation of 940m. This valley is separated from Guatemala's eastern lowlands by the Sierra de Merendón mountain range. The Río Aguán lies at the centre of another big valley in eastern Honduras.

The mountains in the south of Honduras form part of the great Central American volcanic chain, although there are no active volcanoes in Honduras. Volcanic detritus covers much of the southern highlands, but this covering does not extend very far north or east. The Caribbean coastal plain, which is quite narrow in certain places, is flanked by mountain chains with steep slopes and pointy peaks.

Honduras's Mountainous topography, coupled with a paucity of roads in large areas of the country, has contributed through the centuries to a sense of isolation in certain regions. Even today, this continues to hold back economic and social development.

Honduras has a tropical climate, with warm temperatures throughout the year, marked by dry and rainy seasons in the centre and south, and by heavier rainfall along the Caribbean coast and in the Mosquitia jungle. For more information on climate, please see page 38.

Flora and Fauna

In areas with heavy rainfall and high temperatures, particularly in the eastern part of the country, large areas are covered with a heavy growth of tropical evergreen rain forest. In the cooler highland areas, there are forests of oak and pine, but these have been partly destroyed by human depradations. In the drier parts of Honduras, including the area around Tegucigalpa and the lands to the southeast, savannah grasses and low forest have replaced much of the higher forest that existed previously. There were abundant forests of fine hardwoods, especially in the Mosquitia region, but these were razed extensively by the British during the 18th and 19th centuries. On some high mountain ridges lying in moister areas, there remain areas of cloud forest includ-

Black Bear

ing fantastic varieties of epiphytes.

Wildlife remains abundant in Honduras, protected largely by the sparsity of human population and difficult access in many areas. The long list of animals includes black bears, silver-tipped bears, several varieties of deer, many types of monkeys, wild boars and peccaries, tapirs, badgers, coyotes, wolves and foxes. Among feline creatures are jaguars, pumas, lynx, ocelots, black panthers and many smaller varieties. Reptiles include alligators, crocodiles, iguanas and snakes, including poisonous varieties such as the fer-de-lance and barba amarilla. The forests also harbour anteaters, coatis, sloths, armadillos and kinkajous. Birds include wild turkeys, pheasants, parrots, macaws, herons and toucans.

Spider Monkey

try lies near the southeastern edge of Mesoamerica, the zone that begins in central Mexico and includes the territories taken over by the ancient Mayans and Aztecs. It also lies near the northwestern edge of the lands occupied by peoples whose origins can be traced to the forests of northeastern South America. This placed Honduras at the crossroads between two very different groups of cultures.

Those of Mesoamerican descent, living in what are today western and central parts of Honduras, had developed more elaborate social structures and farming practices than their eastern neighbours. People recognizable as Mayans had settled in Honduras by about 1000 BC They left a lasting legacy that includes the ancient city of Copán as well as bold advances in astronomy and mathematics, such as a sophisticated system of numer

als and the development of the concept of zero centuries before it was understood in Europe or the Arab world. For reasons that are still not fully understood, the branch of Mayan civilization that included Honduras went into decline in the ninth century AD, and Copán lay mostly abandoned by the 13th century.

Christopher Columbus sailed past the Honduran coast in 1502 and landed on the island of Guanaja. A series of Spanish military expeditions followed in the 1520s, accompanied by much factional fighting and the depradations of disease. The Spanish made fresh thrusts in the following decade and managed to take control of large parts of Honduran territory, but their progress was halted in the western highlands by resistance forces led by the Lenca Indian chief Lempira (after whom the national currency is named). Lempira and his armies held the Spanish at bay for two years before going down to defeat. Feigning interest in a truce, Spanish officers entered Lempira's fortress and murdered him there. The resistance collapsed in the following months.

History

Indigenous Peoples and Spanish

Various forms of evidence indicate that Honduras has been inhabited by human beings for at least 10,000 years. The coun

Wild Turkey

The Spanish invaders wasted no time in obliterating the existing social order. Indigenous peoples were pushed off the more desirable lands, while disease, enslavement and indiscriminate massacres led to a calamitous drop in population, which some estimates put at 450,000 before the invasion. Many of the survivors interbred with Spaniards, creating the *mestizos* which today form the great majority of the Honduran population. Some remote communities were left largely undisturbed, however, and descendants of various indigenous groups scattered across the country manage even today to retain certain traditions. A presentation of contemporary indigenous groups may be found starting on page 19.

Colonialism and Independence

The Spanish in Honduras devoted themselves largely to extracting gold and silver from mines scattered around the country and to establishing the authority of the Catholic church. Only a relatively small number of settlers arrived from the mother country, and Honduras remained an economic backwater throughout the colonial period, a characteristic which never totally vanished. Administrative arrangements shifted frequently, but during much of the period prior to independence Honduras was part of the captaincy-general of Guatemala, with some chores handled at Comayagua, the Honduran capital from 1537 to 1880. Prior to 1537, Trujillo was briefly the Honduran capital.

Banana Tree

Through much of the 17th and 18th centuries, settlements on the Caribbean coast fell victim to frequent attacks by British and Dutch pirates, including the notorious Henry Morgan who established a base on the island of Roatán. Spain was never able to exert control over the Islas de la Bahía or the Mosquitia region. The British, who had established a protectorate over what was then British Honduras (now Belize), also controlled over much of coastal Honduras until after an 1859 treaty.

The Central American countries declared independence from the crumbling Spanish empire on September 15, 1821, and for a brief period fell under Mexican control. When they reasserted independence in 1823, it was in the form of a loose federation called the United Provinces of Central America. The following years were marked by political and military struggles between conservatives, who wished to retain the Spanish-bequeathed feudal privileges enjoyed by powerful landowners and by portions of the clergy, and liberals, who sought to revoke these privileges. General Francisco Morazán, the Honduran president of the beleaguered federation, fought a constant series of battles against conservative forces which sought to split the federation into its component states. Morazán was eventually defeated, and the federation was formally dissolved in 1838.

Honduras was nominally independent but suffered from a pattern of weak central governments that were undermined by powerful vested interests, by intrigues from neighbouring countries, and by a continuous series of *coups d'état* and military revolts. By one count there were some 85 government chiefs between 1821 and 1876. Starting in the 1890s, banana barons from the United States established vast plantations in northern coastal regions and turned Honduras, for a time, into the world's leading exporter of bananas. The United Fruit Company and the rival Standard Fruit Company ruled parts of Honduras as virtual fiefdoms and also exerted substantial economic and political control over the country as a whole, giving rise to the banana republic tag from which Honduras has managed only recently to emerge.

Modern Honduras

Through most of the 20th century, Honduras has alternated between military and civilian rule. Depression-induced economic calamity caused civil unrest in 1932, leading to disputed elections and the 17-year dictatorship of Tiburcio Carías Andino, followed by fresh coups in the succeeding decades. Meanwhile, however, substantial reforms to the labour code and a gradual process of land reform that began in the 1950s

provided an escape valve. This reduced social tensions and may have played a fundamental part in saving Honduras from the severe convulsions that rocked each of its three neighbours, most intensively from the late 1970s to the middle 1980s.

There have been blemishes, though, on Honduras's record of peace. During the 1950s and 1960s large numbers of Salvadorans, perhaps up to 300,000, entered Honduras to escape overcrowding at home, and many of them took up farming. Like hardworking immigrants anywhere, they created resentment, and in 1969 several hundred were deported to El Salvador, followed, first, by a wave of thousands more who left on their own, alleging mistreatment in Honduras, and then by further involuntary expulsions. Honduran fans at a soccer stadium in San Salvador were attacked during a World Cup qualifying match, and this was the spark that set off what some journalists called the "Football War." Fighting lasted only a little over four days before a truce between the two countries came into effect, but the resulting ill will took many years to subside, and relations are still uneasy. Some Hondurans say the expulsions of 1969 caused a sharp decline in the production of basic grains and

dealt the economy a blow from which it has never recovered.

Honduran politics in the contemporary era have been remarkably peaceable by Central American standards. While El Salvador and Nicaragua were engulfed in insurrection and civil war in the late 1970s and much of the 1980s, and Guatemala for much longer than that, Honduras has known an almost Costa Rican level of tranquility.

We say almost, because there has been some inevitable spillover, starting in 1954 when a U.S.-directed force of right-wing Guatemalan military officers used Honduran territory for an assault that ended Guatemala's brief nine-year period of democratic government. In the early 1980s, U.S.-backed Contra insurgents opposed to Nicaragua's left-wing Sandinista government established base camps inside Honduran territory, displacing several thousand Honduran peasants in the process. For several years, much of the border area was a virtual no-go zone for ordinary civilians. At the same time, the United States beefed up its own military presence in Honduras, mainly at the large air force base at Palmerola in the centre of the country. The United States also established training bases in Honduras for Salvadoran troops fighting a left-wing insurgency.

All of this leads to the inevitable conclusion that, although Honduras has been spared direct political violence, it has been dragged by the United States into playing peripheral roles in conflicts involving each of its neighbours. The anti-Communist doctrine that justified these activities found ready adherents among right-wing politicians and more particularly among Honduran military officers, who saw it as a useful way of getting hefty increases in U.S. government assistance to meet their own spending desires.

For Central America, the 1990s were very different from the 1980s. Rebel groups in El Salvador and Guatemala signed peace agreements that led to a vast reduction in military activity. In Nicaragua, anti-Sandinista contras gradually faded away following the 1990 defeat of the Sandanistas and the election of a more conservative government. For Latin America as a whole, this was a time to start rebuilding economies shattered by recurring debt crises and the slow but necessary adjustments to greater freedom in the international flow of goods. Business people began to take over from military men as the powers behind the

throne in many countries throughout the continent, and the civilian rule was never really threatened very seriously in Honduras or in any of its neighbours. In brief, this was a period of political and economic stability. The birth of the new decade and the new century will bring new developments that, in true Latin American fashion, are bound to take some interesting twists and turns.

Politics

Honduran has two main political parties, the right-wing National Party, which at many times has had close links with the armed forces, and the centre-right Liberal Party. These two parties have alternated in power over most of this century, sometimes sharing it with military overlords, sometimes being excluded altogether. A number of smaller parties have come and gone.

The contemporary era in Honduran politics really began in 1981, when the military dictatorship led by General Policarpo Paz García acceded to pressures from the outgoing U.S. administration of Jimmy Carter and set the stage for elections that were to bring a return to civilian rule. Roberto Suazo Córdova, candidate of the Liberal Party, won the 1981

election, but soon found himself having to contend with the ambitions of General Gustavo Álvarez Martínez. This corrupt and overbearing military commander's staunch anti-Communism and unwavering support for the Nicaraguan Contras brought him the active backing of the U.S. administration of Ronald Reagan. Although General Álvarez never attempted a putsch, he did seize control of virtually all elements of policy related to security. During this period, there were at least 120 documented cases of left-wing activists being disappeared ("disappear" was widely used as a transitive verb in Central America in the 1980s). General Álvarez died a few years later from an assassin's bullet.

Suazo was succeeded as president in 1985 by José Azcona Hoyo, also of the Liberal Party, and in 1989 by Rafael Leonardo Callejas of the National Party. In the 1993 election, Carlos Roberto Reina, who had once headed a left-leaning ginger group within the Liberal Party, was chosen president. Although he continued the orthodox economic policies inspired by the International Monetary Fund-inspired and initiated by his predecessor, Reina took initiatives in other areas, prosecuting military offices responsible for the disappearances of the previous decade, separating the national police from military command, and putting an end to military conscription.

The 1997 election was won by Liberal presidential candidate Carlos Flores. Shortly after his inauguration, jockeying began for the 2001 presidential campaign. One of the top-spending pre-candidates has been businessman Jaime Rosenthal Oliva, a Liberal and former vice-president.

Honduras has a 148-seat, unicameral legislature elected for a four-year term, coinciding with that of the president. The country is divided into 18 departments, although most administrative responsibility lies with the central government. These departments are, in turn, divided into 283 municipalities containing 3,077 villages and about 20,000 smaller settlements.

Economy

For many decades, Honduras bore the dubious distinction of being the poorest country in Central America, but this changed during the 1980s when Nicaragua, bearing the double burden of Sandinista economic mismanagement and implacable U.S. hostility, went into economic free fall and

replaced Honduras at the bottom of the ladder. That shift does not signal any new prosperity for Honduras, which remains poor by almost any measure.

In 1998, gross domestic product was estimated at $630 per person, which rises to about $2,000 when adjusted for purchasing power parities. This poverty is made only slightly more tolerable by the fact that income distribution is not quite as heavily skewed as in the neighbouring countries. The wealthy are not quite as wealthy, and the poor are not quite as poor, as in Guatemala or El Salvador, and this probably helps account for Honduras's political peace, although many visitors may find the gaps quite shocking.

In the 19th century, the Honduran economy was based mostly on subsistence agriculture, with timber being the most important export. Early in the 20th century, however, the two U.S.-based banana giants, United Fruit (known today as Chiquita Brands) and Standard Fruit (which uses the Dole label), colonized

large swaths of land near the Caribbean coast and established huge plantations, primarily for the production of bananas and later for pineapples and other fruits, as well as palm oil. For decades Honduras was the archetypal banana republic, with its economy and politics largely under the sway of foreign-based firms, and with subservient elements in the military fending off challenges to the status quo.

Bananas still play an important role in the Honduran economy, but the growth of other sectors has loosened their dominant role. The coffee industry has grown from modest beginnings in the 1950s, and today Honduras is a significant coffee exporter. Coffee, in fact, has overtaken bananas as the top export. Much of this coffee is grown on small plantations, in contrast to the neighbouring countries where large portions of the coffee-growing lands have traditionally been owned by a small number of very wealthy families and have indeed formed the basis of oligopolies.

Pineapple

Other recent developments have also helped diversify the Honduran economy. Shrimp farming has become big business in the Gulf of Fonseca on the Pacific coast. In several parts of the country, but most particularly in the area around San Pedro Sula, the garment industry grew rapidly in the 1990s. Items are assembled at in-bond plants for re-export under arrangements similar to the *maquiladora* plants that have sprung up along Mexico's border with the United States. Wages are very low at these plants, but for many workers this represents economic progress nonetheless. This adds to the traditional manufacturing base already well established in San Pedro Sula and, to a lesser extent, in Tegucigalpa and La Ceiba. Tourism has also become a significant source of employment.

One money generator that officials prefer not to discuss is the trans-shipment of narcotics. Honduras has a long Caribbean coastline lying about midway between Colombia and the United States, respectively the biggest source of supply and the biggest source of demand. Small numbers of Hondurans have amassed significant wealth as a result.

Society and Culture

To say that Honduras is a multiracial society is something of an understatement. As in much of Latin America, the dominant group is *mestizos*, people of mixed Spanish and Amerindian descent. In Honduras, *mestizos* form an estimated 88% of the population, but they are by no means uniform in appearance or social category.

In Honduras, ethnic group is not the obsessive matter it became in certain other societies and, while it is certainly true that tall, fair-skinned people are overrepresented in the higher reaches of economic and political life, people of different origins appear to mix quite easily.

The remaining 12% of the population is made up of a broad variety of groups, the largest of which are pure-blooded or almost pure-blooded indigenous peoples (see below), while people of pure or almost pure European or Middle Eastern descent also form a substantial group. Small numbers of Chinese help round out the racial mix.

Honduras also has two distinct groups of blacks. Scattered in small towns along the Caribbean coast, with clusters also in the bigger cities, are the Garífunas, sometimes called black Caribs, whose ancestors were expelled by the British from the Caribbean island of St. Vincent two centuries ago. They have maintained a distinct language and myriad other characteristics.

Concentrated on the Islas de la Bahía is the other group, referred to simply as English-speaking blacks. They are the descendants of slaves from the Cayman Islands and elsewhere in the West Indies, and are undistinguishable in many respects from people in English-speaking Caribbean countries, apart from the fact that most of them also speak Spanish.

A brief presentation of Honduran indigenous groups follows below. For readers who want more detailed information and who read Spanish, we can recommend *Pueblos Indígenas y Garífuna de Honduras* by Ramón D. Rivas, 1993, Editorial Guaymuras in Tegucigalpa.

Indigenous Groups

Indigenous peoples (*indígenas* in Spanish) were the undisputed masters of what is today Honduras until the arrival of the first Spanish colonists nearly five centuries ago. After that time, they were pushed off the best lands by brute force, subjected to forced labour, and denigrated in all aspects of their culture and society. Over time the great majority of indigenous peoples intermarried with Spanish settlers to form the dominant *mestizo* race, but some managed to maintain their languages and their distinctive ways until well into the 19th century — and a few up to the present day.

In the 1860s, several decades after independence from Spain, communal land titles were issued to some groups of Amerindians, reversing a key thrust of Spanish policy. But this process was not completed, and even today indigenous peoples in Honduras have various forms of land holding, some of them only tenuous. These include the usufruct that some groups hold over plots of government-owned land.

Honduras lies near the southeastern edge of Mesoamerica, the zone that begins in central Mexico and includes the territories occupied by peoples descended from the ancient Mayas and Aztecs. These groups developed elaborate social structures and achieved advanced forms of agriculture, with a special emphasis on corn. The country is situated at the crossroads between Mesoamerican lands and those occupied by peoples whose origins lie in the jungles of northeastern South America. The forebears of the latter did not achieve the same levels of social or cultural development, with an economy based largely on hunting and gathering. The dividing line runs south from the present-day town of Trujillo on the Caribbean coast to the Gulf of Fonseca on the Pacific side, with a prolongation running inside Nicaraguan territory.

The **Lencas** are the most populous indigenous group in Honduras, with an estimated 90,000 people living in 612 communities scattered mostly through the highlands in the southwestern part of the country, especially in the area around La Esperanza. They are a Mayan-related group, and they live mostly on small plots of unproductive land, forcing many to seek seasonal work harvesting coffee for some of the bigger growers. The Lenca chief Lempira (after whom the national currency is named) led a rebellion against Spanish rule in 1537. The Lenca language all but disappeared in the late 19th century, but some traditional rituals and beliefs remain. They are also distinguished by their production of basketry and ceramics,

little of which has found a commercial outlet.

The **Chortis**, of whom there are only about 3,500 in Honduras, live west of the Copán region near the border with Guatemala. They too are Mayan-related, and they occupied a much bigger territory prior to the Spanish conquest. The Chorti language has disappeared in Honduras but continues to survive among communities on the Guatemalan side of the border. Through much of their history, this group was in continuous contact with the Pipil people, the most important indigenous group in El Salvador.

The **Tolupanes**, also known as **Xicaques**, occupied much of the Caribbean coast prior to the conquest but were pushed into the interior mountains and jungles. Today they number about 10,000 people living in 143 communities, mostly in north-central Honduras in the area around the town of Yoro. A pre-Mayan people, they were hunter-gatherers, and their economic status remains marginal. Their language is thought to be 5,000 years old and, according to conflicting versions, is related either to the Hokan-Sioux group of North America or the Chibcha-Penutia group of South America. Some elements of the language survive, but little remains of traditional social organization. Tolupanes are distinguished by their style of housing and by certain types of handicrafts, particularly basketry.

The **Misquitos** (often spelled Miskitos) live in small communities dispersed over the rivers and lagoons in the vast region of northeastern Honduras referred to as Mosquitia, spilling over into Nicaragua. The origin of the name is unclear. Some historians think it came from musket, a type of firearm introduced by the English in the 17th century and translated into Spanish as *mosquete*. For centuries the Misquitos were allied with the English against Spanish rule. They are descended from the Chibcha tribes of the South American rainforest, with an admixture in the 18th century of African and European elements, which have not affected their strong indigenous identity. Today they number about 35,000 people living in 84 communities, and their language remains widely spoken. Typical dwellings are made of wood or bamboo. In recent decades, the Misquitos have had to cope with an intrusion of *mestizos* onto their traditional territories. They were joined for several years in the 1980s by Mosquito refugees from Nicaragua displaced by

conflicts with the Sandinista government.

The **Pech**, sometimes called **Payas**, live in the western part of Mosquitia, mostly in the basin of the Río Plátano, and number only about 1,600. Some live deep in the mountains and maintain their ancestral customs and Chibcha-related language, while others have lost the language and speak Misquito instead. Their system of beliefs centres around a deep knowledge of and close relationship with nature. The ecological equilibrium of their lands has been harmed by forestry activities, and the dispersal of animals has hurt their diet.

The **Tawahkas**, or **Sumos**, live mostly in the Río Patuca basin in southern Mosquitia and across the border in Nicaragua. Only a few hundred live on the Honduran side. Their language survives in Nicaragua, but in Honduras it has been replaced by Spanish and Misquito. Tawahka communities act as extended families and tend to be isolated and inbred. They suffer serious health and nutrition problems.

The Garífunas

Estimates of the number of Garífunas, or black Caribs, vary widely, some running as high as 300,000, with

perhaps 90,000 of them in Honduras. There are also substantial numbers in Belize and in a small part of Guatemala, but many have emigrated to the United States, and the world's largest Garífuna community, numbering about 50,000, is now found in New York.

They are the descendants of ship-wrecked slaves who mixed with Carib and Arawak Indians in St. Vincent and elsewhere in the eastern Caribbean beginning in the middle of the 17th century. As land disputes intensified, the Garífuna found themselves allied with the French against the British, and they kept fighting even after the French surrender in 1796. In 1797, in a manner similar to the expulsion of Acadians from Nova Scotia to Louisiana several decades earlier, the British deported the Garífuna from St. Vincent and resettled them in the Islas de la Bahía and along the Caribbean coast. Numbering more than 2,500, they became wood-cutters, fishers and smugglers.

The Garífuna have maintained their African roots through dances, stories, drumming and a set of religious beliefs that resembles voodoo. Their language, which remains alive in many of the communities scattered along the Caribbean coast, has a mixture of Arawak,

French, Yoruba and other African roots. Nearly all Honduran Garífunas also speak Spanish. *Punta* is a characteristic dance rhythm.

Religion

The great majority of Hondurans are nominally Roman Catholics, although many cannot be considered practising Catholics. There are many fervent believers, but religiosity appears to be somewhat less pronounced than in some neighbouring countries. In many rural areas, the presence of the church is minimal.

In recent years a number of small evangelical Protestant sects, often U.S.-based, have established large followings. Regardless of denomination, they are referred to as *evangélicos* and practise an exuberant form of worship more akin to the custom in many small churches in the southern United States than to the more traditional strains of Protestantism. *Evangélicos* have been criticized for dividing communities but praised for combatting alcoholism.

Arts and Leisure

Development of arts and letters has been rather limited in Honduras. Several 20th-century painters have achieved a certain prominence within the small circles in which they are known. Their reputation is based heavily on landscape paintings, such as those produced by Carlos Garay, and on portrayals of village scenes, such as the work of José Antonio Velásquez. Another painter, an American who has adopted the name Guillermo Yuscarán, has also achieved some fame as a novelist, with a heavy emphasis on Honduran settings. Among others who have made their mark in Honduran literature are the poet, historian and essayist Rafael Heliodoro, the novelist and short story writer Argentina Díaz Lozano, and the poet and publisher Clementina Suárez.

No particular region or town in Honduras has emerged as a dominant centre of craft production. Carved items of mahogany and other tropical hardwoods are popular items, ranging in size from small wall hangings to elaborate pieces of furniture. While the quality of workmanship can be excellent, the designs may strike some visitors as less appealing than they could be, often based on distorted versions of ancient Mayan themes. Important advances have been made in artistic ceramics, using vases and other objects to portray both Mayan and abstract themes. Among the most common of hand-painted items are porcelain objects in the shape of animals, particularly roosters. More information on crafts is found on page 52.

The marimba is the most important traditional instrument, but it is rarely heard now in Honduras. Salsa, mergengue and other tropical rhythms have emerged as the most popular musical forms, especially in areas toward the Caribbean coast. *Punta*, a distinctive musical rhythm developed by the Garífuna people, is also very popular, and on weekends there are live performances in several coastal communities. For dancing, these are all favoured over American pop and disco tunes, which nonetheless have a certain following. Mexican *ranchero music* is quite popular, especially in the south and the centre of the country. *Peña*, a form of musical expression involving songs of political protest or satire, some-times sad, some-times lively, is performed in select milieus, mostly in Tegucigalpa.

Mayan Pottery

Classical music has only a limited audience in Honduras, but there is an FM radio station in Tegucigalpa whose programming consists mostly of classics.

No survey of Honduran culture is complete without mention of *fútbol* (soccer), by far the most popular sport but, more than that, an obsession. It is a preferred leisure activity for young males who play the game, and for large sectors of the population that listen to soccer matches on the radio or watch them on television. When important matches are being played, the whole country seems to shut down for a couple of hours.

Practical Information

Information contained in this chapter will simplify planning a visit to Honduras. It may even help prevent difficult situations while in the country.

Please take a few minutes to peruse these pages, and pay special attention to some of the warnings, for example concerning the difficulty of exchanging currencies other than the U.S. dollar.

Entrance Formalities

Passports and Visas

All foreign visitors to Honduras must hold valid passports (except citizens of Guatemala, El Salvador, Nicaragua and Costa Rica, who can show national identity cards instead).

Citizens of the United States, Canada and countries in Western Europe can enter Honduras without a consular visa. The same applies to citizens of Australia, New Zealand and Japan.

Citizens of many other countries do require consular visas. The price of the visa varies according to nationality (and seems sometimes to vary also according to the whim of the consular official). Countries whose citizens require visas include most countries in South America and the Caribbean, Mexico, and nearly every country in Africa, Asia and the Middle East.

Visa requirements have been lifted for citizens of Argentina and Chile. Citizens of eastern European countries, most countries in Asia, and certain countries in South America and Africa require not only a consular visa but also approval from the foreign ministry in Tegucigalpa. This is a tedious process and can sometimes take up to two months.

A list of Honduran embassies and consulates appears below. Travellers applying for visas should phone ahead to check on hours of service, requirements for photos or payment, and the amount of time required.

Although the trend in the last few years has been toward a loosening of entry requirements, regulations can change suddenly and without notice. If there are any doubts concerning visa requirements, it is wise to check ahead with a Honduran embassy or consulate.

Length of Stay

Entry stamps for visitors of most western nationalities are valid for 90 days in Honduras. A copy of the entry card is stapled inside the passport by the immigration officer at the point of entry and must be retained until the moment of departure from the country. In some cases, entry visas are valid for only 30 days.

Extensions of 30 days cost $2 and are easy to obtain at any immigration office inside Honduras. There are immigration offices in Tegucigalpa, San Pedro Sula, La Ceiba, Roatán, Utila, Guanaja, Trujillo, Puerto Cortés, Santa Bárbara, Copán Ruinas, Nueva Ocotepeque, Danlí, Choluteca and San Lorenzo. The main office in Tegucigalpa is reputed to have the most cumbersome and time-consuming procedures. It is preferable to obtain extensions elsewhere. The total stay for tourists may not exceed 180 days. Those wishing to stay longer must leave Honduras and re-enter the country.

Entry and Departure Fees

Visitors arriving by air and whose documents are in order are not normally required to pay any fee. Passengers leaving by air must pay a $25 departure tax, payable in U.S. dollars or the equivalent in Honduran currency. (This is a good way to get rid of unspent lempiras, which are nearly worthless outside Honduras.) Credit cards are not accepted. The tax is normally collected at the entrance to the airline check-in counters. Receipts must be shown to the airline clerk.

Those arriving or departing by land are often required to pay a fee of about $2 at the border even if all documents are in order. It pays to keep a supply of small U.S. bills in case border officials claim they have no change.

Customs

Visitors may bring in reasonable quantities of goods for personal use while in Honduras, including cameras and electronic goods. Regulations also permit the import of gifts up to a value of $200, or $100 if the traveller is under 18, as well as up to two litres of alcohol and 200 cigarettes, 50 cigars

or 250 grams of loose tobacco. Beyond these amounts, heavy duties may apply.

Severe restrictions apply to the import of fresh fruits, vegetables, meats and plants. It is probably best not to bother trying. Those wishing to bring pets or firearms must obtain permits beforehand, and this is a very onerous process. Information and the necessary forms may be obtained from Honduran embassies and consulates (but don't count on getting clear answers to your queries).

Motorists entering with their vehicle must have proof of ownership of the vehicle they are driving and a valid driver's licence issued in their country of residence. Insurance is not required. A document called a *pase fronterizo* (border pass) is valid for a stay of up to eight days in Honduras and is issued free of charge (in theory, at least) at border crossings. For longer stays, a vehicle permit costs $20 for up to 90 days and may be extended for a further 90 days. These same requirements apply to motorcycles, but not to bicycles. Selling a foreign-registered vehicle in Honduras entails a lengthy bureaucratic procedure and the payment of customs duties.

Visitors leaving Honduras may take with them almost anything in their possession, but the export of pre-Hispanic items and of certain coral objects is prohibited. It is important also to take account of import restrictions in a traveller's home country, for instance on the tax-free importation of alcohol.

Embassies and Consulates

Honduran Embassies and Consulates Abroad

BELGIUM
Av. des Gaulois 8
Brussels
☎734-0000
⇌735-2626
106101.2432@compuserve.com

BELIZE
91 North Front St.
Belize City
☎02-45889
⇌02-30562

BRITAIN
115 Gloucester Place
London
☎(20) 486-4880
⇌(20) 486-4550
ehlondres@aol.com

CANADA
1650 Blvd de Maisonneuve
Ouest, Suite 306
Montréal
☎514-937-2194

151 Slater St., Suite 805-A
Ottawa
☎613-233-8900
⇌613-232-0193
scastell@magmacom.com

Québec
(honorary consulate)
☎418-681-5070

Toronto
(honorary consulate)
☎416-960-1907

Vancouver
(honorary consulate)
☎604-734-0088

COSTA RICA
Del ITAN 300 metros al este, 200 al norte, 100 al este, Yoses Sur
San José
☎234-9502
⇌253-2209
embhondcr@sol.racsa.co.cr

EL SALVADOR
3 Calle Poniente 3697, Col. Escalón
San Salvador
☎223-2222
⇌223-2221
embbond@es.com.sv

FRANCE
8, rue Crevaux
Paris 16ᵉ
☎47.55.86.45
⇌47.55.86.48
dl.honduras@unesco.org

GERMANY
Uberstrasse 1
Bonn
☎228-356394
⇌228-351981

GUATEMALA
Edificio Geminis, Torre Sur, ofic. 1211
12 Calle 1-25, Zona 10
Guatemala City
☎337-4344
⇌338-2073
embbhon@guatenet.net.gt

ITALY
Via Gian Battista de Vico 40, int. 8
Rome
☎320-7236
⇌320-7973

JAPAN
38 Kowa Bldg. 8F, No. 802
12-24 Nishi Azabu 4 Chome, Minato Ku
Tokyo
☎3-3-409-1150
⇌3-3-409-0305
honduras@interlink.or.jp

MÉXICO
Alfonso Reyes 220, Col. Condesa
México, D.F.
☎5211-5747
⇌5211-5425
embonmex@mail.internet.com.mx

NETHERLANDS
Johan van Oldenbarnevel Tlaan 85
Den Haag
☎703-540-152
⇌703-504-183

NICARAGUA
A.P. 231
Managua
☎279-8233
⇌279-8228

PANAMÁ
Calle 31, Av. Justo Arosemena, Zona 5
Panamá City
☎225-8200
⇌225-3283
hondupma@sinfo.net

SPAIN
Calle Rosario Pino 6, 4º piso A
Madrid
☎579-0251
⇌572-1319
e7610193@teleline.es

SWITZERLAND
13 Charmin de Toverney
Geneva
☎227-336-916
⇌227-100-766

UNITED STATES
4506 W. Fullerton Ave.
Chicago
☎773-342-8281
⇌773-342-8293

4151 S.W. Freeway, Suite 70050
Houston
☎713-622-4572
⇌713-622-3540
bonduras@ix.netcom.com

3450 Wilshire Blvd., Suite 230
Los Angeles
☎213-383-9244
⇌213-383-9306
consulLa@aol.com

300 Sevilla Ave., Suite 201
Miami (Coral Gables)
☎305-447-6375
⇌305-447-9036

2 Canal St., Suite 1641
New Orleans
☎504-522-3118
⇌504-523-0544

80 Wall St., Suite 915
New York
☎212-269-3611
⇌212-509-8391
consulate@msn.com

870 Market St., Suite 451
San Francisco
☎415-392-0076
⇌415-392-6726

1107 E. Jackson, Suite 113
Tampa
☎813-209-3249
⇌813-209-0573

3007 Tilden St. N.W.
Washington
☎202-966-4596
⇌202-966-9751
embbondu@ix.netcom.com

Honduran Embassies are also located in Athens, Bogotá, Brasilia, Buenos Aires, Cairo, Caracas, Kingston (Jamaica), Lima, Quito, Santiago (Chile), Santo Domingo (Dominican Republic), Seoul, Stockholm, Taipei, and Tel Aviv.

Embassies in Tegucigalpa

BRITAIN
Edificio Palmiro, 3er piso, Col. Palmira
☎232-0612
☎232-0618
⇌232-5480

COSTA RICA
Residencial El Triangulo, 1ª Calle, Casa 3451
☎232-1768
☎239-0787
⇌232-1876

EL SALVADOR
Calzada Uruguay 219, Col. San Carlos
☎236-7344
☎236-8045
⇌236-9403

FRANCE
Avenida Juan Linda, Callejón Batres 337, Col. Palmira
☎236-6800
☎236-6432
⇌236-8051

GERMANY
Edificio Paysen, 3ª planta, Boulevard Morazán
☎232-3161
☎232-3162
⇌232-9518

GUATEMALA
Calle Arturo López Redezno 2421, Col. Las Minitas
☎231-1543
☎232-9704
⇌232-8469

ITALY
Avenida Principal 2602, Col. Reforma
☎236-6810
☎236-6391
⇌236-5659

JAPAN
Col. San Carlos, between 3ª Calle and 4ª Calle, near Supermercado Sucasa
☎236-6828
☎236-6829
⇌236-6100

MÉXICO
Avenida República de México 2402, Colonia Palmira
☎232-6471
☎232-4039
⇌232-4719

NICARAGUA
Avenida Choluteca, Bloque M-1, No. 1130, Col. Tepeyac
☎232-7218
☎232-7224
⇌232-4719

PANAMÁ
Edificio Palmira, 2° piso, Col. Palmira
☎232-8147

SPAIN
Calle Santander, Casa 801, Col. Matamoros
☎236-6589
☎236-6875
⇌236-8682

UNITED STATES
Avenida La Paz
☎238-5114
☎236-9325
⇌236-9037

Other countries with embassies in Tegucigalpa include Argentina, Brazil and Colombia. Several countries have honorary consulates in San Pedro Sula. Generally speaking, honorary consulates are able to provide only limited services.

Tourist Information

The Honduran government has confided the task of tourism promotion to the *Instituto Hondureño de Turismo*. In recent years the institute has become more professional in its approach, thanks in part to financing derived from a special tax on hotel rooms, although it still cannot provide the level of service offered by the tourism promotion bodies of many wealthier countries.

Instituto Hondureño de Turismo
Florida Office
toll-free from the United States or Canada:
1-800-410-9608

Queries in Spanish or English can be sent to:

Instituto Hondureño de Turismo
Tegucigalpa Office
open Mon to Fri
8:30am to 4:30pm
in Colonia San Carlos on Avenida Ramón Ernesto Cruz, upstairs from Lloyds Bank in the Edificio Europa, two blocks from the Grupo Taca ticket office on Boulevard Morazán
☎ *220-1600* or *220-1601*
ihturism@hondutel.hn
www.hondurasinfo.hn.

While the Web site may only provide sketchy tourism information, it has data that may be of interest to some business travellers, including lists of trade associations and other contacts in Honduras.

Travel agencies abroad often can provide information on air-and-hotel packages, scuba-diving packages, and fully escorted tour programs in Honduras, but they usually depend for their information on the wholesale tour companies and individual resort hotels that offer these packages. In most cases, they can offer only limited help to independent travellers, although a good travel agent is invaluable in arranging air tickets.

For tourism information within Honduras, the Instituto Hondureño de Turismo can provide some limited assistance at its Tegucigalpa office. The institute closed its branch offices elsewhere in Honduras. Hotel clerks and taxi drivers can often provide useful tips on local points of interest and local services.

For information on excursions around the country, a number of tour companies have offices or representatives in several Honduran cities and can provide an idea of what's on offer. Although some of them are quite generous with information, it should be remembered that they are in business to sell tour programs. Visits to certain places, in particular some national parks and nature reserves, are difficult to arrange on an individual basis, and this is where tour companies are especially helpful. It often makes sense to check with more than one tour company to compare prices and services. Tour companies are listed in the "Outdoors" chapter, (see p 59).

Tour Packages or Independent Travel?

In planning a trip to Honduras (or to almost anywhere else, for that matter), travellers have to decide what they want to do, which in turn will determine whether a tour package or independent travel is more suitable.

Those who are interested mostly in relaxing by the beach will often end up staying at the same hotel and in the same area for most of their visit, and this is where it makes the most sense to consider buying an air-and-hotel package, which in some cases costs only slightly more than air fare alone. Some of these packages are based on the all-inclusive formula with meals, drinks and certain activities included in the price. This option is a useful way to control costs, but on the other hand it may lock you into taking nearly all your meals at hotel buffets whose offerings may soon induce boredom. Air-

Practical Information

and-hotel packages can usually be bought only through travel agencies or, in some cases, from the tour divisions of airline companies.

Those who plan to concentrate on scuba diving will also want to consider prepaid packages, which can be considerably more economical than paying a nightly hotel rate and paying separately for each diving excursion. Single-day packages are offered by some resort hotels, but multi-day packages, often involving a stay of six or seven nights, are more common. In comparing prices, it is essential to check if equipment is included, how many boat dives are provided each day, if there is any charge for shore dives, and if night dives are included. Prices will also depend on the quality of lodgings and on whether meals are offered. Dive packages can be purchased through travel agencies or directly from resort hotels, with air fare covered separately in the latter case.

Visitors who plan to move around within Honduras can choose between package tours, independent travel, or a combination of the two. Fully escorted tours may appeal to older or less experienced travellers or to those who prefer to leave the work to others rather than tackling a foreign country on their own. These tours generally provide well planned itineraries, comfortable vehicles and lodgings, and an overall sense of security. Drawbacks include limits on flexibility, being stuck in the same surroundings with the same group, and a lack of contact with local people. Sometimes travel agencies can provide information on escorted tours. Bear in mind that offerings are rather limited.

Independent travel will appeal to many visitors because it allows almost infinite flexibility in the choice of itineraries and a sense of freedom that no package tour can offer. Travellers also have considerable leeway in choosing accommodations and meal arrangements that suit their budgets and tastes. It is rarely necessary to reserve hotel rooms in advance, although space can be tight at peak travel periods such as Christmas and the week preceding Easter. Travelling independently does require communications skills (see p 47), an ability to deal with the unexpected, and a willingness to put up with occasional inconvenience or discomfort.

Even some independent-minded travellers may want to consider combining package tours with do-it-yourself travel. It is sometimes possible, for instance, to find an air-and-hotel package allowing a two-week stay in Honduras but with the hotel room prepaid for only one week. This enables visitors to spend their first week lounging by the beach and acclimatizing themselves to the country, and the second week travelling around on their own. Another possibility is to arrive independently in Honduras and buy a multi-day tour program from a local agency to see a few of the main sights or perhaps to experience adventure travel in some of the less accessible regions of the country (see p 59-61).

Entering the Country

By Air

Four airports in Honduras receive regular international flights. The busiest is San Pedro Sula, followed by Tegucigalpa. La Ceiba and Roatán see only limited international traffic, with most visitors relying on domestic connections. Landing at Tegucigalpa airport involves a steep descent and an abrupt halt on a short runway. Nervous flyers may choose to land elsewhere.

Is There Competition in the Skies?

Many Hondurans whose livelihood depends on tourism have complained long and loud about high international airfares. From Miami, it is sometimes cheaper to fly to distant points in Europe than to nearby points in Honduras. Grupo Taca, Central America's dominant airline group, is usually cast as the villain. Taca was founded in Honduras in the 1930s but soon shifted its base of operations next door to El Salvador, where it remains to this day. In the 1990s, Taca went on a buying spree, taking over Aviateca of Guatemala and Lacsa of Costa Rica. It also established a small airline in Nicaragua and bought out Isleña, Honduras's biggest domestic carrier. Earlier, it had helped push SAHSA, Honduras's international airline, into insolvency, and it took over several of SAHSA's routes. Grupo Taca, as it now calls itself (*grupo* means group), integrated the services of its various components and became a success on its own terms, but its oligopolistic power created resentment across Central America, nowhere more than in Honduras. Taca's few international competitors on routes into Honduras have generally been content to follow Taca's lead on fares, which have tended to be high, apart from the occasional low-season promotion.

International fares appear especially high when contrasted with Honduras's cheap domestic fares. This has placed the Honduran tourism industry at a competitive disadvantage. In 1999, the Honduran congress was set to pass legislation creating an open-skies policy under which foreign airlines can serve Honduras with no requirement for reciprocal access. At about the same time, the government was preparing to issue an international call for tenders for management of the country's four international airports. Both moves have been widely applauded, but it is unclear to what extent they will affect fares or service.

Practical Information

Honduras has no international airline of its own. El Salvador-based **Grupo Taca** operates the busiest schedule of flights to and from Honduras, with numerous flights from the United States and from several Central American countries, as well as connections from Mexico, South America and the Caribbean. Scheduled service to Honduras is also provided by **American Airlines**, **Continental Airlines**, Panamá-based **Copa** (now a subsidiary of Continental), **Aerocaribe** of Mexico and **Iberia** of Spain. Some charter services also operate to Honduras.

Following is an outline of air service to Honduras. Keep in mind that it is subject to change. Before making plans, it is essential to check with a travel agent or with the airlines concerned.

From the United States

From **Miami**, American Airlines operates daily non-stop flights both to San Pedro Sula and to Tegucigalpa. Taca runs daily nonstop flights to San Pedro Sula and one-stop flights to Tegucigalpa, as well as direct weekend service to Roatán. Taca also provides daily connecting service to Roatán and La Ceiba via Belize. Iberia flies twice a week from Miami to San Pedro Sula.

From **Houston**, Continental Airlines operates daily non-stop flights both to San Pedro Sula and to Tegucigalpa. Taca provides connecting service via El Salvador to San Pedro Sula or Tegucigalpa and via Belize to Roatán and La Ceiba, as well as direct weekend service to Roatán.

From **New York** or **New Orleans**, Taca provides non-stop service to San Pedro Sula several times weekly. From New York or **Washington**, Taca provides daily connections via El Salvador, American and Continental via Miami or Houston. From **Los Angeles** or **San Francisco**, Taca provides daily connections via El Salvador, American and Continental via Miami or Houston with long layovers. Other connections are available via Mexico City, Cancun, or Guatemala City.

From **other points** in the United States, connections are available through the above gateway cities.

From Europe or Canada

There are no direct scheduled flights to Honduras from Europe or Canada. KLM flies five times a week from **Amsterdam** to Guatemala City with connections on Taca to San Pedro Sula and Tegucigalpa. Iberia provides service twice a week

on its own aircraft from **Madrid** to San Pedro Sula with a connection at Miami.

I Grandi Viaggi, a Milan-based travel company, has arranged weekly, year-round charter flights from **Milan** to Roatán. Weekly charter flights from **Montréal** or **Toronto** to Honduras have run some years, on a seasonal basis.

If these suggestions don't work, numerous connections are available via the United States, though in some cases with an overnight layover.

From Latin America and the Caribbean

Grupo Taca dominates most routes to Honduras from other parts of Latin America. Some international flights within Central America are operated using ATR-42 turboprop aircraft rather than jets. Several daily flights operate to Tegucigalpa and San Pedro Sula from Taca's hub in **El Salvador**. Twice-daily direct service is provided to both cities from **Guatemala** and once-daily service from **Costa Rica**. There is no direct service from neighbouring Nicaragua. A daily flight connects **Belize** with Roatán and La Ceiba. Flying from **Mexico City** to Honduras involves connec

Table of distances (km)

Via the shortest route

	Agua Caliente	Catacamas	Choluteca	Comayagua	Copán Ruinas	Danlí	La Ceiba	Puerto Cortes	San Pedro Sula	Tela	Tegucigalpa
Catacamas	721										
Choluteca	641	342									
Comayagua	427	295	216								
Copán Ruinas	411	223	542	327							
Danlí	601	301	226	177	503						
La Ceiba	471	366	531	314	372	489					
Puerto Cortes	331	514	437	219	231	396	267				
San Pedro Sula	268	452	373	156	169	331	201	63			
Tela	367	502	425	211	267	386	102	164	485		
Tegucigalpa	511	209	132	85	411	93	398	304	238	290	
Trujillo	643	297	701	482	541	658	174	438	372	273	566

Example : The distance between Tegucigalpa and Copán Ruinas is 411km.

tions in El Salvador, Guatemala or Cancún. Several countries in South America, extending as far south as **Chile**, are served by Grupo Taca's Costa Rican subsidiary, Lacsa, with connections to Honduras via San José.

Panamá-based Copa runs a daily Panamá City-Guatemala City-San Pedro Sula flight, with connections from South America and several points in the Caribbean via Panamá. Aerocaribe, an affiliate of Mexicana de Aviación, offers direct service from **Cancún** to San Pedro Sula. Occasional charter flights operate from **Guatemala City** to an airstrip on the Guatemalan side of the border not far from Copán Ruinas.

By Car

For information on bringing vehicles into Honduras, please refer to the Customs section (see p 26).

Honduras has two main border crossings with Guatemala, two with El Salvador and three with Nicaragua. From Guatemala City, a highway runs east to Chiquimula and onward to the Honduran border at **El Florido**, 14km from Copán Ruinas and 199km from San Pedro Sula. A more southerly road runs through Quetzaltepeque to Esquipulas and the border village of

Atupala, with the Honduran town of **Agua Caliente** on the other side, 22km from Nueva Ocotepeque. Alternate routes from Guatemala to Honduras go via El Salvador; this is the quickest way to reach Tegucigalpa.

A new road connection is under construction along the Caribbean coast, with **Cuyamelito** as the crossing point, not far from Omoa. This road will provide an important link between Puerto Barrios in Guatemala and Puerto Cortés in Honduras, two of Central America's busiest ports.

From San Salvador, the northern highway reaches the Honduran border at **El Poy**, 9km south of Nueva Ocotepeque and 271km south of San Pedro Sula, while the Panamerican highway runs east through San Miguel to the border town of **El Amatillo** and onward across southern Honduras with a link to Tegucigalpa.

From Managua, Nicaragua, there are three routes to Tegucigalpa. The most southerly route runs via León and Chinandega to the border at **El Guasaule**, continuing via Choluteca on the Honduran side. Another route goes north to Estelí and Somoto, turning west to the border at **El Espino** and onward to Choluteca. The most northerly route goes via

Estelí and Sómoto, continuing north to the border at **Las Manos** and reaching Tegucigalpa by way of Danlí.

Border formalities are considerably faster than they were only a few years ago, but motorists should still be prepared to accept delays, especially on weekends and holidays. A supply of small U.S. bills can sometimes come in handy for the $2 departure tax that seems to be charged arbitrarily. This can be paid in U.S. dollars or in lempiras. There are freelance money-changers at all border crossings waving calculators and wads of cash, but exchange rates are not always favourable and it is best to change only small amounts.

Bear in mind that borders close at night, sometimes as early as 6pm, and do not re-open until 6am. Travellers approaching a border crossing beyond late afternoon should consider staying overnight in a larger town before reaching the border, where lodgings may leave something to be desired.

By Bus

International bus travel in Central America often involves taking a local bus to the border town, crossing the border on foot, and taking another local bus after completing formalities on the other side. This applies, for example, to travel between San Pedro Sula and points in El Salvador or Guatemala. Fortunately, other options exist to and from Tegucigalpa.

King Quality and Cruceros del Golfo jointly offer direct buses twice daily in each direction between San Salvador and Tegucigalpa, with departures at 6am and 1pm for the 6hr trip. Same-day connections are possible to or from Guatemala City via San Salvador. In San Salvador, buses operate from the Puerto Bus terminal inTegucigalpa and from a small terminal on Boulevard Comunidad Europea, not far from the airport. Buses are air-conditioned and comfortable.

The Costa Rican company **Tica-Bus** provides service between Tegucigalpa and Managua, Nicaragua, as well as connections to or from Costa Rica with an overnight stop in Managua.

From Tegucigalpa:
Daily departures at 9am from a terminal in one of the seedier parts of Comayagüela, at the corner of 7ª Avenida and 17ª Avenida
☎*238-7040*
Buses are air-conditioned and comfortable.

By Sea

Several cruise lines have considered calling on Honduras, but as of yet, none do so on a regular basis. The only international seaborne passenger service is provided by small freight vessels that operate infrequently between Puerto Cortés in Honduras and nearby Puerto Barrios in Guatemala, or between Puerto Cortés and ports in Belize. Travel aboard these vessels is suggested only for the adventurous. Information may sometimes be obtained from local port authorities.

Insurance

No insurance is required to enter Honduras, not even for motorists. Nonetheless, before leaving home, it may be a good idea to consider purchasing trip cancellation insurance, supplementary health insurance, life insurance and theft insurance; travellers are also advised to check what kind of allowances their present insurance policies allow for when travelling. Often all three are sold together as a package at moderate cost. These policies can be purchased through insurance brokers or travel agencies.

Motorists may also breathe a little more easily if their vehicles are properly insured.

Cancellation

Trip cancellation insurance comes in handy if a traveller has to call off a trip for valid medical reasons or because of a death in the family. It covers any non-refundable payments to travel suppliers such as airlines and must be purchased at the same time as initial payment is made for air tickets or tour packages.

Health

Supplementary health insurance will cover medical expenses that go beyond what travellers can claim from their regular government or private insurer. When buying insurance, make sure it covers all types of medical costs, such as hospitalization, nurse's services and doctor's fees. A repatriation clause is also a good idea in case the required care is not available on site, and may include the cost of an air ambulance. Furthermore, you may have to pay these costs before leaving the clinic; verify what your policy provides for in this case. Although hospital costs are low in Honduras compared to those in many other countries, the bills can still pile up quickly. Remember always to keep proof of your insurance on your person in case of problems.

Theft

Most residential insurance policies in North America insure your goods from theft, even if the theft occurs while on holiday. To make a claim you must obtain out a police report, which may require a small paymentto the police un charge.

Health

Vaccinations

No vaccinations are required to enter Honduras except for people who have travelled recently in a country where yellow fever is endemic. Travellers who expect to be camping in jungle areas, especially in the Mosquitia, should consider malaria proxylasis and other precautions. Anyone who has special concerns about tropical disease should consult a traveller's clinic before leaving home.

Illnesses

Dengue Fever

Dengue fever is carried by mosquitoes, and can cause discomfort in its more benign forms. Hemorrhagic *dengue*, the most extreme form, is very rare but can be fatal. The main symptom is irritation of the eyes, accompanied by a mild fever.

Malaria

Also called paludism, this illness is caused by a blood parasite. Malaria is transmitted by infected mosquitos; it cannot be passed directly from one person to another. The symptoms of malaria include high fever, chills, extreme lethargy and headaches. Several forms of malaria exist, one of which is very severe. It can take up to eight weeks after being stung by an infected mosquito for symptoms to develop.

Hepatitis A

This infection is generally transmitted by ingesting food or water that has been contaminated by faecal matter. The symptoms include fever, jaundice, loss of appetite and fatigue, and can appear between 15 and 50 days after infection. An effective vaccination can be administered by injection before your departure. Besides the recommended vaccine, good hygiene is important. Always wash your hands before every meal and ensure that the food and preparation area are clean.

Typhoid Fever

This illness is caused by ingesting food that has come in contact (direct or not) with an infected person's stool. Common symptoms include high fever, loss of appetite, headaches, constipation and occasionally diarrhoea, or red spots on the body. These symptoms will appear one to three weeks after infection. There is a typhoid vaccination, which must be administered in two doses to be most effective. Once again, good hygiene is necessary.

Bacterial Disorders

Sanitary conditions in Honduras are poorer than in more northerly climes, and tap water is not safe to drink because of high bacterial levels. Ice cubes made with unpurified water, or raw fruit or vegetables that are rinsed in unpurified water and not peeled before being eaten, will carry the same bacteria. Water that has been boiled or filtered is safer, and bottled water is sold in many food shops and pharmacies. Make sure the seal is not broken.

The most common symptom of bacterial disorder is a mild case of diarrhoea. This usually is not serious, but it is always annoying. Those who are afflicted should drink plenty of liquids to avoid dehydration and avoid most solid foods, especially dairy products. One litre of water mixed with one teaspoon of sugar and three teaspoons of salt will help re-establish the body's fluid balance and rehydrate those who have severe cases. Pharmacists can suggest some remedies that can help control the intestinal discomfort.

If a case of diarrhoea lasts more than a few days, consider seeking medical help. Visitors who come down with something more serious should ask their hotel or a foreign embassy to recommend a doctor.

Different people have different levels of resistance to bacteria. Those whose tolerance is weak should err on the side of caution. At the better hotels and restaurants, purified drinking water is readily available, ice cubes and salads are prepared hygienically, and visitors are generally be kept out of harm's way (though there are never any airtight guarantees).

But not everyone does all their eating and drinking at fancy hotels. At more humble spots, things to avoid include drinks that do not come bottled, drinks with ice cubes, raw seafood (cooked seafood is usually safe), salads, and fruit that may have been rinsed. At many street or market stalls, items are stored without refrigeration or kept warm at unsafe temperatures.

Those who have lived or travelled extensively in tropical places can probably let their guard down a bit. Even so, it never hurts to be aware of the potential hazards.

Water and Alcohol

In warm climates the risk of dehydration is greater, and it is therefore a good idea to drink plenty of water. Bottled water is easy to find, and many hotels provide purified water in the rooms. Heavy alcohol consumption also causes dehydration. Drink plenty of water both before and after consuming large amounts of alcohol. Among other things this will lessen the discomfort of your hangover.

The Sun

Despite its benefits, the sun causes several problems; one hazard faced by many vacationers is sunburn. Doctors warn that heavy exposure to ultraviolet rays also increases the risk of skin cancer later in life. To lessen both these risks, anyone headed for the beach should wear a hat and use sunscreen. Apply sunscreen 20 to 30 before exposure and often during exposure. Do most of your sunning in the early morning or late afternoon, avoiding the stronger midday rays, especially the first couple of days when the skin is most sensitive. Even shaded spots may be bombarded by reflected rays from the sand or water, and cloud cover provides only partial protection against ultraviolet rays. Too much exposure can cause sunstroke (symptoms include fainting, vomiting or fever), especially the first few days. Hikers and boaters should also beware, and remember to wear hats.

Pharmacies and Clinics

Most pharmacies in Honduras carry a broad range of medicines, and some drugs that are sold only by prescription in western countries, including basic antibiotics, are available over the counter. It is easy to find a pharmacy (*farmacia* in Spanish) in any of the larger towns, but a small first-aid kit can also be useful (See below).

Medical clinics are scattered throughout the country. Facilities at those outside the larger cities tend to be rudimentary. On the other hand, the cost of treatment is very low. Medical attention is more sophisticated (and more expensive) at private clinics and

Practical Information

hospitals in Tegucigalpa or San Pedro Sula.

First-aid Kit

A small first-aid kit can prove very useful. Bring along sufficient amounts of any medications you take regularly as well as a valid prescription in case you lose your supply; it can be difficult to find certain medications in the small towns. Other medications such as antimalaria pills and Imodium (or an equivalent), can also be hard to find. Finally, don't forget self-adhesive bandages, disinfectant cream or ointment, analgesics (pain-killers), antihistamines (for allergies), an extra pair of sunglasses or contact lenses, contact lens solution, and medicine for an upset stomach. Though these items are all available in Honduras, having them on hand can certainly make life easier.

Climate

Honduras has a tropical climate with warm temperatures year-round. As in any country, temperatures are highest at low altitudes and more moderate at the higher elevations. Coastal areas are often cooled by sea breezes. Tegucigalpa, situated at an altitude of about 950m, has a pleasant climate year-round with warm temperatures but rarely extreme. San Pedro Sula lies near sea level and away from the coast, making for higher average temperatures. There is only a small variation in temperature from one month to the next. December and January are the coolest months, April and May the hottest.

Rainfall patterns differ enormously by region. In most of central and southern Honduras, there are two seasons, a dry season running from November to April and a rainy season (often called *invierno*, meaning winter) from May to October, with a transitional period of several weeks at each end. Even during the rainy season there are many dry days, and it is often sunny in the morning. The rains are frequently concentrated between the mid-afternoon and early evening hours, often taking the form of brief but intense showers.

Along the Caribbean coast and the Islas de la Bahía, as well as in much of the Mosquitia, it rains throughout the year, with October and November being the rainiest months. But it rarely rains all day, nor does it rain every day. Even during the wettest season there are long periods of sunshine, although mosquitos and sandflies tend to be more abundant.

Packing

A basic rule of thumb for travel almost anywhere in the world is to take half the clothing and twice the money you expect to need. Those who plan to stay put during most of their visit can go ahead and pack that extra outfit or those heavy books. But anyone who expects to be moving around a lot may find that extra weight a burden.

Travellers should think carefully about how much they really need to take with them. The availability of fast and inexpensive laundry service in most towns makes it unnecessary to pack huge amounts of clothing. Honduras's tropical climate eliminates the need for heavy clothing. Even at high altitudes a sweater is sufficient for the cooler evenings. It is best to avoid lugging around a winter overcoat and boots. Try to leave those at home if you can get to the airport without them.

When planning your travel wardrobe, try to strike a balance between the formal and the outrageously informal. Formal clothing is rarely necessary except for business travellers, while clothing that reveals more than the usual amount of flesh is fine for the beach but less acceptable elsewhere. Aim for something in the middle.

Other things to pack include a toiletry kit (again, eliminate unnecessary items or larger sizes of things like toothpaste — the weight can add up), a small first-aid kit, any prescription drugs you normally use (do not put these in checked baggage), a sunhat and sunscreen, a camera and film, a small alarm clock, a reasonable quantity of reading material and, for news buffs, a small short-wave radio.

Two small bags can often be easier to handle than a single big one. Try to leave a little extra space for items purchased during the trip.

Safety and Security

Honduras has consistently been one of the more secure countries in Central America, having experienced little of the political violence that rocked much of the isthmus during the 1980s. It does, however, have its share of the usual assortment of pickpockets, muggers and other nasty sorts. While crime rates are not as worrisome as in some of the neighbouring countries, it does pay to take care. With a few sensible precautions, visitors can generally stay out of trouble.

The larger cities and even a few smaller towns have areas that are dangerous at night. Anyone planning to go out at night to unfamiliar areas or along unfamiliar streets should consider taking taxis. Hotel staff normally can advise which areas are safe and which are not.

Even in the daytime, visitors should use basic common sense. For example, do not wear too much expensive jewellery, do not take large amounts of money or other items of value to the beach, and when possible avoid leaving them in hotel rooms. Some hotels offer individual safety deposit boxes; others can store valuables in the hotel safe. When on the move, a money belt or pouch that fits under your clothes, away from the snip of a pair of scissors, is a good way to conceal cash, traveller's cheques, passport and airline tickets. Though these pouches can be awkward, they are more secure than pouches worn outside the clothing. It is best to avoid wandering into crowds: this can be an invitation to pickpockets or bag-snatchers. Also, cars should be parked in busy areas and the glove compartment left open to show that there is nothing inside worth stealing.

Most Hondurans are honest and hospitable, and travellers who ob-serve basic precautions are unlikely to encounter serious security problems. The national police force has been under military control for several decades, but in 1995 it was brought under civilian control. There have been numerous complaints about a lackadaisical approach to law enforcement. Foreigners who have been victims of crimes involving the theft of property may have to visit a police station to obtain a report for insurance purposes, but expecting a resolution of the case is probably just wishful thinking.

At the Beach

There are no lifeguards on Honduran beaches. A few beaches have strong undertows, that greatly increase the risk of drowning. Bathers should be cautious about going into deep water.

Also, although the temptation may often be strong to wander great distances along deserted stretches of beach, visitors should remember that there is safety in numbers, and solitary beaches may not always be immune from acts of banditry. This is especially true in Tela and Trujillo.

Practical Information

Women Travellers

Women travelling alone should bear in mind that modern feminism has made only limited progress in Honduras. They may encounter attitudes of *machismo* that are seen as anachronistic in North America or Western Europe. On occasion women may find themselves the objects of unwanted male attention. A firm but polite attitude is the best way to indicate that this interest is not shared. On the other hand, women will find many Hondurans, both male and female, to be genuinely protective and concerned for their wellbeing. The usual warnings about avoiding dark streets, rough bars and immodest clothing all apply.

Transportation

By Car

All the larger towns in Honduras, and a few of the smaller ones, are linked by a network of paved highways. It is still rather small in relation to the size of the country but does represent a vast improvement for a country that had scarcely any paved highways before the 1970s. The main roads are built to high standards, with wide lanes and often generous shoulders,

and they are generally well maintained despite rainy-season washouts in a few places. This is not always the case in the rest of Central America.

This said, there remain sizable gaps in the highway network. Travel between certain points entails either very roundabout routings or painfully slow progress along rutted, unpaved roads that test the endurance of vehicles and passengers alike. Some secondary roads, though unpaved, are wide and reasonably well kept, but many others are appalling.

The main trunk roads from south to north consist of the Carretera Panamericana running across Honduras's southern neck between El Salvador and Nicaragua; the busy road linking the Panamericana with Tegucigalpa and continuing north to San Pedro Sula and Puerto Cortés; and the Caribbean coastal highway (whose route lies quite far from the coast over most of its length) connecting San Pedro Sula with Tela, La Ceiba and Trujillo.

Other important roads run east from Tegucigalpa to Danlí and the Nicaraguan border, northeast from Tegucigalpa to Juticalpa and Catacamas, and southwest from San Pedro Sula with branches to Santa

Bárbara, the Copán region, and border points with Guatemala and El Salvador. Good paved highways run to several other points as well, and the network continues to grow.

The Honduran highway network is almost entirely two-lane except for short stretches of four-lane highway radiating from San Pedro Sula. Because of a low level of car ownership, however, traffic is usually quite light, and it is normally possible to maintain reasonable speeds despite mountainous terrain in much of the country. Although the main highways are numbered, these route numbers are rarely used in giving directions. For the most part, the main highways are well signposted, while the secondary roads are not.

Car travel in urban areas presents few problems except in the central part of Tegucigalpa, where narrow streets and heavy traffic lead to serious congestion and difficulty in finding parking.

There are no car ferries to the Islas de la Bahía. Vehicles are shipped there on cargo vessels.

Gas

Several grades of gasoline and diesel fuel are available throughout the country, though lead-free gasoline is comparatively rare.

When heading through any remote area it makes good sense to fill up beforehand; there are long stretches of road with no gas stations. Fuel prices are somewhat higher than in the United States but a good deal cheaper than in Europe. Credit cards are rarely accepted. Except in the more thinly populated areas, it is usually easy to find mechanics.

Car Rentals

Rental cars are available in Tegucigalpa, San Pedro Sula, La Ceiba and Roatán. Lists of rental agencies appear in the respective chapters of this book. Four-wheel-drive vehicles are often available and may be worth considering despite the higher cost. Rental agreements usually bar vehicles from leaving the country.

Both international and local companies are well represented. The local companies often undercut their better known competitors when reservations are made inside Honduras, though it is sometimes cheaper to reserve a vehicle through one of the big international companies before leaving home. Rental rates tend to be higher in Honduras than in the United States, and so-called weekly rates may be equal to seven one-day rentals!

When comparing rates, check to see if tax is included and if the insurance coverage has a big deductible amount. Adequate coverage may entail a hefty supplement (which is usually not covered even when paying with a gold credit card). Check also to see how many free kilometres are included in the rate. Daily rates often provide only 150 free kilometres, with heavy charges for anything beyond that.

By Taxi

Taxis are cheap throughout Honduras are abundant in all the larger towns and even some of the smaller ones (with the notable exception of Copán Ruinas, which has no taxis). Taxis are not metered, so it is important to agree on a price before setting out, especially for those who have not been in the country long enough to have an idea of prevailing rates.

Local trips rarely cost more than $2 except for longer trips in Tegucigalpa and San Pedro Sula. Airport trips tend to be costlier, and fares in Roatán are somewhat higher than on the mainland. In many places, especially the smaller towns, drivers may pick up other passengers if everyone is headed in the same general direction. This helps keep fares low, but sometimes passengers who are travelling together may be charged separately.

Legally registered taxis have different coloured licence plates from private vehicles, and their car numbers appear in large numerals on the side doors. Dome lights are rare. A "libre" sign may show in the windshield in the daytime if the taxi is free, and coloured lights may appear at night. Most taxis in Honduras are small, Japanese-made cars, some of them quite old. A few taxis based at airports and at certain hotels are larger vehicles and charge accordingly.

Many drivers offer hourly rates for travel within urban areas. This is useful for passengers who are making several stops in a short period of time.

Taking taxis on out-of-town trips may seem a huge extravagance for anyone accustomed to North American or European fare levels, but in Honduras it is a more reasonable proposition. A half-day excursion will probably cost less than renting a car, and even a full-day excursion may cost only slightly more. Included in the price is someone who knows his way around. In selecting a taxi, take a glance at the tire tread and at the general appearance of the vehicle. A decaying jalopy with bald tires may be acceptable for a five-minute urban jaunt but not for a longer trip. In negotiating a price, be certain that the driver understands where you want to go and how long you want to stay.

By Bus

Few Hondurans have cars. Most travel by bus. Buses go even to small villages. On busier intercity routes they run several times an hour. Fares are nearly always surprisingly cheap. That said, buses vary enormously in speed and comfort.

Anyone who has ever wondered what happens to old American school buses will find part of the answer in Honduras. These bright yellow vehicles, some of them with the name of a U.S. rural school district still painted on the side, form the backbone of the Honduran bus fleet, on both urban and rural routes. Often devoid of interior luggage racks or convenient exit doors, and with seating that is not well suited to passengers with long legs or weak backs, these vehicles nonetheless provide yeoman service. Fortunately, comfortable Brazilian-built vehicles are found on the main intercity routes.

Most **urban service** routes connect city centres with outlying residential or industrial districts rather than with points of interest to tourists. Most visitors will thus find few opportunities to take city buses. Considering how overcrowded they can sometimes be, this is no huge pity. Baggage-laden travellers who may consider using local transit to get to or from airports or bus terminals should take this paucity of space into account.

Intercity service is a different matter. Buses between the bigger cities are often fast and comfortable, with individual seating aboard modern vehicles and few intermediate stops, although air conditioning and toilets are provided only rarely. Tickets usually must be purchased at the terminal before boarding, and in some cases seats are reserved.

Between Tegucigalpa and San Pedro Sula and also on the Tegucigalpa La Ceiba and Tegucigalpa-Choluteca routes, there are deluxe, premium-fare services with refreshments served on board and film showings. Fast, comfortable buses, minus these extra amenities, handle regular service between most of the larger cities. Seating tends to be fairly tight, with limited legroom, even on some of the luxury services.

Bus travel to smaller cities and within rural areas relies on less comfortable vehicles that make countless stops and seem to take forever to reach their destinations. This is the case, for instance, with most services from Copán Ruinas and from Tela, two spots popular with tourists (an alternative is offered by a minibus service called North Coast Shuttle, but service is infrequent and fares are high, see p 94). On rural services fares are paid on board to a conductor, and seating is sometimes five-abreast, making for a very tight squeeze.

Several cities have central bus terminals, but in Tegucigalpa and San Pedro Sula each company operates from its own terminal. Terminals, like buses, vary in comfort.

By Train

There are scarcely any passenger trains in Honduras. The only regular route is between Puerto Cortés and Tela, with service only a couple of times a week. The scenery is interesting, but the trains themselves are slow and uncomfortable.

By Air

Civil aviation in Honduras is more developed than elsewhere in Central America, in part because some of the key destinations are islands and in part because big gaps remain in the road network. Regular flights connect Tegucigalpa, San Pedro Sula, La Ceiba, Roatán, Guanaja, Utila, Trujillo and several pboints in the Mosquitia region. La Ceiba is the main hub for domestic air service, with most flights to the Islas de la Bahía and Mosquitia radiating from there. Fares are among the cheapest in the world, for example only $19 from La Ceiba to Utila, tax included.

Flying within Honduras is safer than it was not so long ago. For many years domestic service was dominated by SAHSA and LANSA, mostly with venerable DC-3 aircraft. Neither company had an impressive safety record, and both have gone out of business.

A company called **Isleña** later became the biggest domestic carrier in Honduras. More recently it was taken over by **Grupo Taca**. It faces competition from two newer companies, **Sosa** and **Rollins Air**. At the time of writing, all three have unblemished safety records. Grupo Taca dominates the Tegucigalpa-San Pedro Sula route, with four daily flights in each direction using French-built 48-passenger ATR-42 aircraft. The most commonly used aircraft on other routes include the Canadian-built 19-passenger Twin Otter and the Czech-built 15-passenger LET-410.

Tickets may be purchased from airline ticket offices, airport tickets counters and travel agencies. Airport check-in 30 minutes before scheduled departure time is usually more than adequate. Flights are often surprisingly punctual and have even been known to leave a few minutes ahead of schedule.

By Sea

A comfortable passenger vessel operates daily between La Ceiba and Roatán and also between La Ceiba and Utila. For the moment, there are no other regular boat services within Honduras, and there are no car ferries.

Hitchhiking

Hitchhiking is not a common practice in most of Honduras, but it is more accepted in remote regions and in some small villages. Drivers often expect a small monetary contribution.

Addresses

In Spanish, as in many other languages, addresses are shown with the street name first followed by the number. Thus, for example, a street address expressed as 36 Magnolia Street in English would, in Spanish, become Calle Magnolia 36.

Some street addresses are followed by the name of the district. The abbreviation "Col." appears quite often. This stands not for colonel but for *colonia*, which means district or neighbourhood. The synonymous *barrio*, abbreviated "BO", is also used frequently. In suburban areas the terms *urbanización* or *fraccionamiento* sometimes appear. Some areas have a numbering system whereby house numbers are linked not to a particular street but to the neighbourhood as a whole. Thus one may see an address such as Casa #243, Col. Lempira, with no street given.

Often civic numbers are not used at all, and addresses are given instead by referring to the nearest cross streets. Thus an address may be given at "3ª Calle 4ª y 5ª Av.", meaning that it may be found on 3ª Calle on the block between 4ª Avenida and 5ª Avenida. In some places it is street names

Exchange Rates

US$1	=	14.74 lempiras	100 lempiras	=	US$6.78
1 euro	=	13.90 lempiras	100 lempiras	=	7.19 euros
Can$1	=	9.97 lempiras	100 lempiras	=	Can$10.03
£1	=	22.23 lempiras	100 lempiras	=	£4.50
1 DM	=	7.11 lempiras	100 lempiras	=	14.07 DM
1 FF	=	2.12 lempiras	100 lempiras	=	47.18 FF
1 SF	=	8.84 lempiras	100 lempiras	=	11.31 SF
1 guilder	=	6.31 lempiras	100 lempiras	=	15.85 guilders
1000 lire	=	7.18 lempiras	1 lempira	=	139 lire
100 BF	=	34.46 lempiras	1 lempira	=	2.90 BF
100 pesetas	=	8.36 lempiras	1 lempira	=	11.97 pesetas
¥100	=	13.63 lempiras	1 lempira	=	¥7.34

that are not used, with directions given instead in reference to local landmarks. An address may appear, for instance, as "Banco de Occidente 1 cuadra abajo", meaning one block below the bank. This is not as common as in Nicaragua or Costa Rica.

Sometimes addresses are given as the distance along a highway. An address shown as "Km 4, Carretera a Tela" lies 4Km along the highway to Tela.

Money and Banking

The Honduran currency is the **lempira**, named for the 16th-century Indigenous chief who resisted the Spanish conquest. There are bills for 500 (purple), 100 (orange), 50 (blue), 20 (green), 10 (black), 5 (brown), 2 (purple) and 1 (red) lempira and coins for 50, 20, 10 and 5 centavos. Many of them are old and badly worn. The abbreviation for lempira is a capital L, usually followed by a period or with a strike through it.

Prices in Dollars

Prices in this guide are shown in U.S. dollars. There are two reasons for this. The first is that many readers are already familiar with the U.S. dollar and have a good grasp of the value of something expressed in this currency. The second reason is that prices expressed in dollars have remained more constant over the years than prices expressed in lempiras. Inflation, which in 1995 ran at an average rate of about 2% a month, has been balanced by devaluations.

Though prices are shown here in dollars, **most goods and services must be paid for in lempiras**. Exceptions are rooms at higher-priced hotels, whose rates are often set in dollars, and most tours. Even in these cases, customers have the option of paying in lempiras. Taxi drivers are often willing to accept dollars for airport runs or longer trips, and many restaurants and medium-range hotels will do the same, although not always at favourable exchange rates.

Exchanging Money

Official exchange rates are published each day in the newspapers. Banks, casas de cambio and airport exchange counters give better rates than hotels, and most of them change traveller's cheques with little fuss; passports are usually required. Some banks do not handle currency exchange, particularly in the smaller towns, and it is more difficult to change money on weekends and holidays.

In the larger cities, freelance currency dealers cluster on the street at fixed spots. This is referred to as the *mercado negro* (black market), although it appears to be officially tolerated. These dealers wave calculators and large wads of bills, and they pay a marginally higher rate, usually 1% or 2% above the official rate, for U.S. dollars in cash. (Visitors should give wide berth to anyone who purports to offer a substantially higher rate.)

Most of these freelance dealers tend to be honest in counting money, but some of them try to offer less than the going rate for dollars, especially at times when the banks are closed or when only a small amount is being exchanged. If the amount being offered appears unreasonably low, it is best just to walk away. This will sometimes bring a higher offer. Freelance currency dealers abound at border crossings, and they often take advantage of visitors' poor knowledge of the going rates. It is best to change only a small amount with them. In fact most visitors, unless they are truly confident of their

street smarts, would do well to confine most of their dealings to banks or *casas de cambio*. The extra 1% or 2% may not be worth the risk. Moreover, freelance dealers rarely accept traveller's cheques, and if they do it is usually at a poor rate.

It can sometimes be tricky to change lempiras back to dollars except at an unfavourable rate, but even this is likely to be better than the rates that can be obtained outside Honduras. A sensible approach is to limit the quantities of money converted to lempiras in the first place and to use leftover lempiras to pay the departure tax and to buy duty-free goods or gifts before departure.

Canadians and Europeans bound for Honduras are strongly urged to take most of their money in U.S. dollars, in cash or traveller's cheques or both. Canadian dollars, pounds sterling and German marks can be exchanged at branches of Lloyds Bank in Tegucigalpa and San Pedro Sula, although at unfavourable rates. Most other European currencies are nearly impossible to exchange in Honduras. U.S. dollars are far more readily accepted. People from other parts of the world are already well accustomed to the idea of travelling with U.S. dollars and do not need

reminding of the importance of this.

Sending Money

There are several ways to have money sent to you in Honduras from abroad. Telegraphic transfers from bank to bank are an old standby, but they usually take several days and can be expensive and unreliable. Western Union money transfers are faster and more reliable but also more costly. A more sensible solution (unless your accounts are heavily overdrawn or you have lost your card) is to have someone make a deposit to your bank account or credit card account; you can then draw the money directly using an automatic teller machine or obtaining a cash advance through a bank teller.

Should it become necessary to have money sent from home, banks can handle this by telegraphic transfer, but a faster, cheaper and more reliable way to transfer funds is to have the money deposited into a credit card account and withdrawn in the form of a cash advance.

Credit Cards

Credit cards can also come in handy. They are accepted by many hotels and by some restaurants and shops.

Practical Information

Inflation and Exchange Rates

For many decades, the Honduran lempira was maintained at a fixed exchange rate of two to the U.S. dollar, giving it a value of $0.50 US. Once, during a period of financial instability in the 1950s, the central bank imported large quantities of $0.50 US coins to replace one-lempira notes as a way of bolstering confidence in the local currency. After this crisis blew over, most of these coins were shipped north and lempira notes were put back into circulation. Tight fiscal policy and low inflation kept this parity sustainable until the early 1980s, when inflation raced ahead of U.S. levels and a sizable black market developed in U.S. currency. Finally, the central bank relented and began a series of devaluations. By early 1996 the lempira was worth only $0.10 US, and in 1999 it slipped below $0.07 US. During most of the 1990s, devaluations have been intended roughly to match the differences between U.S. and Honduran inflation rates, but the pace of devaluation slowed. In the latter part of the decade prices expressed in dollars were creeping up at more than 4% a year. Even today, however, the Honduran 20-centavo and 50-centavo coins are the same size as their $0.10 US and $0.25 US counterparts, a throwback to the old two-to-one parity.

They can also be used to pay for car rentals or airline tickets. Visa and MasterCard are the most widely accepted, followed by American Express.

These same cards can come to the rescue of travellers who run short of cash. Some bank branches and automatic teller machines provide cash advances. **Credomatic**, which processes **Visa** and **MasterCard** transactions for Honduran banks, can help in case of problems and will also take reports of lost or stolen cards:

Tegucigalpa
☎*238-6570*

San Pedro Sula
☎*557-4350*

La Ceiba
☎*443-0668*

It is essential to bring your passport as well as your credit card. **American Express** cardholders should check before leaving home about arrangements for obtaining cash advances or transfers in Honduras.

Automatic Teller Machines (ATMs)

Automatic teller machines have been popping up in Honduras, mostly in larger cities but also in some of the smaller towns. They are normally located at banks or gas stations

and are usually accessible at all hours. Bank cards and credit cards issued by many banks outside Honduras are accepted at Honduran ATMs, but it is not a sure bet. While ATMs can be a useful way of obtaining cash (in lempiras) without having to carry it from home or worry about finding an exchange dealer, backup plans are essential. Some cards may be rejected, and no machine is infallible. Also, at some ATM locations there may be security problems.

A useful alternative, especially for large sums of money, is to take a cash advance (in Spanish, disposión en efectivo) at a bank. Some banks, but not all, provide this service. Ask one of the employees seated at a desk and then go to the teller with your credit card and passport. Normally it is quite a simple procedure. You receive cash in lempiras, and your account is debited in your home currency.

Taxes

A sales tax of 12% applies to many goods and services in Honduras. This includes hotel rooms and restaurant meals. An additional 4% tax applies on hotel rooms, for a total tax of 16%. Cheaper hotels tend to include the tax in their rates, while more expensive hotels add it on top of their quoted rates. International air travellers face a $25 departure tax, while at some airports there is a $2 departure tax on domestic flights. At retail establishments the prices shown normally include the tax.

For purposes of honest comparison, **all hotel rates shown in this guidebook already include the tax**. The same applies to restaurants and bars.

Tipping

Tipping in Honduras is practised less widely than in North America but more widely than in Europe. Taxi drivers do not expect tips, but a small amount is appreciated if the driver helps with baggage or takes you to an out-of-the-way or hard-to-find spot. Bellhops should get about $0.50 per bag, but this will vary according to the size and weight of the bags and the distance they have to be carried. Chambermaids should get about $0.50 a day, but again this can vary.

At restaurants and bars, an amount equal to about 10% of the bill is usually more than adequate. A larger percentage can be offered if the service was exceptionally good, if the amount of the bill is small, or if payment is made by credit card, in which case management will take part of the tip. At some restaurants a 10% tip is added automatically to the bill.

Language

Spanish is the sole official language of Honduras and is spoken nearly everywhere. In villages and small towns in some more remote parts of the country, Indigenous languages are also spoken. English remains the majority language on the Islas de la Bahía, settled during the British protectorate, although many Spanish-speakers from the mainland have migrated there in recent years, and most people are bilingual. On the mainland itself, English is spoken at some hotels and restaurants, by members of the country's educated elite, and by emigrants who have returned from the United States.

Apart from the Islas de la Bahía, anyone who steps outside the cocoon of a tour group or resort hotel will almost certainly be thrust into situations where a knowledge of Spanish is useful. That does not mean they will be totally lost if they do not speak Spanish. What it does mean is that they will have to show patience, grace, good humour and the odd bit of ingenuity. Sign language combined with a few key words is often useful, and hav-

Practical Information

ing pen and paper at the ready can help in some situations. The glossary at the end of this guide may come in handy.

Pronunciations

In a few places in this book, pronunciations of some difficult words or names are shown phonetically, with accented syllables in upper case. "A" is pronounced as in cat, "ay" rhymes with day, "ee" rhymes with see, "oo" rhymes with too, and "ow" rhymes with cow. The "ah" sound does not exist in Spanish; some people imagine, mistakenly, that it makes them sound erudite. The letter "j" (as well as "g" when followed by an "e" or "i") has a guttural sound not found in English; "kh" will be used here to show that sound.

Mail and Telecommun- ications

Mail

Postal service in Honduras is exceedingly slow. Both inbound and outbound letters can take many weeks to reach their destinations.

Telephone

Telephone service is provided by a government-owned company called **Hondutel**, which operates telephone centres for local and long distance calls throughout the country, including most small towns. Hours of operation vary. To place a call at an Hondutel office, it is necessary to give a clerk the number being called and, usually, a deposit for the desired number of minutes. When a line is free, normally after a few minutes' wait, the caller will be directed to one of several telephone booths along the wall, which are identified by number. Accounts are settled after the call is completed.

International rates tend to be quite high, running at more than $2 a minute to the United States, with a three-minute minimum, and much higher to most other countries outside Central America. It may often be cheaper to call collect. Telephone subscribers in the United States can use special toll-free numbers to place collect calls to the United States, with calls routed through a U.S. operator. These numbers are 800-0123 for AT&T, 800-0122 for MCI, 800-0120 for Netcom and 800-0121 for Sprint. For the moment, similar arrangements do not

exist with other companies or for other countries.

International calls placed from hotels often entail hefty surcharges. Before calling, it is best to check with the hotel operator to see how high the charge will be.

There are very few public telephones in Honduras, and those that exist are mostly in the larger cities. They require 20-centavo or 50-centavo coins. The new public phones are equipped to operate with prepaid cards, but there's just one hitch: prepaid cards were not available long after the new units were installed and it is uncertain whether they will be accepted for international calls.

All telephone numbers have seven digits. There are no city codes or area codes. The international telephone code for Honduras is 504. To call Honduras from abroad, first enter the international access code, then 504, then the seven-digit local number.

Fax

Fax machines have come into common use in Honduras. Many hotels can provide fax service for their guests. Some Hondutel offices and stationery stores also provide fax service. though only the

Hondutel offices in Tegucigalpa and San Pedro Sula offer international fax service.

Internet

A select group of Hondurans have latched onto the Internet with great enthusiasm, and several of them have opened Internet cafés (the café part is usually an afterthought) where members of the public can have access to computers and Internet links for just a few dollars an hour (often there is a half-hour minimum). Some also offer to receive E-mail messages, normally for a charge of about $1. Internet cafés are found in nearly all towns that attract significant numbers of tourists, and details are provided in the respective chapters covering these towns. A handful of hotels make Internet services available to their guests.

Accommodations

A full range of hotel accommodations, from the deluxe to the dismal, is available in Tegucigalpa, San Pedro Sula, the Islas de la Bahía and Copán Ruinas. Even in many less travelled places, there is a decent choice. For instance, there are comfortable places to stay in Choluteca and Jícaro Galán in the south and, along the Caribbean coast, in Trujillo, La

Ceiba, Tela, and near Puerto Cortés. A frequent complaint among visitors to Central America has been the dismal state of lodgings in many smaller towns, particularly in Nicaragua and parts of El Salvador. This is less true in Honduras, where standards seem generally to be higher, although not everywhere, of course.

Hotels

In choosing hotels that appear in this guidebook, we have looked for places in varied price categories that offer reasonable levels of appeal, good standards of cleanliness and convenient locations. We have not attempted to provide comprehensive lists, preferring to take a more selective approach. Prices that appear here include taxes and were valid at the time each establishment was visited. Needless to say, they are subject to change.

Many hotels and *hospedajes*, in big towns and small, have been left out because often they are places that are seriously lacking in comfort or charm. This does not mean that travellers who want to stay overnight in a town for which we provide no hotel listing should immediately give up on the idea, but it does mean they

may have to settle for something rather basic.

Hospedajes and Hotelitos

The term *hospedaje* is often used to designate a modest and very simple hotel. There is nothing pejorative about the term, and some *hospedajes* are reasonably pleasant, but many really are quite bleak. The same applies to the term *hotelito*. In certain towns it would be nice to have a choice extending beyond what these terms imply but this isn't always possible. Some of the better ones are listed in this guidebook.

Camping

Formal campgrounds are not very common in Honduras, though several of the national parks have areas set aside for campers with only basic amenities that may include drinking water, latrines and cooking grills, but sometimes not even that. Trailer and RV parks are virtually unknown.

Restaurants

Dining out is one of the pleasures of travel, in Honduras as elsewhere. Although there are many restaurants where visitors can eat well, it would be an exaggeration to say that Honduras is a place people visit specifically because of the food. For many well-to-do Hondurans, a restaurant meal means sitting down to a big steak. This is reflected in the menus even at some of the better spots, which often lack originality, sticking mostly to simple, tried-and-true preparations. Still, there are interesting regional specialties to sample (notably the wonderful coconut-scented seafood soups on the Caribbean coast) and enough good restaurants around that the intrepid gourmet will not leave disappointed.

Toward the lower end of the price range, there exist countless small restaurants and *comedores* offering ordinary fare at very reasonable prices. At many public markets, rows of stalls offer varied meals, while customers often sit all together at long benches and tables. Visitors can simply point to something that looks appealing in a steaming cauldron, and it will be served. Chinese restaurants dot the landscape in the larger towns and even some of the smaller ones. Although many have broad menus, customers at the cheaper spots often seem to prefer the economical and filling fried rice or chow mein dishes with chicken or shrimp.

Menus are nearly always in Spanish only except at some of the fancier spots, where English may be added. Besides salt, condiments usually found on restaurant tables include hot pepper sauce (*salsa picante*), with Worcestershire sauce (called *salsa inglesa*, or English sauce) sometimes an added option.

Bread is an area that needs some work: even some of the best restaurants offer limp, industrial-style dinner rolls, served with margarine rather than butter. Hondurans of most social classes, however, are more likely to accompany their meals with pancake-shaped cornmeal *tortillas*, which tend to be thicker and doughier in Central America than the version many travellers will recall from Mexico. Fresh vegetables are lamentably rare except, it seems, at the more expensive spots and at Chinese restaurants.

Fast-food culture has not yet caught on in a big way, but several of the big U.S. chains, notably Burger King, Wendy's and Pizza Hut, have established a small presence, as has Pollo Campero, a Guatemala-based chain of fried-chicken restaurants. For hamburgers, however, a better bet may be the Honduran chain Bigos, with many branches in Tegucigalpa and a few elsewhere. Although not as

slick as its U.S. rivals, Bigos simply has better hamburgers and offers customers the option of beer with their meals.

Honduran Cuisine

The *plato típico* (typical meal) offered at many restaurants and *comedores* consists of varied combinations of any or all of the following: a small piece of steak, a fried or scrambled egg, salty white cheese, black beans, fried plantain or sweet banana, heavy cream, avocado and, in a few cases, a slice of grilled mortadella. Variations on this theme are offered morning, noon and night, with a heavier emphasis on eggs in the morning and on meat thereafter. The *plato típico* is usually accompanied by *tortillas* rather than bread, and a cup of steaming coffee is often included in the price, which may be surprisingly modest.

Pinchos, or brochettes, are a popular item at many restaurants, consisting of pieces of meat grilled on skewers with slices of onion, sweet pepper and tomato. Although beef is most common, it may occasionally be substituted by chicken, pork sausage or shrimp. *Pupusas* are a Salvadoran-inspired snack food (good for meals too) made from cornmeal *tortilla* stuffed with cheese, black beans, pork rinds or other fillings and topped with pickled cabbage. The meatless varieties provide a good respite for vegetarians, as do *baleadas*, concoctions of cornmeal, beans and cheese. Popular soups (seen more commonly in private homes and at market stalls than in formal restaurants) include tripe soup, called *mondongo*, and a meat and vegetable soup called *tapado*.

Nobody should leave Honduras without sampling Garífuna-style seafood soups. The Garífuna are a people who inhabit villages along the Caribbean coast, and they do wonders with rich, coconut-scented broths filled with fish, shrimp, crab or other seafood, either mixed or alone. Fortunately, the popularity of these soups (which are often hefty enough to constitute a full meal) has spread far and wide, and they may be found at restaurants in many parts of the country. (The Garífuna are also noted for their coconut bread, which ought to be making its way into more restaurants.)

Desserts are rather limited, but only those who are morbidly obsessed with concerns about saturated fat should turn up their noses at *flan de coco*, egg custard with coconut.

Drinks

Coffee is an important crop in Honduras, and it is also a popular drink. Unlike some of their neighbours in other coffee-producing countries, Hondurans seem to be pretty good at brewing the stuff. Coffee here is dark and rich, not at all watery, and it is served *negro* (black) or *con leche* (with milk).

Soft drinks are also very popular. The usual international favourites are available, along with banana soda which, to put it gently, is an acquired taste. Among the less sugary flavours are grape (*uva*) and ginger ale (called by its brand name, Canada Dry). *Agua mineral* (mineral water) normally refers to carbonated water even if it does not come from a mineral source.

Honduras has four locally produced beers. *Nacional* and *Salva Vida* are watery, American-style lagers, while *Imperial* and *Port Royal* are richer and fuller in body. (The author's favourite is *Port Royal*. Lest we be accused of commercial favouritism, let us point out that all these beers come from the same brewery.) Beer is served at most restaurants and is generally inexpensive.

Wine selections (where they exist) tend to be rather modest, although a few restaurants offer some decent Chilean or Spanish vintages. Prices of wines are quite high because of import duties. The same applies to liquors imported from outside Central America. Rum is the most popular liquor in Honduras, and the locally produced *Flor de Caña* is reasonably good, although some people prefer *Botrán* rum from Guatemala. Dominican and Puerto Rican rums are also widely available.

Entertainment

Evening leisure activities in most places in Honduras centre around restaurants and bars, but there are other options as well, especially in the bigger cities.

Cinemas present a variety of American films, many of them in the original English version with subtitles or dubbed in Spanish. There are also a smattering of European or Latin American films. Admission is cheap.

In Tegucigalpa and San Pedro Sula there are occasional **cultural performances**, including plays, classical concerts and dance recitals. Tegucigalpa also is noted for **peña** shows, with politically tinged folk songs and satire presented in intimate surroundings. In several

Practical Information

places along the Caribbean coast **Garífuna dance troupes** give weekend shows at local dance halls. There are **discotheques** in the larger towns, which come to life mostly on weekends.

Fútbol

Lovers of soccer (known as football everywhere outside North America) should have a good time of it. *Fútbol* is practically the national religion, and there is scarcely a village in the country without a heavily used playing field. For the dates and times of professional matches, check the newspapers or, better still, ask taxi drivers or hotel clerks when their favourite team is playing. Tickets are inexpensive, so try for the better seats.

Festivals

Most towns and villages in Honduras have annual local festivals marking the day of the local patron saint, often with processions and dances and nearly always with plenty of drinking and revelry. Some towns put on a better show than others, and the celebrations may stretch several days, beginning before or ending after the actual saint's day.

In some cases the festivities are in honour of an important local commodity (for example, the potato festival in La Esperanza the fourth week of July, the corn festival in Danlí the last week of August, or the mango and mamey festival in Yuscarán the third Sunday in June).

A full list of these festivals, titled *Listado General de las Ferias, Festivales y Otras Celebraciones Populares de Honduras*, is available from the Instituto Hondureño de Turismo.

Shopping

Honduran handicrafts are greatly varied, and many items are cheerful and well crafted. Perhaps the most commonly found items are carvings made of mahogany or other tropical woods, often with a Mayan motif. These range from small wall hangings to enormous pieces of furniture carved with a wealth of detail. Visitors to Honduras may find some of the designs unappealing, but the execution of the work is generally excellent.

Another trademark category of items are the ceramic figurines depicting roosters and other animals. In fact, the rooster has been adopted as a symbol of Honduran handicrafts in general. Other ceramic items include vases and similar objects of glazed pottery presenting Mayan imagery or colourful abstract designs.

Among other objects produced by Honduran artisans are many items of silver or bronze jewellery, leather items ranging from simple belts to elaborate handbags, reproductions of ancient Mayan stone carvings, baskets in a variety of shapes and sizes, straw hats, colourful hand-painted wooden objects presenting rural scenes, and of course the naive paintings for which Honduras is famous. Some of the paintings are quite small, making them easy to carry.

In addition to Honduran items, some handicrafts shops also carry selections of Guatemalan and Salvadoran handicrafts, including wonderful highland Indian textiles, decorative beach towels, and hand-painted jewellery boxes.

Handicrafts can be found in market or street stalls and also in some city centre or hotel gift shops. Places to look are indicated in this book in the chapters covering each of the regions of Honduras. When buying at a public market or from street merchants, it is essential to bargain to obtain the best price. It is easier to get a discount when making more than one purchase at the same place.

Honduran rum is also a good buy and costs no more at grocery stores than at airport duty-free shops. Honduran coffee of excellent quality is sold in foil bags at the airport departure lounges in San Pedro Sula and Tegucigalpa.

Press and Broadcasting

Honduras has five daily newspapers, all in Spanish and all published in Tegucigalpa or San Pedro Sula. All are available in the larger towns on the day of publication. *La Prensa* is arguably the best of the Honduran papers, with the broadest political and economic coverage, followed by *El Heraldo*. *La Tribuna* has tended to put more of an emphasis on social news. *Tiempo* has the most interesting editorial page. *El Nuevo Día* is the newest of the five. There is no financial paper, but *La Prensa* and *El Heraldo* publish interesting financial supplements on Tuesdays. These papers are all printed in tabloid format and are remarkably similar in their focus, with an emphasis on local political disputes, criminal acts, road accidents and social news. All carry selections of international news as well.

Honduras This Week is published in English each Saturday and provides, among other things, an indispensable roundup of cultural events. It also contains interesting commentaries on the passing scene in Honduras. It is available at some shops and hotels.

There are countless radio stations in Honduras, and this is the most pervasive means of communication, reaching far more people than television or newspapers. There are several television channels in Honduras, and these are supplemented by channels from the United States and Mexico that are distributed by cable. Many hotels offer a small selection of U.S. channels, often, but not always, including CNN International.

Miscellaneous

Business Hours

Office hours vary in Honduras but tend to start early, with some government offices opening as early as 7am and most other offices open by 8am, with closing times ranging from 3:30pm to 6pm. The most common time for lunch break is between noon and 1pm. Some offices close completely at lunch time, while others stay open but with limited service.

Many Hondurans tend to be more casual than people from northern latitudes in matters of punctuality, and meetings often start late. It is always a good idea to bring reading material.

Shopping hours vary tremendously. Stalls in public markets often open shortly after dawn and may start shutting by early afternoon, especially in rural areas, while in other places they may stay open until dusk. Regular shops open around 8am and close between 5pm and 6pm, although a few, including many pharmacies, stay open until later. Saturday hours tend to be shorter, with closing times between noon and 2pm. Many shops are shut all day Sunday.

Banking hours also vary from place to place. Opening times are usually 8am or 9am and closing hours between 3pm and 5pm, with many bank branches closing for an hour or two at midday. In a few places banks also open Saturday mornings.

Holidays

Official holidays are:

January 1
New Year's Day

Variable
Easter Sunday and the three days preceding it

April 14
Day of the Americas

May 1
Labour Day

September 15
Independence Day

October 3
Francisco Morazán Day

October 12
Christopher Columbus
Day

October 21
Army Day

December 25
Christmas Day

Several of these holidays, notably Day of the Americas and the three October holidays, are less important than the others.

Time Zone

Honduras stays on Central Standard Time year-round. This is one hour behind Eastern Standard Time in North America and two hours behind Eastern Daylight Time. It is six hours behind Greenwich Mean Time, seven hours behind Winter Time in most of western Europe, and eight hours behind European Summer Time.

Weights and Measures

Honduras uses a mixture of metric and U.S. measures though some old Central American measures are also used occasionally. These include the *vara*, a measure of distance slightly less than a metre, and the *manzana*, a measure of area roughly equal to a city block.

Electricity

For electrical appliances, nearly all of Honduras uses the 60-cycle, 110-volt system, the same as in North America. Appliances sold in North America can be used without voltage converters. But take note: a few localities, including parts of Tegucigalpa, were using the 220-volt system. Most of these have been converted to 110 volts, but it is important to check before using any of your own electrical equipment. Wall sockets take the flat-pronged plugs without the third, round grounding prong. Anything with three-pronged plugs may require a plug adaptor, available at hardware stores. European appliances require voltage converters **and** plug.

Weights and Measures

Weights
1 pound (lb) = 454 grams (g)

Linear Measure
1 kilogram (kg) = 2.2 pounds (lbs)
1 inch = 2.2 centimetres (cm)
1 foot (ft) = 30 centimetres (cm)
1 mile = 1.6 kilometres (km)
1 kilometres (km) = 0.63 miles (mi)
1 metre (m) = 39.37 inches (in)

Land Measure
1 acre = 0.4 hectares (ha)
1 hectare (ha) = 2.471 acres

Volume Measure
1 U.S. gallon (gal) = 3.79 litres
1 U.S. gallon (gal) = 0.83 imperial gallons

Temperature
To convert °F into °C:
subtract 32, divide by 9, multiply by 5

To convert °C into °F:
multiply by 9, divide by 5, add 32

Outdoors

Among the outdoor activities for which Honduras has enjoyed the most widespread fame are the fabulous diving and snorkelling off the Islas de la Bahía, endowed with reefs that are part of a series of formations second in extent only to the Great Barrier Reef of Australia.

With its long Caribbean coastline (as well as a rather less enticing Pacific shore), Honduras also boasts many kilometres of idyllic white sand beaches. Both along the coasts and deep in the interior are national parks and nature reserves, most of them still in early stages of development, that will enchant bird-watchers, hikers and many others besides.

Honduras is just beginning to reveal its rich storehouse of rivers, mountains and coastal marshes that are well suited to so-called ecotourism. We tend here to shy away from the term ecotourism because it suggests that groups of tourists who go trampling through sensitive zones that shelter rare animal or plant species are somehow more virtuous and more environmentally beneficent than the lazier sorts who just like to hang around beaches. Yes, many of the people who visit nature reserves behave with suitable restraint, and yes, it is worth emphasizing that tourism-related revenues can help stave off the depradations of logging or slash-and-burn agriculture, but at the same time it should be borne in mind that ecotourism has become an important commercial buzzword and that certain types of "ecotourism" are anything but ecologically helpful. Any visitor who is enticed by brochures that use this term too liberally should take a closer look.

Parks, beaches and various other sites

for outdoor activities are outlined in the chapters covering each region of the country, but here is a brief summary of what to expect.

Outdoor Activities

Diving and Snorkelling

The Islas de la Bahía got a head start over the rest of Honduras in matters of tourism development. This is due mostly to the coral reefs that are part of a formation extending all the way from Belize. Divers have been visiting the Islas de la Bahía for decades to enjoy what connaisseurs have long recognized as some of the finest dive sites in the world. Beginners are just as welcome as experienced divers. For safety reasons, it is not a good idea to go diving without first having taken a course. Dive shops throughout the islands offer courses year-round, including four-day courses leading to certification. Prices are very reasonable, and it is not normally necessary to reserve in advance.

Where there is diving, snorkelling is usually not very far away.

Snorkelling requires no special training and no expensive equipment. Snorkels, masks and fins are available for rent at many dive shops.

Beaches and Swimming

The finest beaches in Honduras – some of the finest in the world, really – are situated along the Caribbean coast, with fine white sand, swaying palms and gentle waves. Of these, some of the best are on the outskirts of Tela and Trujillo, while others lie just east of La Ceiba or just west of Puerto Cortés. There are fine beaches also on the Islas de la Bahía; these tend to be somewhat smaller.

The Pacific shoreline is shorter and rockier. Sandy beaches, where they exist, tend to be of the dark volcanic variety. Probably the most enticing spot on the Pacific side for swimming or beachcombing is Amapala, on Isla del Tigre, which has several small, secluded beaches (see p 196).

Rivers and lakes also offer swimming opportunities, most notably Lago de Yojoa in the central part of the country. In several places scattered around Honduras, river chan-

nels (either on their own or with human assistance) have formed pools suitable for swimming. Such spots may be found in or near Trujillo, Danlí, the Pulhapanzak falls, Santa Bárbara and Gracias. They are usually referred to in Spanish as *balnearios*. The pools near Gracias are called Balneario Aguas Termales and, as the name suggests, the water is heated naturally. There are also hot springs near Trujillo; the pools there are suitable for soaking but not for swimming. Finally, most excursions that offer river rafting or hiking next to rivers also offer bathing opportunities.

Nature Reserves

As mentioned above, we prefer to avoid the often deceptive term ecotourism, but visitors looking for what the term implies in its more positive sense will be far from disappointed. Honduras has been developing a broad network of nature reserves and national parks on mountain, river and sea, all with rich varieties of plant and animal species whose protection helped motivate their creation. Central America, with just 1% of the planet's land area, accounts for about 10% of all living species, some of them endangered. Many of the parks cover mountainous terrain and present different types of vegetation depending on elevation, including cloud forest near the top.

People familiar with national parks in wealthier countries, with their well developed road networks, carefully signposted trails, selections of food and lodgings, and general holiday camp atmosphere, will be struck immediately bythe relatively pristine and primitive state of the Honduran park network. For the most part, facilities for visitors at parks and reserves are very limited (some parks have visitors' centres at main entrances, while other parks are scarcely even signposted). Some supposedly protected areas have fallen to encroachment from agriculture or logging. But Honduras has the beginnings of what seems destined to become some of the finest nature tourism in Central America and beyond.

National Parks

Parque Nacional La Tigra, near Tegucigalpa (see p 80)

Reserva Natural Monserrat, near Yuscarán (see p 82)

Parque Nacional Cusuco, near San Pedro Sula (see p 109)

Parque Nacional Santa Bárbara, near Santa Bárbara (see p 110)

Parque Nacional Celaque, near Gracias (see p 110)

Parque Nacional Punta Sal, near Tela (see p 134)

Refugio de Vida Silvestre Punta Izopo, near Tela (see p 135)

Jardin Botánico Lancetilla, near Tela (see p 135)

Parque Nacional Cuero y Salado, near La Ceiba (see p 136)

Parque Nacional Pico Bonito, near La Ceiba (see p 137)

Parque Nacional Capiro-Calentura, near Trujillo (see p 137)

Refugio de Vida Silvestre Laguna Guaymoreto, near Trujillo (see p 138)

Parque Nacional La Muralla, in Olancho department (see p 184)

Parque Nacional Sierra de Agalta, in Olancho department (see p 186)

Biósfera del Río Plátano, in the Mosquitia (see p 186)

Outdoors

The list above is by no means exhaustive: additional reserves and parks have been created. But it does outline the spots that are most accessible and most interesting. Each of them is presented later in this guide. The Cusuco, Celaque, Pico Bonito and Sierra de Agalta national parks all encompass areas of cloud forest at higher elevations. The Punta Sal and Cuero y Salado national parks face the sea and offer enticing beaches in addition to rich varieties of marine, bird and plant life. The Biósfera del Río Plátano is the most important draw in the Mosquitia, with its rivers, varied ecosystems and indigenous villages.

Hiking

Many of the parks listed above cover mountainous terrain and offer networks of hiking trails lead to fine vistas and access to areas of interest to naturalists. Some of these parks have seen scarcely any human development, while others have simple campsites and visitor facilities. La Tigra, although not among the bigger parks, has some of the better de-veloped and more challenging trails. Cusuco, Celaque and Pico Bonito also offer good hiking possibilities, while Santa Bárbara, Capiro-Calentura and La Muralla all have great potential but only limited networks of existing trails. Hikers should, of course, wear solid footwear, bring extra clothing for higher altitudes, and carry an adequate supply of water.

River Rafting

Honduras is something of a paradise for river rafting, with plenty of options for those who enjoy the white-knuckle excitement of white-water rafting as well as for those who prefer to paddle sedately past luxuriant vegetation or varied wildlife habitats. Several of the tour companies listed in this chap-ter offer rafting programs, including transport, guides and the provision of kayaks. Ríos Honduras, based in La Ceiba, is the acknowledged specialist in the field, with the greatest variety of programs.

Río Cangrejal, near La Ceiba, is the most popular spot in Honduras for white-water rafting, and several tour companies offer single-day programs there. Río Sico, at the edge of La Mosquitia, and Río Plátano, deep inside La Mosquitia, are other favourites; these rivers have some light rapids but also long stretches where participants can relax amid vivid scenery as part of a multi-day program. Other rivers with organized rafting tours include Río Chamelecón near San Pedro Sula, Río Mame deep inland from La Ceiba behind the coastal mountains, and Río Humuya flowing from the Cajón dam near Lago de Yojoa.

Several rivers in La Mosquitia, besides those already mentioned, offer possibilities, although special arrangements are usually necessary. These include Río Patuco and Río Coco.

As always, river conditions vary with rainfall. Too much rainfall, and the river can become too wild for safe passage. Too little rainfall, and the river practically dies. Specialized tour companies can advise on the best times of year for particular rivers.

Cycling

Cycling is not often regarded as a leisure activity in Honduras, although it is a common means of transport in many rural zones as well as in some of the larger towns, including Puerto Cortés, La Ceiba and Danlí. Long distance cycling is seen as exotic, but it is by no means unheard of. Some stretches of highway have paved shoulders, and on most of the highway network (the Tegucigalpa-San Pedro Sula road being an obvious exception) traffic is light enough that cyclists can enjoy a good measure of peace and safety.

Since most of Honduras is mountainous, cyclists venturing beyond the coastal plains must be

in good shape. Bear in mind also that many secondary roads are poorly surfaced. Some rural buses have roof racks that can accommodate bicycles, but most do not, meaning this is not a reliable means of supplementing pedal power. Simple bicycles are available for rent in the principal resort areas. Fancier bicycles are a target for thieves and should be watched or stowed carefully.

Boating, Tennis and Golf

Honduras is a poor country, and these activities are accessible only to a very small number of people. The same seems to apply even to visitors, which means that somebody looking to centre a holiday around golfing, for instance, should be looking elsewhere. Some luxury resorts make certain types of water craft available to guests, and a handful of hotels boast tennis courts. There are nine-hole golf courses at San Pedro Sula and La Ceiba.

Outfitters

Honduras's attractions include spots that are hard to reach and activities that require special equipment or difficult

logistical arrangements. This is where specialized tour companies can make a real difference. There are wild and beautiful parts of the country that even self-reliant travellers will have trouble reaching otherwise.

Tour companies operate programs that can take visitors to secluded nature reserves or to remote zones such as the Mosquitia. Others offer specialized activities such as river rafting or railway trips through banana country. Most also offer programs that stick to the beaten track, handling arrangements for travellers who prefer not to do it on their own.

Because the number of visitors to Honduras is still fairly small, many tours operate only at irregular intervals and only when a minimum number of participants has been assembled. Often the tour company will not know until a few days before the planned departure whether a particular program will be operating, and for single-day programs they may not know until the night before. Most tour companies deal with travel agencies or wholesalers abroad as well as with local walk-in business.

Tour groups are mostly small. Participants travelling to more remote spots should be aware that lodgings and other facilities may be more rudimentary than those to which they are accustomed. Before paying it is important to verify if meals, drinks and admission fees are included in the price. It rarely hurts to shop around to compare prices and offerings. Tour prices are usually quoted in U.S. dollars, with the option of payment in lempiras. Prices tend to be well beyond the reach of budget travellers, though they usually stand up well when compared to similar programs in other countries.

The list below is far from comprehensive and is provided for purposes of information only. The author and publisher have reason to believe that all companies listed here operate in a competent and ethical manner, but we offer no guarantees.

La Moskitia Ecoaventuras
Avenida 14 de Julio
La Ceiba
☎442-0104
moskitia@laceiba.com
The name says it all. This company offers the most varied selection of hiking and rafting tours in the Mosquitia, ranging from three days to two weeks. Some of the longer tours start deep in the interior near the headwaters of the Río Plátano. Besides expeditions in the Río Plátano and Tawahka reserves, programs include bird-watching tours, rafting on the Río

Sico, and sport fishing in the Caratasca lagoon. Itineraries outside the Mosquitia region cover areas that include Parque Nacional Sierra de Agalta, known for its cloud forest.

C.B. Tours
Hotel Plaza Flamingo
La Ceiba
☎443-2738
☎443-3149
This firm arranges tours covering several of Honduras's national parks. It also provides guides to accompany groups or individuals anywhere in Honduras.

Trek de Honduras
Avenida Julio Lozano Díaz
between 12ª and 13ª Calles
Colonia Alameda, frente a
Salven los Niños
Tegucigalpa
☎239-826
☎239-0743
This company operates conventional tour programs in some of the more heavily visited parts of Honduras and also offers five-day and seven-day programs in the Biósfera del Río Plátano in the Mosquitia. Customers stay at the comfortable company-run Río Tinto Jungle Lodge in Palacios, starting point for the Mosquitia tours.

Adventure Expeditions
1020 Altos de la Hoya
Tegucigalpa
☎237-4793
Run by Ricardo Madrid, a Louisiana-born Honduran, this company specializes in adventure tours in the Moskitia, including six-day tours of the Río Plátano Bio-

sphere Reserve. It also runs fishing and bird-hunting programs in several parts of Honduras.

Cramer Tours
4ª Avenida near 3ª Calle S.O.
San Pedro Sula
☎557-082
This small agency organizes visits to the Parque Nacional Cusuco.

Go Native Tours
1 ½ blocks from the plaza
Copán Ruinas
☎651-4432
Programs include six-day and 10 day tours of the Biósfera Río Plátano in the Mosquitia, visits to several of Honduras's national parks including Parque Nacional Celaque, and five-day beach treks between Puerto Cortés and Tela. René Hernández, who runs the company, is an excellent source of information.

Garífuna Tours
near the central plaza
Tela
☎448-1069
garifuna@bondutel.ca
Single-day and half-day excursions take visitors to explore the Parque Nacional Punta Sal and to canoe in Laguna de los Micos or Punta Izopo wildlife reserve, all near Tela.

Eurohonduras
Edificio Gran
Hotel Italia,
Avenida 14 de Julio
La Ceiba
☎443-0933
This company is known for its excursions in the

area around La Ceiba, including hiking in Parque Nacional Pico Bonito, white-water rafting on the Río Cangrejal, and exploring in the Cuero y Salado wildlife reserve.

Programs include a 4hr hike through rain forest leading to a gorgeous waterfall with a natural pool for swimming. The company also makes arrangements for tours elsewhere in Honduras.

Turtle Tours
Hotel Villa Brinkley
Trujillo
☎ 434-444

Programs include rain-forest hikes in the Parque Nacional Capiro-Calentura, boating in the Laguna Guaymoreto, and road trips to banana plantations and Garífuna villages.

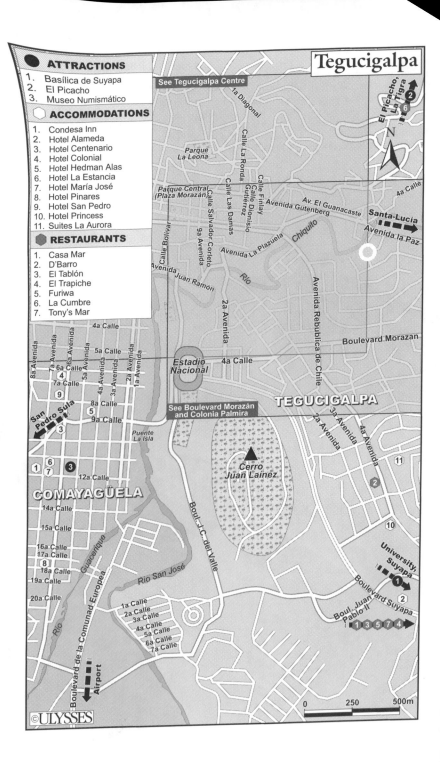

Tegucigalpa

ATTRACTIONS
1. Basílica de Suyapa
2. El Picacho
3. Museo Numismático

ACCOMMODATIONS
1. Condesa Inn
2. Hotel Alameda
3. Hotel Centenario
4. Hotel Colonial
5. Hotel Hedman Alas
6. Hotel La Estancia
7. Hotel María José
8. Hotel Pinares
9. Hotel San Pedro
10. Hotel Princess
11. Suites La Aurora

RESTAURANTS
1. Casa Mar
2. D'Barro
3. El Tablón
4. El Trapiche
5. Furiwa
6. La Cumbre
7. Tony's Mar

See Tegucigalpa Centre

El Picacho, La Tigra

Santa-Lucia

Parque La Leona

Parque Central (Plaza Morazán)

1a Diagonal

Calle La Ronda

Calle Las Damas

Calle Finlay

Calle Dionisio Gutiérrez

9a Avenida

Avenida Gutenberg

Av. El Guanacaste

Avenida la Paz

Avenida La Plazuela

Calle Salvador Corleto

Calle Bolivar

Avenida Juan Ramón

Río Chiquito

4a Calle

Avenida Rebública de Chile

Boulevard Morazan

TEGUCIGALPA

See Boulevard Morazán and Colonia Palmira

Estadio Nacional

4a Calle

2a Avenida

Cerro Juan Lainez

3a Avenida

2a Avenida

4a Avenida

8a Avenida

7a Avenida

6a Avenida

5a Avenida

4a Avenida

3a Avenida

2a Avenida

1a Avenida

4a Calle

5a Calle

6a Calle

7a Calle

8a Calle

9a Calle

San Pedro Sula

Puente La Isla

12a Calle

COMAYAGÜELA

14a Calle

15a Calle

16a Calle

17a Calle

18a Calle

19a Calle

20a Calle

Boul. J.C. del Valle

Río San José

Guacerique

Boulevard de la Comunad Europea

Río

Airport

1a Calle

2a Calle

3a Calle

4a Calle

5a Calle

6a Calle

7a Calle

University, Suyapa

Boulevard Suyapa

Boul. Juan Pablo II

0   250   500m

©ULYSSES

Tegucigalpa and Surroundings ★★★

The Honduran capital

is a quirky sort of place, with narrow streets twisting up the hillsides, an abundance of old pastel-hued buildings, and a friendly bustle that rises above the city's widespread economic squalour.

It is a place that alternately enchants and depresses, all the while hiding plenty of little surprises.

Central America has been somewhat of a backwater since colonial times, and Tegucigalpa is the capital of one of the region's less eminent countries. The seat of government was shifted from Comayagua only in 1880. Even then, Tegucigalpa was deemed so unimportant that the railway-building frenzy of the early 20th century bypassed it entirely, and paved roads were not created until much later. The banana industry that

was to dominate the Honduran economy for many decades developed near the north coast, far from the capital, and the city of San Pedro Sula emerged as the country's most important centre of industry and commerce, a position it still retains today.

All this to say that visitors should not come to Tegucigalpa expecting to find the

trappings of a major world capital. What visitors can count on finding is a city (population 1,000,000) with charming pockets of colonial architecture, a decent selection of hotels and restaurants, and imposing hills on three sides. Even if Tegucigalpa has been capital for little more than a century, it is an old city, founded in 1578 to serve nearby gold and silver mines.

Its name is derived from Amerindian words meaning "silver hill" and is often shortened to Tegus in casual conversation, with the first syllable stressed.

As tourism development in Honduras began to accelerate in the mid-1990s, it appeared Tegucigalpa might be bypassed again. It seemed certain that gowth would be focused near the beaches of the Caribbean Coast, the diving sites of Islas de la Bahía, the nature reserves in the northern part of the country and, of course, Copán with its splendid Mayan ruins. Tegus, some distance by road from the Caribbean Coast and without even a direct highway to Copán, looked like it would be left out of the loop. This would be a pity. Even if the city cannot truly claim any must-see attractions, it is worth a visit for itself and is close to several delightful old towns whose physical aspect has scarcely changed since colonial times. It is also near La Tigra national park.

Plaza Morazán, also known as the Parque Central, lies in the heart of the city. Apart from the area near the diminutive colonial cathedral with its delightful white-washed facade, the park is not especially attractive at first sight. But what it lacks in physical charm it makes up for in atmosphere, from the shoeshine men offering their services in one corner to the great bustle of humanity spanning the well-heeled and the humble. Most of the surrounding architecture is mediocre, the trees and fountains could use some care, and the vegetation is a bit sparse, but the surrounding hills provide enchanting vistas and at dusk, it seems that every songbird in Tegucigalpa gathers in the park's few trees to put on a performance. It is very Central American.

Avenida Paz Barahona, commonly known as the Calle Peatonal (pedestrian street), runs in both directions from the park, and on the side across the plaza from the cathedral it is a lively three-block-long pedestrian mall with countless shops and stalls. Streets heading in the opposite direction lead up toward Colonia Palmira and other swank neighbourhoods. Most of the city's better restaurants, and many of the more fashionable shops, are found along Boulevard Morazán and other suburban boulevards. The city centre, however, remains vibrant throughout the day and into the early evening hours, having escaped the sort of neglect that left the centres of San Salvador or Managua so badly scarred. At night things become quieter, and those who have not yet developed a feel for the place would be wise to consider getting around by taxi.

The Río Choluteca runs past the centre of Tegucigalpa, winding its way to the Pacific Ocean. Because much of its water is diverted for irrigation and other purposes, the river bed is dry most of the year, creating space for makeshift soccer fields. Across the river lies Tegucigalpa's twin city, Comayagüela (pronounced co-MY-a-GWAY-la), a lively but

The Garífunas have maintained various aspects of their African roots. Their distinctive rhythmic musical style, *punta*, adds another dimension to this country's diverse culture. - *Vicente Murphy*

Tegucigalpa, surrounded by towering hills, is located in a magnificent natural setting.
- *Claude Hervé-Bazin*

rather grubby place with bustling markets, many cheap hotels. This is where many of the poorer people live and work, and there is a serious safety problem here at night. Most of the intercity bus terminals are located in Comayagüela, and the airport lies a little farther along.

A day or a day-and-a-half should suffice to see Tegucigalpa's main tourist points of interest, including the anthropological museum, colonial churches, and the lookout along the slopes of El Picacho. But a stay in Tegucigalpa should be extended by a couple of days to visit some of the outlying towns and parks. Santa Lucía is a delightful hillside village that has scarcely changed throughout the centuries, and Valle de Angeles, a little farther in the same direction, has a good selection of handicrafts. Other towns within easy striking distance of Tegucigalpa that are noted for their colonial charm include Ojojona and Yuscarán. Anyone with an interest in agriculture will want to drop

by the Escuela Agrícola Panamericana, the agricultural school in El Zamorano. Parque Nacional La Tigra, located in the hills above Tegucigalpa, offers fine possibilities for hikers and nature-lovers.

Finding Your Way Around

By Air

Toncontín airport, situated 6.5km from the centre of Tegucigalpa, is a relic from another era, with a terminal building straight out of the 1950s (although there were some superficial renovations in the 1990s). The approach by air is thrilling, to say the least. Arriving flights skim low enough over a nearby hillside for passengers to almost feel they can reach out and pluck the fruit. The plane then swoops down at a sharp angle like a dive bomber, coming to an abrupt halt on a short landing strip beyond which lies a sharp drop. Crashes, although mercifully few in number, have been known to occur. Anybody who is nervous about flying should consider arriving at San Pedro Sula instead. Departures, incidentally, are a lot less scary. There have

been many proposals over the years to build a new airport, but the only suitable sites lie a very long distance from the city.

Domestic air service to San Pedro Sula is provided by Grupo Taca with four daily flights, and by Isleña, Sosa and Rollins to La Ceiba, each with two or three daily flights and connections from there to Islas de la Bahía. Connections at La Ceiba for Trujillo and the Mosquitia often require an overnight layover on the outbound journey, though not on the return. Tegucigalpa has direct international links from Miami, Houston, Guatemala, El Salvador and Costa Rica. For more information on international service, please see page 32.

Airline Reservations

American Airlines
Edificio Palmira, near Hotel Honduras Maya
☎232-1414

Continental Airlines
Edificio Palic, Colonia Palmira
☎220-0999

Grupo Taca
Edificio Interamericana
Boulevard Morazán
☎239-0148

Isleña
Galería La Paz
Avenida La Paz
☎237-3410

Rollins Airport
Rollins Airport
☎234-2766

Sosa Airport
Sosa Airport
☎233-7351

By Highway

Besides having no railway links, Tegucigalpa also has the distinction of being one of the few western hemisphere cities of its size with no highways wider than two lanes connecting it with anywhere else. For the moment, traffic is light and highway congestion has not become too serious a problem, although traffic along the road to San Pedro Sula, two lanes most of the way, is approaching its full capacity. At times, getting around a slow-moving truck can test the patience of drivers due to the density of oncoming traffic, but there are passing lanes in a few places. Because this highway passes through mountainous terrain, doubling its width would be a very expensive project.

Well-maintained highways run south from Tegucigalpa to Choluteca and the southern border crossings with El Salvador and Nicaragua, as well as east to Danlí. They also lead to alternate routes to Nicaragua, and northeast to Olancho department, including the cities of Juticalpa and Catacamas. Reaching the Copán area requires a more roundabout route, however. Many motorists choose to go via San Pedro Sula despite the extra distance since the roads are better. Another possibility is to take the San Pedro Sula highway as far as Siguatepeque, and then go west to Santa Rosa de Copán via La Esperanza and Gracias. The problem here is that the road is rough and unpaved between the two latter towns, and some of the countryside is very isolated, making emergency help hard to come by.

This may seem curious, but the highways running north to San Pedro Sula and northeast to Olancho actually run from the southwest of the city. They make long loops, allowing for more gentle climbs and avoiding the almost sheer slopes north of the city.

Intercity Buses

Intercity bus services are operated by a profusion of bus companies. There is no central terminal: companies operate from their own terminals, and in some cases from public markets. Most are scattered across Comayagüela. Different companies compete on some busier routes. Tickets may often be purchased in advance, and it is always wise to check ahead on departure times, which can change without notice.

A new deluxe category of air-conditioned express buses, with snacks and drinks served on board and comfortable seating at terminals, leave from Tegucigalpa on routes to San Pedro Sula, Puerto Cortés, La Ceiba and Choluteca, as well as on international routes to San Salvador and Managua. During busy holiday periods and on Sundays, it can be useful to book in advance. The international services, in particular, can fill up rather quickly. Several other points, including Danlí, Trujillo and Catacamas, are served by reasonably comfortable buses. Most smaller towns are connected by less adequate vehicles, in some cases former American school buses, that run on slow schedules and are often overcrowded. On certain busy routes travellers can choose between several categories of buses.

To **San Pedro Sula**, Viana and Saenz both offer top-of-the-line service, each with four to six daily departures and fares of about $9 for a 3.5hr journey.

Viana
Boulevard Fuerzas Armadas
☎239-8288

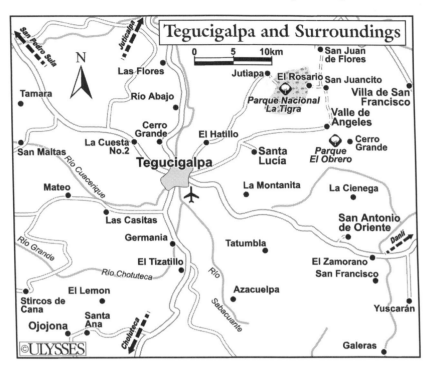

Tegucigalpa and Surroundings

0   5   10km

San Juan de Flores
Las Flores
Jutiapa   El Rosario   San Juancito
Tamara
Río Abajo
Parque Nacional La Tigra   Villa de San Francisco
Cerro Grande
El Hatillo   Valle de Angeles
La Cuesta No.2
San Maltas
Tegucigalpa   Santa Lucía   Parque El Obrero   Cerro Grande
Mateo   La Montanita   La Cienega
Las Casitas   San Antonio de Oriente
Germania   Tatumbla   Danlí
El Tizatillo   El Zamorano
Río Chotuteca   San Francisco
El Lemon   Azacuelpa
Stircos de Cana   Yuscarán
Santa Ana
Ojojona   Galeras

©ULYSSES

Saenz
Centro Comercial Perisur, near the airport
☎233-4229

Hedman Alas is a notch lower, with about a dozen daily departures, including some express services, and fares averaging about $6.

Hedman Alas
11 Avenida between 13 and 14 Calles
Comayagüela
☎237-7143

Several other companies offer slower, cheaper service, with frequent departures and journey times of 4.5hrs or more:

El Rey
☎237-1462

El Rey Express
☎237-8561

Norteños
☎237-0706

El Rey and Norteños make intermediate stops at the highway junctions for several points including **Comayagua** and **Siguatepeque**.

For the two latter towns, there are also slow local services running into the town centres, with service about once an hour.

To Copán:

La Sultana
8ᵃ Avenida between 11 and 12 Calles
Comayagüela
☎237-8101
La Sultana runs through to San Rosa de Copán about three times a day via San Pedro Sula, with connections at La Entrada for Copán Ruinas. Total travel time varies widely, depending on connections. To Copán Ruinas it should average around 8hrs.

Tegucigalpa and Surroundings

To Puerto Cortés:

Maya Express
Hotel Alameda
Boulevard Suyapa
☎232-6855
Maya Express runs a
deluxe service once
daily, with an afternoon
departure from Teguci-
galpa and a morning
return. Otherwise, con-
nections are usually
required at San Pedro
Sula.

To Tela
5.5hrs; $5
and La Ceiba:
6.5hrs; $6

Etrusca
12 Calle between 8ᵃ and 9ᵃ
Avenidas
Comayagüela
☎220-0137

Cristinas
8ᵃ Avenida between 12 and 13
Calles
☎220-0117
Each run several times
a day with fast, com-
fortable buses.

Viana
Boulevard Fuerzas Armadas
☎239-8288
Viana operates a luxury
service to La Ceiba
(6hrs; $17) twice daily,
with no stop at Tela.

To Trujillo:
8hrs; $7

Cotraipbal
7ᵃ Avenida between 10 and 11
Calles
☎237-1666
Cotraipbal goes twice
daily with comfortable
buses via La Unión
(near Parque Nacional
La Muralla).

To Juticalpa
3hrs; $2.50
and Catacamas:
4hrs; $3.50

Discovery
7ᵃ Avenida between 12 and 13
Calles
Comayagüela
☎222-4256

Aurora
8ᵃ Calle between 6ᵃ and 7ᵃ
Avenidas
☎237-3647

To Danlí:
2hrs; $1.50

Discua Litena
near the Jacaleapa market
☎230-2739
Discua Litena runs ev-
ery 40min or so.

Dandy
6ᵃ Avenida
Comayagüela
☎232-7939
Dandy runs less fre-
quently. Some buses
continue to San Marcos,
near the Nicaraguan
border.

To Choluteca:
2.5hrs; $2

Mi Esperanza
6ᵃ Avenida between 23 and 24
Calles
Comayagüela
☎225-1502
Mi Esperanza provides
frequent and reason-
ably comfortable ser-
vice to Choluteca and
the main intermediate
points. The same com-
pany operates a deluxe
service (2hr, $5) from a
small building behind
the main terminal, with
departures at 2hr inter-
vals and no intermedi-
ate stops. If space is
not available, buses

operated by other com-
panies can be flagged
outside the terminal
along 6ᵃ Avenida,
though these tend to be
slow and uncomfort-
able. Some buses con-
tinue to points near the
Nicaraguan border.

To San Salvador:
6hrs; $17-$25

Crucero del Golfo and
King Quality
Boulevard Comunidad Europea
☎225-5415
Twice daily on a joint
basis. The earlier of the
two departures allows
for same-day connec-
tions to **Guatemala City**
($45).

To Managua:
8hrs; $20-$23

King Quality and **Tica Bus**
16 Calle between 5ᵃ and 6ᵃ
Avenidas
Comayagüela
☎220-0590
Each company offers
one daily departure.
Tica Bus continues to
San José, in Costa Rica,
with an overnight stop
in Managua. (Tica Bus
no longer operates
from Tegucigalpa to El
Salvador or Guate-
mala.)

In the City

The first thing to re-
member when trying to
get around the city is
that the metropolitan
area also includes
Tegucigalpa's twin city
of Comayagüela, linked
by a number of bridges
across the Río
Choluteca. Together

Mitch's Legacy in Tegucigalpa

When Hurricane Mitch pounded Honduras with six straight days of heavy rains starting on Oct. 30, 1998, the Río Choluteca swelled from its usual narrow trickle and became a fearsome torrent racing through the heart of the capital. It tore away bridges and swamped portions of the city centre both on the Tegucigalpa and Comayagüela sides. A year later, damage was still highly visible.— and will probably remain so for years to come. Several buildings on the Tegucigalpa side are conspicuous by their absence, with foundations and portions of walls serving as reminders. The headquarters of the education ministry was one notable casualty. On the Comayagüela side, damage was more severe. Nearly every building facing a long stretch of 1ᵃ Avenida, lying parallel to the river, was simply wiped out. A portion of San Isidro market was also carried off. Today the bridges are mostly back in operation, and life has returned more or less to normal in most parts of the city. Looking at the river on most days, it is hard to imagine it could ever overflow its banks.

Damage was not limited to areas along the river, however. The rains also caused landslides that devastated more than a dozen mostly poor hillside neighbourhoods, some of which may never recover. In one area, dozens of houses and a soccer field literally slid down the hill, and there were numerous casualties. An article in *The New York Times,* titled "Honduras's Capital: City of the Dead and the Dazed," related how "hundreds of vultures swirled overhead, apparently attracted by the faint but fetid scent of corpses buried in the rubble created by an avalanche." The vultures are long gone, but portions of the city's decrepit sewerage system burst under the strain triggered by Mitch. Some poorer areas, far from the gaze of most foreigners, faced sanitary hazard as streets were turned into open sewers, with funds promised by international aid agencies providing the only relief in sight.

Tegucigalpa and Surroundings

they form an administrative unit called the *Distrito Central*.

What is commonly considered the centre of Tegucigalpa actually lies near the northern part of the urban area. Because of the topographical restraints caused by the high hills, the city has spread mostly to the east and southeast. Comayagüela lies to the southwest. There are many little hills which are not always evident on maps, leading to some surprising twists and turns.

Plaza Morazán, also known as the Parque Central, is the focal point of the traditional city centre. Although many of the streets follow a rectangular grid pattern, others go off at irregular angles, especially in the hills just north of Plaza Morazán and down toward the river.

In 1991 the municipality restored traditional names to many of the streets in the city centre and gave new names to a few others. Even today many maps do not show the revised names or, worse yet, show the system of numbered *calles* and *avenidas* that had been in use for a while. Some residents remain unfamiliar with the current nomenclature and when giving directions will use points of reference rather than actual street names.

The most important street for many pedestrians is Avenida Paz Barahona, more commonly referred to as the Calle Peatonal (pedestrian street). Over a length of several blocks, and spanning Plaza Morazán, this street is closed to motor traffic and has become a lively area for commerce and conversation.

Most other areas on the Tegucigalpa side that are of interest to visitors are situated to the southeast of the so-called centre. Colonia Palmira is an upscale residential, office and commercial area whose most important landmark is the Hotel Honduras Maya, situated a little over 1km from Plaza Morazán. Another important orientation point is the stadium (Estadio Nacional), located next to the river south of the city centre. A bridge to Comayagüela is situated nearby, and two of the city's most important boulevards begin just on the other side of the stadium. Boulevard Morazán runs east past shopping centres and the city's biggest concentration of restaurants, while Boulevard Suyapa runs southeast to the suburb (formerly village) of Suyapa, past the campus of the Universidad Nacional Autónoma de Honduras. Another important boulevard, Juan Pablo II (named after a famous Polish pope) runs

parallel to Boulevard Suyapa over a short distance.

Streets in Comayagüela, the tougher, grittier part of the metropolitan area, follow a more rigid rectangular grid pattern. Streets (*calles*) and avenues (*avenidas*) have numbers rather than names, making it easy for visitors to find their way around, which is just as well because this is not a part of town where one wants to get lost, especially at night. *Calles* run east and west, *avenidas* run north and south. Most of the intercity bus terminals are located on this side of the river. Avenida Centenario is one of the few roadways that runs diagonally to the others, and it forms one of the entrances to the northern highway. Boulevard de la Comunidad Europea runs south from Comayagüela, linking with entrances to most of the important highways connecting the city with the rest of Honduras. This same boulevard runs past Toncontín airport.

The rate of car ownership in Tegucigalpa is climbing. As a result, traffic congestion has become much worse. Streets are narrow in the city centre, and bottlenecks can develop when approaching the bridges. Clearly, these parts of the road system were not designed to cope with current vehicular flows. The only solution is to be patient and allow plenty of extra time for trips at rush hour.

Urban Buses

Nearly all parts of the metropolitan area are served by frequent buses from 5am to 9pm. Service continues later on a few routes, but at greatly reduced frequencies. Fares are very cheap, only a few pennies, although it can get very crowded. Travelling by city bus with a large amount of baggage is not recommended. In addition to drivers, most buses have conductors to collect the fares.

Finding the right bus can be a real problem. There is no route map or central directory to steer passengers in the right direction, and asking around is the only way to find out which route to take and where to catch the bus. Hotel clerks can sometimes be of help.

In a controversial move, in 1998 the mayor of Tegucigalpa banned buses from the city centre. Although this has resulted in lower noise and pollution levels, it has also created greater inconvenience for bus users, who must make their way to spots, mostly near the river, where buses are now stationed. Several collective taxi routes link

these spots with collection points in the city centre. During the evening rush hour taxi queues can be quite long.

By Taxi

Collective taxis supplement buses on several fixed routes, leaving from assigned spots. Although the fare is several times higher than the bus fare, it is still cheap, and passengers are guaranteed a seat even if they are jumbled tightly together.

Most visitors, however, will find regular taxis more useful. Even some inveterate public transit users will find that they have little occasion to take buses or collective taxis within the city. Most points in the central area are within walking distance.

Taxis are cheap and abundant in Tegucigalpa, and it rarely takes more than a couple of minutes to hail one in the city centre or along the main thoroughfares. They are the most useful way of getting around. Taxis that are free will often display a "libre" sign in the window or an interior purple or red light at night. The licence plates of authorized taxis have different colours from those of private vehicles, and the taxi's registration number is displayed in

big yellow and black figures on the door.

Fares are very low, as little as $1 for a short trip and rarely more than $4 for a longer haul. One exception is for trips to or from the airport, for which the fare is about $8. By walking one short block down to the main road from the airport, arriving passengers can shave a couple of dollars off the fare.

Taxis do not have meters and, while most drivers are honest, there can sometimes be cause for argument. After a day or two, visitors should get an idea of the general level of fares. To avoid arguments and overcharging, it makes sense to establish the fare before getting in. A few large yellow vehicles, found at certain hotels, offer a supposedly premium service and charge higher fares.

Drivers do not expect tips, but those who help with baggage or who take passengers to hard-to-find or out-of-the-way places should get a little extra. Fares should normally be paid in lempiras, but for trips from the airport or special excursions out of town, drivers will usually accept U.S. dollars, although they are not obliged to.

Some visitors may want to consider using taxis for excursions outside the city. This is not as extravagant as it may seem for someone accustomed to North American or European fare levels. For half-day excursions it is usually cheaper than renting a car, and even for full-day excursions it may not cost much more. In return, passengers get a driver service and avoid the hassles associated with car rentals. It is essential to agree on a price beforehand and to clearly say where you want to go and how much time you plan to spend in each place. It is also a good idea to look for a newer vehicle which is more likely to be in good condition.

By Foot

Tegucigalpa is fairly compact, and in most areas it is safe to walk during the day. Walking is certainly the most practical way for visitors to get around the city centre. After dusk, large parts of Comayagüela are unsafe for pedestrians because of the threat posed by muggers, and late at night the central area of Tegucigalpa can be a little dodgy as well. Certain streets away from the centre have plenty of night-time activity and are safer as a result. Even so, taxis are usually a better idea.

By Car

There is no special advice to offer visitors who want to see Tegucigalpa by car, except that they should take into account that the city centre is very congested during the daytime and parking can be scarce. When parking in certain areas, motorists may be approached by children or even by adults offering to guard their vehicle. Usually they only ask for a very modest sum, and it rarely hurts to agree to their proposal.

Car Rentals

Rental cars are available at Toncontín airport and in town, with a cluster of agencies near the Hotel Honduras Maya. Four-wheel-drive models are often available. When comparing prices, it is important to check on the deductible amount of the insurance coverage, which can often be quite high. It is also wise to check if tax is included and how many kilometres per day are free. Here is a list of car rental agencies and telephone numbers:

Avis
Edificio Palmira
☎232-0088
☎239-5711
Airport
☎233-9548

Budget
Boulevard Suyapa
☎233-5161
☎235-9528
Airport
☎233-6927

C&B
Boulevard Centro América
☎239-1373

Hertz
Centro Comercial Villa Real,
Colonia Palmira
☎239-0772
Airport
☎234-3784

Maya
Avenida República de Chile,
Colonia Palmira
☎232-0682

Molinari
1ª Avenida at 2ª Calle,
Comayagüela
☎237-5335
Airport
☎233-1307

Thrifty
Colonia Prado Universitarios
☎235-6077
Airport
☎233-0922

Practical Information

Money Exchange

Casas de cambio, or exchange dealers, have popped up next to certain hotels, offering the same exchange rates as the banks but with longer hours and faster service. Freelance money-changers also tend to cluster along the Calle Peatonal and at the far end near the Hotel Plaza. There is also a *casa de cambio* next to the Hotel Plaza, making this a good spot to compare rates. Traders in the street tend to shun traveller's cheques. There have not been many reports of short-changing, but it pays to be vigilant.

Long-Distance Telephone and Fax

The main office of Hondutel is situated in an imposing pink stone building on Avenida Cristóbal, parallel to and one block north of the Calle Peatonal, between Calle Los Dolores and Calle El Telégrafo. Long-distance telephone service is available around the clock. Fax service is offered until 4pm on weekdays only.

Internet Service

Internet Café
Mon to Sat 9am to 8pm
Avenida Jerez
half block from Hotel La Ronda

Galaxy Net
Mon to Sat 9am to 7pm
Plaza Crystal
Calle Hipólite Matute between Avenidas Jerez and Colón

Internet Planet
Mon to Sat 8am to 7pm
Avenida Cervantes at Calle La Plazuela

Post Office

The main post office is situated at the corner of Calle El Telégrafo and Avenida Paz Barahona, just beyond the end of the Calle Peatonal.

Exploring

Tegucigalpa

Tegucigalpa is blessed with a magnificent natural setting, surrounded on three sides by towering hills, most notably the peak known as El Picacho. The hills are clearly visible from Plaza Morazán in the very heart of the city and from many other points. One of these hills, covered in a thin coat of vegetation, is located very near the city centre, just across the river, and is steep enough to have resisted attempts to build housing more than a short way up its impressive flank.

To truly appreciate Tegucigalpa's majestic topography and the intriguing roofscape of the older part of the city with its colonial churches and spires, it is best to seek a higher vantage point. **Parque La Leona**, within easy walking distance of Plaza Morazán or a short hop by taxi,

provides a sweeping view of the city's central area and some of the nearby bluffs. Perched high on a hillside, it is reached by a series of narrow, steep and twisting streets. (The park is also a favourite hangout for teenaged couples.)

For a truly stunning vista of the Tegucigalpa basin, the place to go is the wide observation deck in Parque Naciones Unidas, partway up **El Picacho ★★**. This is the commanding peak that is visible from most parts of the city. Getting there involves a long climb along the paved road to El Hatillo. A cutoff from the El Hatillo road leads along two very bumpy kilometres to the observation area which stretches some distance along the crest. Buses go regularly to El Hatillo but take this cutoff only on Sundays, so private vehicles or taxis are more suitable options. The views of Tegucigalpa and its surroundings are truly magnificent, making it well worth the time and effort of getting there, and on a clear day it seems you really can see forever.

A recent addition to this same hillside, clearly visible from the city centre, especially at night, is a 2,500-tonne illuminated statue of Christ, inaugurated in 1998 and standing more than 30m tall.

● ATTRACTIONS

1. Calle Peatonal
2. Catedral
3. Congreso Nacional
4. Galería Nacional de Arte
5. Iglesia de San Francisco
6. Iglesia El Calvario
7. Iglesia La Merced
8. Iglesia Los Dolores
9. Mercado San Isidro
10. Museo del Hombre Hondureño
11. Museo Histórico de la República
12. Museo Nacional
13. Parque La Concordia
14. Parque La Leona
15. Plaza Morazán (Parque Central)
16. Teatro Nacional Manuel Bonilla

◯ ACCOMMODATIONS

1. Gran Hotel Krystal
2. Hotel Excelsior
3. Hotel Fortuna
4. Hotel Granada 1
5. Hotel Granada 2
6. Hotel Granada 3
7. Hotel Iberia
8. Hotel Imperial
9. Hotel Istmania
10. Hotel La Ronda
11. Hotel MacArthur
12. Hotel Plaza (R)
13. Hotel Prado
14. Hotelito Goascarán No. 1
15. Hotelito Goascarán No. 2
16. Nuevo Hotel Boston

● RESTAURANTS

1. Al Natural
2. Café El Greco
3. Café Paradiso
4. La Terraza de Don Pepe
5. Pepe Chalet
6. Mediterraneo
7. Mirawa
8. Picadeli
9. Repostería Duncan Maya

Back in the centre of town, **Plaza Morazán** ★★, often referred to as the Parque Central, is the starting point for many visits. This is the traditional heart of the city, and from early morning to mid-evening it is a buzzing hive of activity. At dusk, thousands of songbirds congregate and entertain. It is a magnificent time of day.

In the centre of the plaza is an equestrian statue honouring General Francisco Morazán, a national hero who led the fight for Central American unity in the 1830s. Of the buildings surrounding the plaza, most are shabby and uninteresting, with one exception, the 18th-century **Catedral de San Miguel de Tegucigalpa** ★ with its whitewashed facade. It is not a particularly imposing structure, but its simple lines and pleated columns are quite pretty. Inside, there is an elaborate pulpit as well as a profusion of altarpieces and religious paintings. Doors close shortly after 5pm. Three blocks behind the cathedral, facing a small square called Parque Valle, is the **Iglesia de San Francisco**, the oldest church in Tegucigalpa. Its construction began in the 16th century and altered extensively in the 18th. Those who arrive during the irregular moments when the church is open can see colonial-era art and an ornate gold-plated altar.

Several noteworthy buildings are situated between Plaza Morazán and the Puente Mallol (pronounced ma-YOL), the oldest of the bridges crossing the river to Comayagüela. Facing a small square called Parque Merced are the 17th-century **Iglesia La Merced**, with religious paintings and an elaborate altar, and a building that once housed the national university. This is now the home of the **Galería Nacional de Arte** ★★ (*$1.50; Tue to Sat 10am to 4:30pm, Sun 10pm to 2pm*). Downstairs are

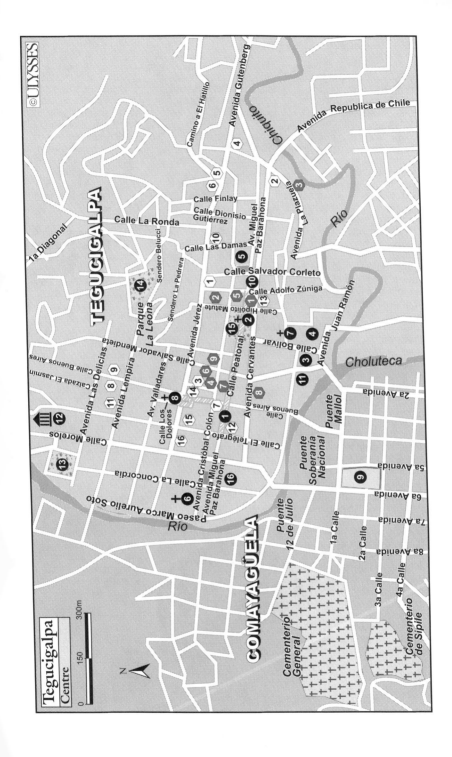

exhibits devoted to the pre-Hispanic era, including stone and ceramic art from the Mayan period. On the same floor is a fine collection of paintings, sculptures and religious art from the colonial era, including gold and silver objects. Rooms upstairs display an interesting selection of paintings and sculptures by modern Honduran artists including José Antonio Velásquez, Pablo Zelaya Sierra and Carlos Zúñigua Figueroa. Directly adjacent is the building of the **Congreso Nacional**, Honduras's legislature, a modern structure set on high metal stilts with the space below left stylishly empty. A little beyond is the former presidential palace, now home to the **Museo Histórico de la República** (*$1.50; Tue to Sat 9am to noon and 1:30pm to 4pm*) is housed in the gorgeous structure that used to be the presidential palace, situated about midway between Plaza Morazán and the river. The building itself is more interesting than the exhibits, which consist mostly of portraits, documents and knicknacks relating to former government leaders from the 18th century to the present. The former presidential office, cabinet room and ballroom are worth brief glimpses. This grandiose turreted structure has a garden and wooded area in the

back and is painted in subdued beige tones, a contrast to its former bright pink.

Returning to Plaza Morazán, crossing the square half way and then turning left, one enters Avenida Paz Barahona, more commonly known as the **Calle Peatonal ★**, (pedestrian street) and describes three blocks of its length, lined with shops and stalls. Two blocks west, Calle Los Dolores leads north from the Calle Peatonal to a plaza facing **Iglesia Los Dolores ★**, with gold-plated altars and religious paintings and sculptures. The interior of its capacious dome is painted in an ornate gold and blue pattern. Calle Los Dolores is also closed to cars over part of its length with many stalls selling leather goods and other handicrafts items.

Teatro Nacional Manuel Bonilla ★, facing Parque Herrera two blocks beyond the end

of the Calle Peatonal, has a handsome pink exterior and a horseshoe-shaped gold and white interior. Regular performances are held at this restored turn-of-the-century treasure. On the other side of the park is the 18th-century **Iglesia El Calvario**.

The **Museo Nacional ★** (*$1.50; Wed to Sun 8:30am to 3:30pm*) houses anthropological and ethnological exhibits. It forms part of the *Instituto Hondureño de Antropología e Historia* and occupies the Villa Roy, a large mansion set in an extensive wooded estate just a few blocks from the centre of the city.

On display is a small but interesting collection of objects from Honduras's pre-Hispanic past, including some pieces made of obsidian, jade or precious stones. There are animal heads carved in stone and even some musical instruments. Most of this collection consists of ancient Mayan items covering the early to late classical periods.

The ethnological section depicts the day-to-day lives and the traditional cultures of contemporary indigenous groups living in Honduras. Downstairs is the natural history section, featuring paleolithic objects. Another section presents religious

Lempira, Indigenous Hero

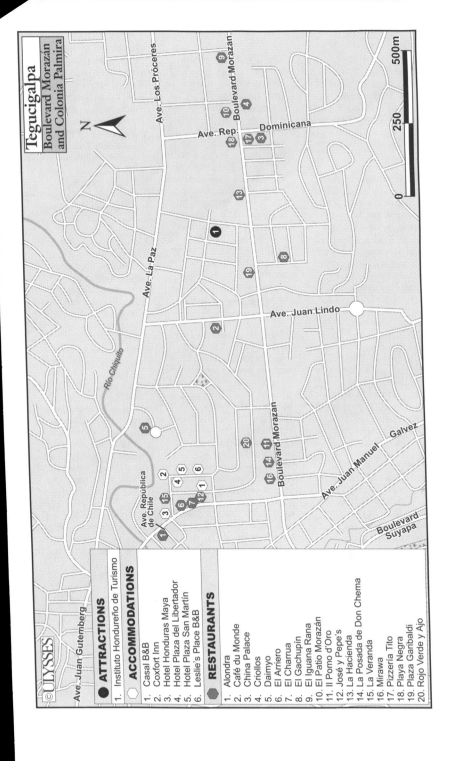

Tegucigalpa
Boulevard Morazán and Colonia Palmira

© ULYSSES

N

0   250   500m

Ave. Juan Gutemberg
Ave. Los Próceres
Ave. Rep. Dominicana
Boulevard Morazan
Ave. La Paz
Ave. Juan Lindo
Ave. República de Chile
Río Chiquito
Boulevard Morazan
Ave. Juan Manuel Galvez
Boulevard Suyapa

● ATTRACTIONS
1. Instituto Hondureño de Turismo

⬡ ACCOMMODATIONS
1. Casal B&B
2. Coxfort Inn
3. Hotel Honduras Maya
4. Hotel Plaza del Libertador
5. Hotel Plaza San Martín
6. Leslie's Place B&B

⬡ RESTAURANTS
1. Alondra
2. Café du Monde
3. China Palace
4. Criollos
5. Daimyo
6. El Arriero
7. El Charrua
8. El Gachupín
9. El Iguana Rana
10. El Patio Morazán
11. Il Pomo d'Oro
12. José y Pepe's
13. La Hacienda
14. La Posada de Don Chema
15. La Veranda
16. Mirawa
17. Pizzería Tito
18. Playa Negra
19. Plaza Garibaldi
20. Rojo Verde y Ajo

objects from the colonial period, many of them gold or silver. Outside the museum is a small collection of antique luxury automobiles belonging to former Honduran presidents.

The entrance to the grounds lies one block over and one block up from **Parque La Concordia**, a pleasant tree-shaded park adorned with imitation Mayan relics, including stelae, carved heads and a small pyramid. From the centre of the city the park is a few blocks up Calle Morelos, which lies one block past the end of the Calle Peatonal. Taxis are a good way of getting there. Even after entering the grounds of the museum, it is a steep climb to Villa Roy, the mansion housing the displays.

Museo del Hombre Hondureño ★ (*donation; Mon to Fri 9am to 6pm, Sat 9am to 1pm*) is housed in the small former Supreme Court building on Avenida Cervantes, a couple of blocks behind the cathedral. It displays paintings, lithographs and photos, including some interesting shots of Tegucigalpa taken in the early 20th century.

The **Basílica de Suyapa** ★ draws many pilgrims and is noted for a 15cm statue of the Virgin of Suyapa which many worshippers credit with miraculous powers.

The feast day of the Virgin is February 2, and you can always find large crowds around that date. The current structure, which replaced an older, smaller church, is an impressive edifice with two big bell towers that are plainly visible from a great distance along Boulevard Suyapa, running past the campus of the national university. Suyapa is a suburb, formerly a separate village, 8km east of the centre of Tegucigalpa.

Comayagüela

The Comayagüela side is scruffy and bedraggled yet full of life, with several bustling markets. The most important of these is **Mercado San Isidro**, a beehive of activity from dawn until just after dusk. It stretches several blocks along 5^a and 6^a Avenidas and may seem intimidating at first because of its sheer sprawl and crowded, chaotic conditions. Food and a cornucopia of cheap industrial goods are displayed in great profusion, and some handicrafts items can also be found. Although the market is not dangerous during daylight hours, it is best to keep objects of value carefully hidden.

Inside the tall, intimidating pink-hued office building at 12ª Calle and 6ª Avenida housing the Banco Central de Honduras (this oversized building really sticks out like a sore thumb) is the **Museo Numismático** (*free; Mon to Fri 9am to 4pm*), with collections of coins and banknotes from across Central America.

Santa Lucía

This former mining town comes straight out of another century. With its stone-paved streets, red-tile roofs and whitewashed 16th-century church filled with religious art, the town centre is utterly unspoiled and has an almost medieval feel. There is not a lot to do here except stroll along the steep, winding streets, enjoy gorgeous views of the surrounding valleys from a lookout near the Palacio Municipal, and enjoy the pine-scented air, not a bad way to spend a couple of hours. There is a small lagoon on the outskirts. Some interesting restaurants and handicraft shops have popped up.

Santa Lucía lies 17km northeast of Tegucigalpa and is reached by a cutoff from the highway leading to Valle de Angeles. Twice-hourly buses leave from the Mercado San Pablo next to Bar El Manchén in Tegucigalpa. It is feasible to visit Santa Lucía and Valle de Angeles in the same day without being unduly rushed.

Valle de Angeles

This attractive old town has become something of a Mecca for handicrafts shoppers, with several large markets and many independent shops. The largest of the markets is run by the Asociación Nacional de Artesanos de Honduras and offers a very broad selection. Two smaller markets lie nearby. Several of the independent shops in town offer artwork and fine items not found at the markets, (see p 88).

Valle de Angeles (pronounced BA-yay day AN-khay-lays) has an attractive tree-shaded plaza facing a rather less attractive church. There are several small restaurants around the plaza, situated a couple of blocks from the market area. The town is reached by a paved highway running 28km northeast from Tegucigalpa. Buses to Valle de Angeles leave from Hospital San Felipe in Tegucigalpa.

Ojojona

The physical aspect of Ojojona (pronounced o-kho-KHO-na) has not changed much over the centuries. This quiet town has broad streets and plazas, large grassy areas and many trees, interspersed with meadows and orchards and bisected by a narrow brook. The scent of wood smoke pervades its crisp, clean air. There are several churches, including the 1823 cathedral and the churches of El Carmen and Sangre de Cristo.

Lately Ojojona has become a centre of handicrafts production, mostly simple items of pottery, sometimes in animal shapes and spray-painted in lurid colours. This is not the highest-quality work to be found in Honduras, though the quality has been improving, and the town has begun to draw residents who regard themselves as artists rather than humble artisans. Objects including the *papier mâché* roosters that have become almost a national symbol abound at local shops, but more sophisticated items are also available.

The town is located 32km from Tegucigalpa, 7km west along a poorly paved cutoff from the main highway to Choluteca. Buses run hourly from 7ª Avenida and 4ª Calle, next to the San Isidro market in Comayagüela.

Yuscarán

This is a former mining town of steep, narrow, stone-paved streets with an attractive Parque Central, a simple whitewashed church and wooden balconies overhanging some streets. Surrounded by lofty mountains and idyllic valleys, Yuscarán is noted now for the production of *aguardiente*, a form of unmatured rum. The **Reserva Natural Monserrat** (see p. 82) is situated nearby.

The **Casa Fortín**, across from the Bancahsa branch, is an 18th-century mansion that once belonged to a prominent local family. It houses only a few exhibits, including information about the town's natural surroundings, mineral samples, farming tools, and old mining records. To gain access, ask around town for Señor Oscar Lezana, who has the keys.

Tegucigalpa and Surroundings

Yuscarán is situated 65km from Tegucigalpa, the last 17km running southeast along a paved but rockslide-prone cutoff from the highway to Danlí. Buses from Tegucigalpa leave the Mercado Jacaleapa at 2hr intervals, with the last bus back at 3pm.

San Antonio de Oriente

This pristine former mining town, founded in the 17th century, has whitewashed buildings with red-tile roofs, stone-paved streets, and a twin-spired church that has inspired some of the finest work of renowned naïve painter José Antonio Velásquez. Although only about 30km from Tegucigalpa, San Antonio de Oriente remains partly isolated by poor roads and thus has remained largely unspoilt.

The town is not accessible by regular car and there is no regular bus service. A four-wheel drive vehicle, high truck or mule is required. An alternative is a delightful 90min hike from the Tegucigalpa-Danlí highway, involving steep climbs through pine forest with fine valley views.

El Zamorano

This tiny town 36km east of Tegucigalpa on the road to Danlí is home to the **Escuela Agrícola Panamericana** (Panamerican Agricultural School), where an average of 700 students from 18 countries throughout Latin America learn farming techniques from a teaching staff from 22 countries. The school opened in 1942 and is a legacy of Sam Zemurray, founder of the United Fruit Company. (Some of his other legacies are often seen as less charitable.) In its early years the school depended entirely on United Fruit for its financing, but in more recent times governments, private foundations and corporations have chipped in. Thirty per cent of enrolments are reserved for students from poor peasant families. Newer programs include studies in the fields of women and agriculture, environment, and agribusiness development. Some 220 species of plants and animals are raised on a commercial or semi-commercial basis.

For the casual visitor, there is not really very much to see apart from the school's vast, orderly grounds. Some areas are finely landscaped, and most buildings are sheathed in an attractive white stone, quarried nearby. A leaflet available from the school outlines a 90min self-guided tour. A shop along the highway, open until 3pm, sells a variety of fresh produce and meats as well as fruit and vegetable preserves and other items produced by students at the school.

For anyone interested in agriculture, there will be much more to see, and the school's administrators are happy to receive visitors. The site was selected in an area with only marginal agricultural potential to show what can be done with hard work and suitable technology. The grounds also include a 7,000ha biological reserve that is maintained in pristine state and accessible only to specialists.

Parks

Parque Nacional La Tigra

This great expanse of parkland climbs through cloud forest to the peak of El Picacho, 2,290m above sea level. The **Parque Nacional La Tigra** (*free admission; every day 7am to 4pm; day visitors must leave by 5pm*) plays an important part in safeguarding a substantial portion of Tegucigalpa's water supply and provides refuge for many plant and animal species. Although agricultural encroachment has penetrated deeply into the buffer zone surrounding the protected area, there has been sufficient political will in recent years to evict, for instance, the cousin of a former president who had attempted to establish a coffee plantation within the park. The protected area comprises about one-third of the park's 23,000ha span.

The park's main attractions are its luxuriant vegetation, waterfalls and abandoned mines, and you may also get to glimpse some rare wildlife here. La Tigra has a network of hiking trails, and maps are available at the visitor's centres. A long circuit favoured by some hikers requires an early-morning start to be sure of completing it before closing time, as well as good physical condition to cope with the many rises and descents. A shorter and more popular hike takes visitors 90min each way from the Jutiapa entrance to the largest waterfall (waterfalls here do not seem to have names). Visitors are urged to stay on the trails and to take warmer clothing than they would need in Tegucigalpa.

La Tigra lies near the continental divide (to the east of which waters flow to the Caribbean and to the west, to the Pacific) and abundant year-round rainfall in some of the higher areas of the park assures cloud forest conditions, with many broad-leafed plants, a proliferation of vines and mosses, and a high canopy of vegetation that filters much of the natural light. Pine forest is common at lower elevations.

Tapir

Among the rare animal species that can sometimes be spotted is the almost mythical quetzal, with its long tail and magnificent plumage. Other birdlife abounds, and jaguars, tapirs and ocelots have also been spotted.

The park is run by a private foundation called Fundación Los Amigos de la Tigra. There are entrances near Jutiapa, each with a visitor's centre. For those who plan to make a longer trip, simple camping facilities are available without charge inside the

park and can be reached from either entrance. Campers must bring tents, food supplies and water purification tablets, and they should notify the park ranger at the entrance that they intend to stay overnight. Alternatively, simple lodgings are available at the El Rosario entrance (see p 86).

The more convenient entrance for those arriving from Tegucigalpa can be reached by the all-weather road through El Hatillo. The total distance is 22km; the town of El Hatillo is about halfway along, past the cutoff for the popular El Picacho observation deck. The nearest village is Jutiapa, 4km from the park entrance. Buses to Jutiapa run twice an hour from Parque Herrera in Tegucigalpa starting at 6am. The last bus back is at 5pm, but it is best to double-check with a bus driver or with the park ranger at the visitor's centre to avoid being stranded. You will have to walk the final 4km up the park entrance. For serious hikers it is possible to make a day excursion of it even without access to a private vehicle. An alternative is to take a taxi and pay the driver for the waiting time. Vehicles must be parked at the entrance.

The other entrance is located at the abandoned mining village of El Rosario, 44km from

Tegucigalpa. El Rosario lies 4km along a very bad road from the town of San Juancito, which lies beyond Valle de Angeles along an unpaved road.

tables, a restaurant and swimming pool. It is popular with family groups and rather crowded on Sundays.

Reserva Natural Monserrat

Reserva Natural Monserrat lies near the outskirts of the town of Yuscarán, 65km east of Tegucigalpa, and forms an important part of the watershed for a wide area. This reserve is not formally a park, and access is not restricted. There are walks of up to 2hrs each way along a rough road (accessible also to sturdy vehicles) past pine forests, waterfalls and abandoned mines, with some splendid views along the way. For the more ambitious, a trail climbs farther up toward the peak of Monserrat. Limited information can be obtained at the Casa Fortín in Yuscarán.

Parque El Obrero

Parque El Obrero (*$0.50, half price for children; every day 8am to 4pm*) is situated near Valle de Angeles 2km off the main highway, entailing a bit of walking for those arriving by bus. This is a big pine-forested area with sheltered grills and picnic

Accommodations

Tegucigalpa offers a full range of hotels, from the five-star to the truly dismal. Most top-of-the-line hotels are situated in Colonia Palmira, a short distance from the city centre. Hotels in the city centre cover the gamut from upper-middle-range to very cheap. Immigration officers occasionally stage sweeps at some of the cheaper hotels looking for travellers without valid documents.

Across the river in Comayagüela are a proliferation of mostly small, cheap hotels, some of them catering to customers who rent by the hour rather than by the night. We provide information here on several of the more suitable hotels in Comayagüela, with the triple warning that surrounding streets can be dangerous at night, restaurants are mostly poor, and little of interest lies nearby apart from the bus terminals. Most travellers, even those arriving by night, will do better to take a taxi to the Tegucigalpa side.

We also include information here on hotels in Valle de Angeles, Ojojona, El Zamorano and Yuscarán. Although most visitors to these towns arrive on day trips from Tegucigalpa, reasonable lodgings are available for those who choose to stay longer.

Tegucigalpa

Several cheap hotels and *hospedajes* are clustered in the area around Los Dolores church.

Hotelito Goascarán No. 1
$3 with sb
Calle Los Dolores
☎*238-1903*

Hotelito Goascarán No. 2
$3 with sb, $6 with pb
Calle El Telégrafo near Avenida Jerez
☎*238-1907*

Hotel Imperial
$4 with sb, $6 with pb
Calle Buenos Aires near Avenida Lempira
☎*222-1973*

Hotel Fortuna
$4 with sb, $7 with pb
Los Dolores near Avenida Jerez
no phone
Each of these spots offers between 10 and 20 clean but rather rudimentary rooms that may vary in size. Hotel Imperial is slightly better than the rest.

Hotel Iberia
$8 with sb, $11 with pb
Calle Los Dolores between the Calle Peatonal and the church
☎*237-9267*
The 20 rooms here are plain but decently

furnished and face a bright lounge with big tables and sofas. The entrance is almost hidden by street stalls.

Hotel Granada 1
$10 with sb, $17 with pb
☎222-2654

Granada 2 and **Granada 3**
$18, with pb
☎237-7079

These three hotels are clustered along or near Avenida Gutenberg near the Cine Aries. Granada 1 is very basic and suffers from street noise. Granada 2, on a side street, is quieter, but rooms are dark and very simple. Granada 3 is also basic but more spacious and appealing.

Nuevo Hotel Boston
$20-$25
Avenida Jerez near Calle Morelos
☎237-9411
The 19 rooms at this centrally located spot vary enormously, some small and a bit dark, others bright and spacious, all with nice decorative touches. Many guests appreciate the family atmosphere. Rooms facing the street have balconies but can be noisy.

Gran Hotel Krystal
$21
≡, tv, ☎
Avenida Jerez at Calle Salvador Mendieta
☎237-8804
The 60 rooms in this modern, centrally located two-storey hotel are dark and somewhat dingy.

Hotel MacArthur
$27 with ⊗, $37 with ≡ tv, ☎
Avenida Lempira between Calle Buenos Aires and Calle El Telégrafo
☎237-5906
Rooms are fresh and modern although fairly ordinary in this elevatorless three-storey hotel, located in a quiet area beyond Los Dolores church.

Hotel Istmania
$39
≡, tv, ☎
Calle Buenos Aires near Avenida Lempira
☎237-1639
Situated a short way north of Los Dolores church, this six-storey, 34-room hotel has carpeted rooms that are bright and adequate. Larger suites are available.

Hotel Plaza
$45
≡, tv, ☎, ℜ, bar
near the end of the Calle Peatonal
☎237-2111 to 2118
≠237-2119
Well-situated along the Calle Peatonal, this modern 83-room hotel offers very good value, with friendly staff and pleasant rooms, each with a desk and chairs. Car parking is difficult.

Suites La Aurora
$58
≡, tv, ☎
Avenida Luís Bográn
Colonia Tepeyac
☎232-9891 or 232-0245
≠232-0188
Situated on a quiet suburban street not far from Avenida Juan

Pablo II, this 47-suite establishment has pleasant furnishings and a homey feel. Suites vary in size, and a few face an interior shaft.

Coxfort Inn
$64 bkfst incl.
reductions for longer stays
≈
facing Plaza San Martín
Colonia Palmira
☎ 239-1254
This friendly bed and breakfast spot, near the much bigger Hotel Plaza San Martín, has a small pool and 10 bright, cheerful rooms, some of them with good views.

Hotel La Ronda
$72
≡, tv, ☎, ℜ, bar, valet P
Avenida Jerez
☎237-8151 to 237-8155
≠237-1454
U.S. and Canadian reservations 800-446-2747
Suites in this centrally located 72-room hotel are spacious but ordinary, and rooms are rather small, decorated in modern and not very appealing style. Many rooms have tiny windows, some facing an interior shaft. The hotel does have a pleasant open-air breakfast area.

Leslie's Place Bed and Breakfast
$82 bkfst incl.
≡, ℜ
facing Plaza San Martín
Colonia Palmira
☎239-641 or 239-0642
≠231-2957
www.lesliep.com
Set on a quiet side street near the much bigger Hotel Plaza San

Tegucigalpa and Surroundings

Martín, this place offers a pleasant family atmosphere and classical music in the lobby. Big, bright rooms are whitewashed and simply furnished. There is a sitting area in front of the hotel, as well as a shaded concrete patio in the rear. Included in room rates is a good choice of breakfasts, including fruit plates.

Hotel Prado
$78 bkfst incl.,
≡, *tv*, ☎, ℜ, *bar*, ⊛, *P*, ◻
Avenida Cervantes just behind the cathedral
☎*237-0121* to *237-0127*
⇌*237-2221*
elprado@netsys.bn
Very centrally located, this hotel has 72 small but pleasantly furnished rooms and brightly carpeted corridors.

Hotel Alameda
$80
≡, *tv*, ☎, ℜ, *bar*, ≈
Boulevard Suyapa
☎*232-6920* or *232-6902*
⇌*232-6932*
This very suburban spot has a big pool and a huge parking area. Its 75 modern rooms, set on three levels, are greatly overpriced. Furnishings are nondescript, and lighting is so dim that reading can be difficult. Taxi drivers sometimes take unsuspecting customers here, but there are better choices elsewhere.

Hotel Excelsior
$93
≡, *tv*, ☎, ℜ, *bar, indoor P*
Avenida Cervantes near the bridge over Río Chiquito
☎*237-2638*
⇌*238-0468*
Following a thorough and elegant renovation, this hotel has a total of 78 rooms in two wings. It is well situated, easy walking distance both from the heart of the city and from Colonia Palmira. All rooms are big and spacious, which is unusual in Tegucigalpa. Furnishings are attractive, and floors are covered in white tile, far more suitable than carpeting in a tropical climate. In a few rooms the windows face inside corridors.

Hotel Plaza San Martín
$127
≡, *tv*, ☎, ℜ, *bar*
facing Plaza San Martín, Colonia Palmira
☎*237-2928* or *232-8268*
⇌*231-1366*
Set on a quiet side street facing a tiny park, this white, yellow and blue building has 110 rooms and suites set on nine floors. Rooms are small but comfortable with pleasant decor in shades of green, grey and pink and original Honduran artwork. All have balconies, many with good views of the city and the surrounding hills. The hotel has a gym and sauna but no pool. Service is friendly and efficient. Sheltered parking is available.

Hotel Plaza del Libertador
$139 (promotional rate: $103)
ℜ, *bar, gym*, ◻, ≡, *tv*, ☎
Plaza San Martín
Colonia Palmira
☎*220-4141*
⇌*220-4242*
libertad@netsys.bn
This elegant new 14-storey hotel prides itself on the Honduran artwork decorating guest rooms and public areas. Its 80 rooms are tastefully and comfortably appointed, with mahogany furniture and fine views over the city. Amenities include a business centre and conference rooms.

Hotel Honduras Maya
$160
≡, ☎, ℜ, *bar*, ≈, ⊛, *convention facilities*
Avenida República de Chile, Colonia Palmira
☎*220-5000*
⇌*220-6000*
www.hondurasmaya.bn
This 10-storey landmark hotel has 180 rooms and an octagonal shape that makes for more corner rooms and better views. Executive floors offer private lounges with breakfast service, fax machines and computer jacks. Shopping and travel services are available within the hotel, as is a small casino. Rooms are elegant but small and rather nondescript. The lobby is impressive.

Comayagüela

Hotel Pinares
$4 with sb, $6 with pb
6ª Avenida between 17 and 18
Calles
☎238-4663
Located just 50m from
the Tica Bus terminal,
this hotel has 38 sim-
ple, basic rooms set
around a narrow three-
storey atrium.

Hotel San Pedro
$4 with sb, $7 with pb
tv, fan
6ª Avenida between 8ª and 9ª
Calles
☎222-8987
⊷222-7783
This 40-room hotel
offers good value for
travellers on tight bud-
gets. Rooms, simple but
clean, are set around a
scruffy terrace. Ground-
floor rooms have
lounge chairs outside.

Hotel Colonial
$7
≡, ℜ
6ª Calle
between 6ª and 7ª Avenidas
☎237-5785
The 15 rooms at this
friendly spot are small
and clean, providing a
basic level of comfort.

Hotel La Estancia
$7 with pb
⊗
7ª Avenida between 11ª and 12ª
Calles
☎237-3564
The 10 rooms all face a
small courtyard with
potted plants. Rooms
vary enormously: some
are bright and pleasant,
others are dark and
claustrophobic. Staff are
very friendly.

Hotel María José
$12 with ⊗ $16 with ≡
all with tv
12ª Calle at 7ª Avenida
☎237-7292
Each of the 17 rooms
are fresh, bright and
pleasant with private
bath and bedside
lamps. Not only is this
a good value, but the
atmosphere is welcom-
ing.

Condesa Inn
$14-$19
most rooms with ⊗
a few with ≡ and tv
12ª Calle at 7ª Avenida
☎237-7857
Rooms in this 35-room
hotel are basic but
clean, all with private
bath. Some rooms are
rather stuffy, and a few
have no window or
face an indoor corridor.
Most are quiet.

Hotel Hedman Alas
$17
tv, ☎, ⊗
4ª Avenida between 8ª and 9ª
Calles
☎237-9333
☎237-1479
This friendly spot, affili-
ated with the bus com-
pany of the same name
but not near its termi-
nal, has 20 small and
darkish but comfortably
furnished rooms as well
as a bright, pleasant
sitting area.

Hotel Centenario
$23
tv, ⊗
6ª Avenida between 9ª and 10ª
Calles
☎222-1050 or 237-7729
⊷222-7575
This reassuring 42-
room hotel is probably
the most comfortable in
Comayagüela. Rooms

are simple but clean,
though some are dark
and others are noisy.
Entry is through a pro-
tected parking area.

Valle de Angeles

Los Tres Pinos Bed &
Breakfast
$14 per person
Just outside town along the
highway to San Juancito
☎766-2148
This quiet spot is set on
spacious grounds
shaded, as the name
suggests, by pine trees,
with four comfortable
guest rooms in a big
house. Room rates
include a light break-
fast. Horseback riding
can be arranged.

Hotel Posada del Angel
$28 per person
≈, *tv*, ℜ
in the centre of town
☎766-2233
This 30-room hotel has
simple but pleasant
rooms facing an agree-
able pool area with
many plants. It tends to
fill up on weekends
and holidays.

Ojojona

Posada Joxone
$3 per person
ℜ; *no phone*
Although rooms are
nothing special, this
homey five-room estab-
lishment has plenty of
whitewashed stucco,
wooden ornaments and
red tile floors, as well
as a luxuriant garden
and orchard. Excellent
value. Meals in the
small restaurant are

Tegucigalpa and Surroundings

cooked on a wood fire. Most dishes are $2.

Yuscarán

Hotel Carol
$5 per person
☎881-7143
This eight-room hotel has bright, simple rooms with wood ceilings and carved doors. There are fine mountain and valley views, but only a narrow ledge runs in front of the rooms, leaving no room to sit and enjoy the vista.

El Zamorano

Centro de Desarrollo Rural W.K. Kellogg
$38
ℜ, tv
just off the Tegucigalpa-Danlí highway, to the left approaching from Tegucigalpa
☎776-6140 ext. 2528
≈766-6140
Part of the Escuela Agrícola Panamericana, this hotel and conference centre is sometimes used for special courses and seminars. Because of this, advance reservations are strongly suggested. A handsome two-storey stone building houses 53 simple but bright and comfortable rooms. The restaurant is open for all three meals, but hours are short and very early, timed to fit in with the school's schedule. There is a games room.

Parque Nacional La Tigra

Simple lodgings are available near the El Rosario entrance. An old building has been converted to a so-called Ecoalbergue (eco-inn) with simple dormitory-style lodgings for up to 30 people (no phone). Arrangements should be made in advance in Tegucigalpa through:

Los Amigos de la Tigra
Edificio Italia,
Colonia Palmira
☎232-6771
Camping is possible inside the park.

Restaurants

Tegucigalpa

For many people in Tegucigalpa, eating out in style means digging into a big steak. As a result steak houses figure prominently among the city's more elegant restaurants. But that is far from the whole story, for there is a profusion of restaurants offering Chinese, Mexican and other cuisines, and several spots, although not many, specialize in seafood.

The dining scene in the central part of the city is dominated by the usual fast-food joints offering hamburgers,

fried chicken or pizza. A number of other restaurants offer broader but not especially interesting menus. There are not many restaurants in the centre that really can be recommended for a relaxed evening meal.

Those who are staying or awaiting buses in Comayagüela may find that some of the small Chinese restaurants dotting that area offer the best bets.

Boulevard Morazán (sometimes referred to simply as *el boulevard*) has by far the biggest concentration of restaurants in Tegucigalpa, and most are contained within a strip about 2km long. They cover the gamut from casual open-air taco or *pincho* joints to elegant air-conditioned dining rooms. Prices also follow a broad range, although few spots are truly expensive. Some are open very late.

There are several noteworthy restaurants in Colonia Palmira, in the area around the Hotel Honduras Maya. Other restaurants may be found in the suburbs along Avenida Juan Pablo II and Boulevard Suyapa. We also mention here restaurants found in some of the towns just outside Tegucigalpa.

Dress is casual at most spots, but shorts and t-shirts are frowned upon at the fancier establishments. Reservations are rarely required, although at the more elegant restaurants it may sometimes be a good idea to call ahead, especially on weekends.

Downtown

As an alternative to the ubiquitous fast-food restaurants, **Salman's** has several branches, including one on the Calle Peatonal, with breads, pastries, coffee, and a wide variety of ready-made sandwiches that can be taken out or eaten in.

Café El Greco
$
Mon to Sat 8:30am to 7pm
Hipólite Matute between Jerez and Colón
☎220-0441
With tables set in a small, pleasant courtyard, this spot offers selections of coffee, cakes and other items such as *empanadas*.

Café Paradiso
$
Mon to Fri 9am to 8pm, Sat 9am to 6pm
Plazuela Calle Los Horcones casa 1351
☎222-3066
In a new location near the city centre, this is a delightful spot for coffee, dessert or a light meal. It also houses a bookshop, art gallery and handicrafts shop.

Al Natural
$-$$
Mon to Fri 8am to 7pm Sat 8am to 3pm
On the narrow side street behind the cathedral, Al Natural has a delightful garden terrace that provides a quiet oasis in the city centre. A fruit and vegetable stall guards the entrance. Besides an interesting variety of fresh fruit shakes, the menu offers many salads, soups, meat dishes, omelettes, sandwiches, tacos and fruit platters.
The premises are now shared by the Tobacco Road Tavern, open afternoons and evenings.

Restaurant Picadeli
$-$$
Mon to Fri 7am to 4pm
Avenida Cervantes
1½ blocks north of the plaza
☎237-9226
This spot, with a simple dining room and small outdoor terrace, serves breakfasts and lunches cafeteria-style, offering a big selection of hot dishes, including economical daily specials.

Mirawa
$-$$
every day 10am to 9pm
along the Calle Peatonal
Mirawa is one of the better choices in the city centre for Chinese food. Although most customers seem to go for the cheap and filling fried rice or chow mein, this brightly decorated restaurant offers a broad menu, including special preparations of steamed fish.

Mediterraneo
$$
Mon to Sat 9:30am to 9:30pm
Avenida Salvador Mendieta one block up from the Calle Peatonal, across from Pizza Boom
Mediterraneo offers the usual paella, meats, sandwiches and pasta, as well as a small selection of Greek specialties. The dining area is a bit dingy.

Hotel Plaza
$$
every day 7am to 8pm
near the end of the Calle Peatonal
Hotel Plaza has a dining room with a rather conventional menu, but it is comfortable and air-conditioned, and there are excellent lunches on weekdays for $5.

Colonia Palmira

Café du Monde
$$
Mon to Sat 11am to 7pm
3ª Calle
☎239-0334
Café du Monde is an elegant tea room facing a lovely garden. Sandwiches are offered on baguette, bagel or croissant, and a variety of soups, salads, quiches, juices, coffee and ice cream are also available, in addition to cheese platters. Classical music plays in the background, which seems appropriate since this spot is run by a grand-niece of French composer Hector Berlioz.

Tegucigalpa and Surroundings

El Arriero
$$$
Mon to Sat 11:30am to
3pm and 5:30pm to 11pm
Sun 11:30am to 10pm
☎*232-5431*
El Arriero offers attentive service in several small, inviting dining rooms with blue and white tablecloths. Appetizers at $5 to $6 include seafood cocktails and ceviche, grilled kidney, grilled sausage, and pickled tongue. Main courses lean heavily to steaks and also include brochettes and mixed grills.

La Veranda
$$$$
every day; Hotel Honduras Maya
La Veranda is an elegant hotel dining room with an enticing selection of appetizers including cream of pepper soup and duck salad. Linguine with shrimp, mixed seafood grill and roast suckling pig are among the main courses.

Elsewhere in Tegucigalpa

D'Barro
$
8am to 7pm
until 2am on weekends
Avenida Juan Manuel Gálvez, Colonia Alameda
☎*236-6905*
D'Barro is a courtyard café combined with a small bookshop, handicrafts store, and performance space on Friday and Saturday evenings. The menu contains light Mexican and Central American specialties.

Santa Lucía

Donde El Francés
$$
everyday 8am to 8pm
1 km before the entrance to the town
no phone
Donde El Francés is a delightful little tree-shaded outdoor restaurant with a small indoor dining room as well and a simple but appealing French menu that includes rabbit, goat and kidneys. Crepes and fruit drinks are among the other offerings.

Parrilla Miluška
$$
Tue to Sun, 10am to 8pm
at the edge of town
☎*237-0472 or 231-3905*
Parrilla Miluška is a big open-air shed offering a Central European menu with schnitzel, goulash and mixed grills.

Valle de Angeles

Several small, simple restaurants around the central plaza offer grilled *pinchos* and sausages as well as local breads and sweets.

Restaurant El Papagayo
$-$$
Tue to Sun 9am to 5pm
in the centre of town
☎*766-2152*
El Papagayo has a series of small dining-rooms decorated with artwork. The menu features Honduran dishes such as beef or sausage with the usual accompaniments, tripe soup and *tapado criollo*.

Il Pomodoro Pizza
$$
Mon to Thu 10am to 8pm
Fri to Sun 10am to 10pm
Half a block from the plaza
☎*766-2895*
A large variety of pizza is offered here. The front part of the restaurant is attractive, though the rear is quite gloomy.

Entertainment

Teatro Nacional Manuel Bonilla offers a variety of musical and theatrical programming. Unfortunately, notices rarely appear in the newspapers, making it necessary to visit the box office to find out what is on. The theatre, with its handsome pink exterior, faces Parque Herrera, situated two blocks beyond the end of the Calle Peatonal. Ticket prices are usually very cheap, except for certain foreign performers. It is worth the price of admission just to see the horseshoe-shaped, white and gold interior of this restored turn-of-the-century treasure.

There are many **cinemas** in the city centre and along Boulevard Morazan. The daily newspapers contain full listings. Most foreign-language films are presented in the original version and subtitled rather than dubbed in Spanish, which makes them more accessible to visitors. Ticket prices are cheap, although the choice of films tends to be rather narrow, with a preponderance of year-old Hollywood blockbusters and older action films.

A popular form of weekend entertainment, especially among young, sophisticated audiences, is an art form called **peña**, which consists of folk singing with a strong political or social character, often mixed with theatrical works of satire. Peña performances are presented at several venues on Friday and Saturday evenings. Among them are **D'Barro** (*Avenida Juan Manuel Gálvez, Colonia Alameda*) and **La Mancha** (*Boulevard Suyapa, near the university*). La Mancha has a big windmill in front and, in a separate area, offers **dancing** to a tropical beat every night. It is open late, until dawn on weekends. Peña performances usually begin late in the evening. There is a small

cover charge, and drinks are served.

For something noisier and less sophisticated, Tegucigalpa has its share of discotheques. Two or three others are clustered together along a single block of Avenida Juan Pablo II.

There are several night-clubs offering a blend of striptease, *ranchero* singing, juggling and various other acts. These clubs (taxi drivers know them well) are scattered around several parts of the city. Shows usually start shortly before midnight. Visitors should take note that the young women working at these spots often invite themselves to patrons' tables and order themselves many drinks, courtesy of the sometimes unsuspecting customers.

Casino Royale
every day 1pm to 2am
in the Hotel Honduras Maya
Casino Royale is Tegucigalpa's lone legal spot for gamblers. It consists of one small room with slot machines and gaming tables. There is no cover charge, but visitors must show passports to prove they are not Honduran. Doors close at 2am, but those already inside may stay until 5am.

Last but far from least, soccer, known in these parts as *fútbol*, is practically the national religion. Professional ga-

mes are played at the Estadio Nacional. Taxi drivers and hotel clerks can tell you when their favourite teams are playing. Amateur soccer also thrives, and in virtually any working-class neighbourhood games can be seen going full tilt in the hours before dusk and almost all day long on weekends and holidays.

Shopping

Tegucigalpa

The central area of the city is dotted with shops and outdoor stalls offering a wide variety of handicraft items from Honduras and neighbouring countries. **Tikamaya**, along Avenida Cervantes behind the cathedral, offers a fine selection of leather items, ceramics, textiles, wood objects and jewelry, mostly Honduran but also including some Guatemalan and Salvadoran products. A cluster of shops lies further east along Avenida Cervantes toward the Hotel Excelsior, offering similar items. Several more handicrafts shops can be found in the streets surrounding the Hotel Honduras Maya.

A number of movable street stalls make a daily appearance on the Calle Peatonal, with wood and leather objects in particular. More stalls can be found along the pedestrian-only stretch of Calle Los Dolores, a block north of where it intersects with the Peatonal. On the Comayagüela side, you can find some good bargains at the Mercado San Isidro, where selections of handicrafts are sold alongside the much bigger sections devoted to food and general merchandise. As well, there is a busy Saturday market adjacent to the Estadio Nacional, where some handicrafts items are sold. When buying something on the street or in a market, it is usually necessary to bargain to obtain the best price, and chances of getting reductions are improved if several purchases are made at the same spot.

Café Paradiso, on Avenida Paz Barahona three blocks behind the cathedral in Tegucigalpa, offers a small selection of original paintings. **D'Barro**, on Avenida Juan Manuel Gálvez in Colonia Alameda, is also part café, part shop with original paintings and some creative items of pottery and ceramics.

For books, **Librería Guaymuras**, on Avenida Cervantes a couple of blocks behind the cathedral, offers a good variety of books in Spanish, with the best selection anywhere of

books dealing with Honduran topics.

Santa Lucia

Local ceramic work is sold at several shops near the entrance to the town. **Cerámicas Santa Lucía** has some very pretty glazed pieces, while **Alfarería Ucles** offers larger pieces, many in animal or human shapes. **Artesanías Flor de Barra** has simple but pleasing items.

Valle de Angeles

The main handicrafts market, run by the Asociación Nacional de Artesanos de Honduras, offers a broad variety of wood carvings, ceramics, jewellery, leather items, naïve paintings and brightly coloured ceramic objects, especially the roosters which have almost become a national symbol. As well, there are reproductions of Mayan sculptures, bronze items, colourful baskets and straw hats.

A smaller market to the right of the main handicrafts market offers mostly cheaper objects, as well as simple items of furniture. The nearby municipal market also has handicrafts stalls in addition to the usual food items.

A row of shops across from the main market offers leather, wood and ceramic items as

well as naïve paintings and a selection of clothing and textiles from Guatemala and El Salvador. There are more shops along the road leading to the central plaza, including **Contrastes**, with fine wood and pewter objects. **Artesanías del Valle**, across from Restaurant El Papagayo, has a selection of Lenca masks in addition to some of the more common items. **Casa Yarumela**, one block below and marked by a big sign, offers a small but interesting collection of contemporary Honduran painting.

Souvenirs La Carrera, behind the church, offers a good selection of tropical wood items, including carvings and hand-painted objects, as well as ceramics and textiles. **Lessandro Leather**, near the market, provides a fine choice of handbags and other leather items.

Ojojona

Ojojona has an abundance of handicrafts shops, but most seem to concentrate on simple, locally produced items of pottery, many of them in animal shapes and spray-painted in lurid colours.

Western Honduras

The fabulous Mayan ruins of Copán evoke Central America's mysterious past and constitute the most stunning sight in western Honduras, if not the whole country.

These ancient ruins are memorable for their spectacularly carved stelae and majestic stairways. Few visitors fail to come away impressed. The adjacent town of Copán Ruinas is friendly and pleasing in its own right, with cobbled streets and plenty of traditional architecture.

But there is much more to western Honduras. The picturesque colonial towns of Santa Rosa de Copán and Gracias lie farther south. The latter is situated near the Parque Nacional Celaque, which encompasses Honduras's highest peak, Monte Celaque. Northeast of the Copán region, and reached by a different road, is the pleasant town of Santa Bárbara, known for its straw hats. Parque Nacional Santa Bárbara lies nearby.

Finally, there is the big industrial city of San Pedro Sula, which will give many visitors their first glimpse of Honduras. This is a mixed blessing. Although San Pedro Sula is a reasonably clean and prosperous place offering a decent range of services, it might also be described as stiflingly hot and decidedly boring, with little to retain tourists for more than a few hours. Business travellers, on the other hand, may come away with a more positive impression. Nevertheless, it is a good base for visits to other areas, notably Parque Nacional Cusuco, with its cloud forest at higher elevations. The port city of Puerto Cortés, 58km north of San Pedro Sula, has good beaches nearby and is covered in the Caribbean Coast chapter (see p 117).

Even visitors with only a passing interest in archaeology should make the ruins of Copán a priority. For nature lovers and hikers, Cusuco and Celaque national parks both deserve serious consideration. And those with a little extra time will have no trouble putting it to good use elsewhere in the region.

Finding Your Way Around

By Car

The first thing to remember when planning an itinerary in western Honduras is that points on the map that appear to be close as the crow flies may actually be quite far apart once Honduras's paucity of roads is taken into account. For example, someone bound from Tegucigalpa to Copán Ruinas will quickly discover that roads only extend a short distance west from the capital. A glance at the map suggests that the next most likely route leads northwest to Siguatepeque and west from there to Santa Rosa de Copán, except that a long stretch of this road is rough and unpaved. Even after reaching Santa Rosa, it becomes necessary to take a long jog north to La Entrada and then to

head southwest from there. What most travellers in this circumstance end up doing is heading north almost all the way to San Pedro Sula and then doubling back in a southwesterly direction, making for a long trip. And this is not the only such example.

It is an exaggeration, but only just, to suggest that in western Honduras all roads lead to San Pedro Sula. One of the most heavily travelled highways in the country leads south from San Pedro Sula past Lago de Yojoa and then southwest to Tegucigalpa. Another runs north from San Pedro Sula to Puerto Cortés and yet another goes east to El Progreso, Tela and La Ceiba. All are four-lane roads leaving San Pedro Sula, narrowing later to two lanes.

The most important road for the points covered in this chapter leads southwest from San Pedro Sula. At the village of Canoa, a branch runs south to Santa Bárbara and provides an alternate route to Lago de Yojoa. The main road continues southwest to La Entrada, where another branch goes southwest to Copán Ruinas and to the Guatemalan border at El Florido. Highway improvements on the Guatemalan side between the border and the city of Chiquimula are expected to reduce travel times between

San Pedro Sula and Guatemala City via Copán. From La Entrada, the main highway runs south to Santa Rosa de Copán, Nueva Ocotepeque and El Poy on the border with El Salvador. From Nueva Ocotepeque another road leads to the Guatemalan border crossing at Agua Caliente.

All these roads are paved and well-constructed for the mountainous terrain they traverse, but they are prone to occasional washouts or landslides during the rainy season, particularly in spots toward Copán Ruinas and Nueva Ocotepeque. The same applies to the road from Santa Rosa to Gracias. East from Gracias to La Esperanza, the road is rough and unpaved.

Car Rentals

San Pedro Sula

Avis
1ª Calle at 6ª Avenida N.E.
☎ *553-0888*
☎ *553-3716*
Airport
☎ *668-1088*

Blitz
Gran Hotel Sula, 1ª Calle between 3ª and 4ª Avenidas
☎ *553-2405*
Airport
☎ *668-3171*

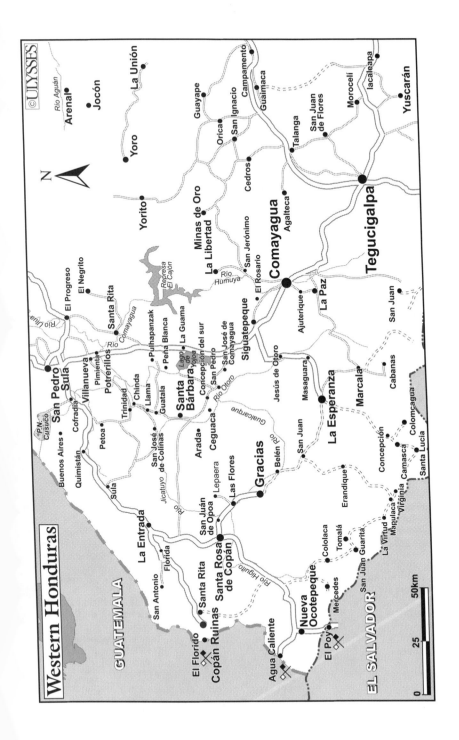

Budget
1ª Calle at 7ª Avenida N.O.
☎552-2295
☎552-6749
Airport
☎668-3179

C&B
1ª Calle toward the highway to
La Lima
☎552-4910

Dollar
3ª Avenida between 3ª and 4ª
Calles N.O.
☎557-0820
☎552-7626
Airport
☎668-3211

Hertz
Airport
☎668-3156
☎668-3157

Maya
3ª Avenida between 7ª and 8ª
Calles
☎552-2670
Airport
☎668-3168

Molinari
Gran Hotel Sula, 1ª Calle between 3ª and 4ª Avenidas
☎553-2639

National
4ª Avenida between 2ª and 3ª
Calles N.O.
☎557-2644

Thrifty
Airport
☎668-3153

Toyota
3ª Avenida between 5ª and 6ª
Avenidas N.O.
☎552-2666
Airport
☎668-3174

By Bus

All points mentioned
here are linked by
buses that are frequent,
if not particularly fast
or comfortable. On
many routes, seating is
five abreast, making for
a tight squeeze, and
numerous stops make
for long travel times.
On the other hand,
fares are very cheap.

There are few direct
services between Tegu-
cigalpa and points in
western Honduras
other than San Pedro
Sula. This has much to
do with the shape of
the highway network,
described above. It
seems that even if
you're going to heaven
you have to change
buses in San Pedro
Sula. Making things a
little trickier, there is no
central terminal in San
Pedro Sula; each com-
pany has its own small
terminal, although most
are clustered within
several blocks of one
another.

From San Pedro Sula

To Tegucigalpa:

Viana
Avenida Circunvalación
200m from Wendy's
☎556-9261

Saenz
8ª Avenida between 5ª and 6ª
Calles S.O.
☎553-4969
Viana and Saenz both
offer top-of-the-line
service, each with four

to six daily departures
and fares of about $9
for a 3.5hr journey.

Hedman Alas
3ª Calle between 7ª and 8ª
Avenidas N.O.
☎553-1361
Hedman Alas is a notch
lower, than Viana and
Saenz with about a
dozen daily departures,
including some express
services, and fares aver-
aging about $6.

El Rey
☎553-4262

El Rey Express
☎550-8355

Norteños
☎552-2145
Several other compa-
nies, including El Rey,
El Rey Express and
Norteños offer slower,
cheaper service, with
frequent departures and
journey times of 4.5hrs
or more. El Rey and
Norteños make inter-
mediate stops at high-
way junctions for sev-
eral points including
Lago de Yojoa,
Siguatepeque and
Comayagua. For the two
latter towns, there are
also slow local services
running into the town
centres, with service
about once an hour.

To La Entrada and Santa Rosa de Copán:

Toritos y Copanecos
11 Calle between 6ª and 7ª
Avenidas
☎553-4930
Toritos y Copanecos
runs local services
about twice an hour

and express services several times a day.

Congolón
8ª Avenida between 9ª and 10ª Calles
☎*553-1174*
Additional service is provided by Congolón, which continues onward to **Nueva Ocotepeque** and **Agua Caliente**.

To Copán Ruinas:

Casarola
6ª Avenida at 6ª Calle S.O.
☎*558-1378*
Gama
6ª Calle between 6ª and 7ª Avenidas S.O.
☎*552-2861*
Casarola and Gama each provide direct mid-afternoon departures, with return trips from Copán in the morning. Alternately, go to La Entrada and connect there for local service to Copán Ruinas, leaving at 40min intervals until late afternoon.

To Santa Bárbara:

Cotisba
4ª Avenida between 9ª and 10ª Avenidas S.O.
☎*552-8889*
Cotisba operates buses 45 to 60min apart until 6pm, on this slow 2.5hr trip.

To Puerto Cortés:

Impala
2ª Avenida between 4ª and 5ª Calles S.O.

Citul and Expresos del Atlántico
6ª Avenida between 7ª and 8ª Calles S.O.
Impala, as well as Citul and Expresos del Atlántico each run several times hourly *(45min, $1)*.

To Tela
1hr15min, $2
and La Ceiba:
2.5 hrs, $2

Catisa, Tucsa and **City**
2ª Avenida between 5ª and 6ª Calles S.O.
☎*553-1023*
Catisa, Tucsa and City run a coordinated service with departures every 30 to 60min from 5:30am to 6pm. Local service to Tela *($1, 2 hrs)* departs at 30min intervals.

Cotraipbal
1ª Avenida between 7ª and 8ª Calles Oriente
☎*557-8470*
Additional express service is provided four times daily by Cotraipbal, continuing on to **Trujillo** *(5hrs, $5)*.

From Copán Ruinas

To San Pedro Sula:

Casarola and Gama each provide one daily direct service to San Pedro Sula *(3hrs, $4)*, with early-morning departures.

To La Entrada:

Alternatively, slow local buses run at 40min intervals to La Entrada *(1.5 hrs, $1)*, from

where there are frequent connections north to **San Pedro Sula** or south to **Santa Rosa de Copán** and points beyond.

To El Florido:

Minibuses and pickup trucks provide service to El Florido on the Guatemalan border, with bus connections until mid-afternoon to **Chiquimula**.

From Santa Rosa de Copán and Gracias

From a terminal along the highway, there are departures at least twice an hour north to **La Entrada** (for connections to **Copán Ruinas**) and **San Pedro Sula**. Buses from Santa Rosa south to **Nueva Ocotopeque** run about an hour apart, with some of them continuing to **Agua Caliente**. Service between Santa Rosa and **Gracias** runs hourly and takes about 1.5hrs. From Gracias to **La Esperanza** there are one or two buses a day.

International Service

King Quality
6a Calle between 7a and 8a Avenidas S.O.
San Pedro Sula
☎*553-3443*

Monarcas Travel
1.5 blocks north of Banco de Occidente
Copán Ruinas
☎*651-4361*

Monarcas Travel, a Guatemalan company, provides daily minibus service between **Copán Ruinas** (*1.5 blocks north of Banco de Occidente* ☎*651-4361*), **Guatemala City**, and **Antigua Guatemala**. Travel time between Antigua and Copán is about 9hrs, with a one-way fare of $35. Departure time from Antigua is 4am, with the return trip leaving Copán at 2pm.

By Train

Passenger service between San Pedro Sula and Tela was suspended after Hurricane Mitch destroyed a bridge near the outskirts of San Pedro Sula. Twice-weekly service continues between Puerto Cortés and Tela.

By Taxi

As elsewhere in Honduras, taxi fares are quite cheap for travel both within and between cities. Fares for most trips within San Pedro Sula are $1 to $2, but $10 to the airport. There are few taxis in Santa Bárbara and none in Copán Ruinas. Taxis are readily available at La Entrada, Santa Rosa de Copán and Nueva Ocotepeque.

By Air

Aeropuerto Internacional Ramón Villeda Morales is located 17km east of **San Pedro Sula**, near the banana town of La Lima. Taxis between the airport and San Pedro Sula cost about $10. Local buses run along the main highway every few minutes, but the airport is 15 to 20min by foot from the highway, and security is a problem. The modern terminal building has restaurants, bars and duty-free shops. There is a currency exchange counter inside the building, while freelance money-changers operate just outside, near the taxi stand.

Grupo Taca operates four daily flights to **Tegucigalpa**. Isleña, Sosa and Rollins compete on the route to **La Ceiba**, with connections there to the Islas de la Bahía. There are also connections at La Ceiba for Trujillo and the Mosquitia, although in the eastbound direction this may require an overnight layover.

The airstrip at **Copán Ruinas** was closed many years ago. A small airstrip about 20km away on the Guatemalan side of the border receives occasional charter flights. There has been talk of a possible agreement to waive border formalities. Meanwhile, the Honduran government has indicated that it favours construction of a new airport somewhere nearby on the Honduran side. For the moment, San Pedro Sula has the nearest airport with scheduled service.

Airline Reservations

San Pedro Sula

American Airlines
16 Avenida between 1ª and 2ª Calles
☎*558-0524*
☎*558-0525*
Airport
☎*668-3241*

Continental Airlines
Gran Hotel Sula, 1ª Calle between 3ª and 4ª Avenidas
☎*557-4141*
☎*557-4142*
Airport
☎*668-3208*

Copa
Gran Hotel Sula, 1ª Calle between 3ª and 4ª Avenidas
☎*5505583*
Airport
☎*668-6776*

Grupo Taca
Avenida Circunvalación at 13 Avenida N.O.
☎*557-0525*
☎*550-5264*
Airport
☎*668-3112*

Iberia
Edificio Quiroz, 2ª Calle at 2ª Avenida S.O.
☎*550-1604*
Airport
☎*668-3217*

Isleña
Airport
☎*668-3186*

The San Miguel Cathedral, with its whitewashed facade,
is the highlight of Plaza Morazán, in Tegucigalpa. - *Claude Hervé-Bazin*

With its 16th-century church, the former mining town of Santa Lucía seems to belong to another era. - *Claude Hervé-Bazin*

Sosa
Airport
☎*668-3223*

Practical Information

Tourist Information

The **San Pedro Sula** branch of the Instituto Hondureño de Turismo is closed. Hotel clerks and taxi drivers are often the best sources of information. At **Copán Ruinas**, booklets and other forms of information are available at the entrance to the archeological site.

Banks

Most banks and *casas de cambio* exchange U.S. dollars in both cash and travellers' cheques. *Casas de cambio* offer similar rates as well as faster service and longer hours. Lloyds Bank, in San Pedro Sula, exchanges Canadian dollars, U.S. dollars, pounds sterling and German marks. There is an exchange counter at the airport that closes at 5pm and is closed on weekends.

Freelance money-changers operate just outside the airport terminal and sometimes in the *parque central*

where it meets the pedestrian-only portion of 4ª Avenida. Some of them offer poor rates, especially when the banks are closed.

Telecommunications

To avoid often excessive hotel surcharges, the best places for long-distance telephone calls or fax service are the offices of **Hondutel**. The main San Pedro Sula office is situated near the corner of 4ª Avenida and 4ª Calle S.O., a block and a half beyond the pedestrian-only section of 4ª Avenida (open 24hrs, but the immediate area is unsafe at night).

Hondutel also has centrally located offices in each of the other towns covered in this chapter. Hours of operation vary, and not all of them offer fax service. **Internet** service is available in **San Pedro Sula** at Yupichat *(Mon to Sat 9am to 8pm, 1a Calle at 10a Avenida N.O.,* ☎*550-8365)*, and in **Copán Ruinas** at Maya Connections *(every day 7am to 7pm, 1 block down from Banco de Occidente,* ☎*651-4077)*.

Language Schools

Ixbalanque Escuela de Español
☎*651-4432*
ixbalan@hn2.com
Ixbalanque Escuela de Español in Copán Ruinas, offers one-on-one Spanish courses, with 4hrs of daily instruction.

Exploring

San Pedro Sula

Honduras's second largest city is the country's most important centre of business and industry. With a population estimated at nearly two-thirds of a million, San Pedro Sula lies at the centre of Honduras's booming garment industry and is also home to other industrial sectors ranging from food processing to plastic goods and cement. The city is situated near an important banana-growing region, and this contributed significantly to its growth during much of the 20th century. The Sampedranos, as the city's residents are known, have cultivated and been shaped by a business mentality that stands in contrast to the lethargic pace and evident poverty of Tegucigalpa, the centre of government to the south.

Lying near the fertile valley of the Río Ulúa in the northwest corner of Honduras, San Pedro Sula is mostly flat, rising gently toward the west. The imposing Merendón mountains loom nearby. Though the city is situated close to sea level, it does not benefit from sea breezes, and the climate is mostly hot and humid throughout the year, moderated by occasional heavy showers from June to October. The hottest months are from March to May.

It would be a serious exaggeration to describe San Pedro Sula as a tourist mecca, but it has the country's busiest international airport, and many visitors funnel through here on their way to other places. Parque Nacional Cusuco, with its cloud forest and birdlife, lies nearby. Highways radiate to the Mayan ruins of Copán, to the beach resorts and nature reserves of the nearby Caribbean coast, and to Lago de Yojoa en route to Tegucigalpa.

San Pedro Sula's own attractions are more limited, although it does boast a new and interesting archaeological and historical museum, a substantial handicraft market, many hotels and restaurants (most budget-range hotels are quite unpleasant, however), and tour companies offering excursions to points throughout Honduras.

The city was founded in 1536 by Spanish conquistador Pedro de Alvarado, but fires, earthquakes and wanton demolition have erased virtually all traces of the past, leaving a place with little sense of its history. The Sula in the name is thought to come from an alternate pronunciation of Ulúa, the nearby river, whose name in turn may have come from an Aztec word for birds. San Pedro Sula really came into its own in the late 19th and early 20th centuries with the building of railways, the development of huge banana plantations nearby, and the arrival of families from the Middle East whose descendants continue to play an important role in the city's business life.

The central area of San Pedro Sula, encircled by a ring road called Avenida Circunvalación, is laid out in a rectangular grid pattern with streets and avenues identified by numbers and by quadrant. Streets (*calles*) run east and west, avenues (*avenidas*), north and south. The intersection of 1ª Calle and 1ª Avenida marks the dividing point of the four quadrants, which go by the Spanish initials N.E., N.O., S.E. and S.O. (standing for *noreste, noroeste, sureste* and *suroeste*, corresponding to the secondary points of the compass; *sur* means south and *oeste* means west, by the way).

Primera Calle (1ª Calle) forms a spine through the city centre, passing the *parque central* between 3ª and 5ª Avenidas Suroeste and serving also as the main approach to the city from the airport and other points to the east. Most points in the city centre are within easy walking distance, although taxis are often advisable at night to ensure of personal security. Even in the daytime, all but the most impecunious foreign visitors will find taxis more useful than city buses, which are generally oriented to outlying residential and industrial districts.

The *parque central* is the focal point of outdoor life in San Pedro Sula, though not as busy or picturesque as its Tegucigalpa equivalent. In the park is a statue of General Manuel Bonilla, a champion of public education. The pedestrian-only portion of 4ª Avenida Suroeste extends only one block from the park, but it has several restaurants and numerous shops and street stalls offering a variety of handicrafts. These stalls spill over into the park itself.

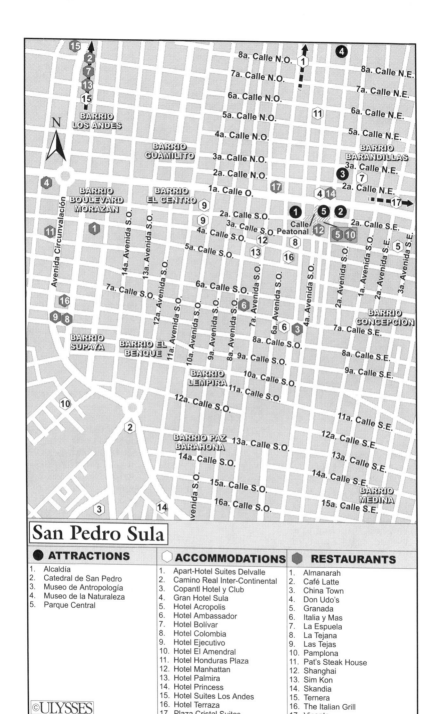

San Pedro Sula

©ULYSSES

Among the landmark buildings facing the *parque central* are the Gran Hotel Sula, the handsome Art Deco **Alcaldía** (city hall), and the big, modern, and very austere **Catedral de San Pedro**, built in the Gothic Revival style over a period of several years starting in 1949.

The **Museo de Antropología e Historia de San Pedro Sula** ★★ (*$0.70; Tue to Sun 10am to 4:15pm; 3ª Calle at 3ª Avenida N.O.*) is housed in a bright, pleasant terra cotta building that opened in 1994 and was financed in large part by a local industrialist who is also a keen amateur anthropologist and collector. The pre-Hispanic collection, drawn mostly from western Honduras, includes ceramic items, jade and obsidian carvings, and ancient utensils. Although items are well displayed, little information is provided on their origins. Another section of the

museum presents large canvasses and diverse objects depicting San Pedro Sula's history from the Spanish conquest to the present. The museum includes a garden café and an auditorium, used sometimes for plays or recitals.

The **Museo de la Naturaleza** (*free; Mon to Fri 8am to 5pm, Sat 8am to 12 noon; 3ª Avenida at 9ª Calle N.O.*, ☎552-5060) is a science and natural history museum oriented mainly to children and students, with most notations in Spanish only. Exhibits cover plants, animals, forests, conservation, volcanoes, and astronomy. Located a short distance from the city centre.

The **Mirador Capri**, on a hillside at the western edge of town, consists of an observation deck with views over San Pedro Sula and, on clear days, a wide swath of surrounding countryside extending to the hills near Lago de Yojoa. It is accessible by private car or by taxi.

East of San Pedro Sula, near the town of **La Lima** just beyond the airport, it is possible to visit **banana** plantations and processing plants operated by the local subsidiary of Chiquita Brands (formerly the United Fruit Company).

Technically, it is necessary to secure permission beforehand from the company office in La Lima, but it is often possible merely to show up during normal working hours (early morning to midafternoon) and take a brief look around. A private car or taxi is required. Passengers at the airport who have a couple of hours to kill before flight time can hire a taxi for a short excursion.

Other excursions from San Pedro Sula include **Parque Nacional Cusuco** (see p 109), **Lago de Yojoa** and **Pulhapanzak falls** (see p 186).

★

Santa Bárbara

Situated 108km south of San Pedro Sula, Santa Bárbara is a pleasant town with many colonial-era buildings, an attractive, tree-shaded central plaza, and a lively public market near the plaza. The town is noted for the production of hats and other items made of junco (pronounced KHOON-co), a straw-like fibre. The remains of a 19th-century castle, **Castillo Pográn**, are perched on a hillside outside the town. The **Parque Nacional Santa Bárbara** and **Balneario La Torre** (see p 110) are situated nearby.

La Entrada

La Entrada, whose full name is La Entrada de Copán, is a dusty, sprawling crossroads town situated 126km from San Pedro Sula, 59km from Copán Ruinas, and 44km from Santa Rosa de Copán. It is a place where passengers change buses and motorists pass through, rarely stopping, on their way to somewhere else. There are several restaurants here and a variety of accommodations.

The **Museo de Arqueología** (*$1.50; every day 8am to 4pm; 300m north of the highway junction*) has a small pottery collection and stone carvings as well as a recreation of a Mayan burial site. Tickets from the museum are also valid for the **Parque Arqueológico El Puente**, (*$2, 8:30am to 4:30pm*), an archaeological site situated 9km from La Entrada, mostly along a newly paved road. Taxis charge about $15 for the round trip, including waiting time. The site has a lavish Japanese-financed visitors' centre. The main group of ruins is 1km from the visitors' centre, through an area which is in the process of being reforested. The ruins, poised near the edge of a river, consists of a medium-sized pyramid and several smaller structures, harmonious but not in

Ruins of Castillo Pográn

any way impressive. There is simply no comparison with the ruins of Copán, and El Puente is best left to true archaeology buffs or visitors with ample time.

★★★

Copán Ruinas

The town of Copán Ruinas (pronounced co-PAN roo-EE-nas) is perched at a pleasant altitude, 1km from the majestic Mayan ruins that most visitors come to see. The town itself has a charming colonial air with traditional low-slung buildings and hilly, cobbled streets. The central plaza is tree-shaded and lively, and was recently extensively refurbished. A big rise in tourism in the last few years has led to the opening of more hotels, restaurants and gift shops, somehow without really

marring the town's peaceful character.

The **Museo Regional** (*$2, 8am to noon and 1pm to 4pm*) faces the central plaza and provides an introduction to the ruins, with historical information and exhibits of pieces taken from the site, including jewellery, ceremonial objects, some clay figures, and a reconstructed tomb. This museum has been eclipsed by the far grander museum **Museo de Esculptura de Copán**, which houses a truly magnificent collection, including some of the finest pieces excavated at the site. When opened in 1996, it was hailed as Central America's most splendid museum. The building itself celebrates Maya symbolism, shaped inside like a winding serpent, with visitors entering through a stylized mouth. Unfortunately, structural flaws forced the closing of the building a couple of years after it opened. It is currently open on an irregular basis while extensive repairs are being conducted. The number of visitors is limited due to safety concerns. This truly is a huge pity. The well preserved Altar Q, renowned for its sculptural beauty and for its series of glyphs and

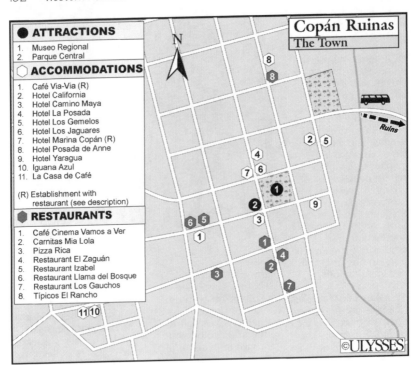

ATTRACTIONS

1. Museo Regional
2. Parque Central

ACCOMMODATIONS

1. Café Via-Via (R)
2. Hotel California
3. Hotel Camino Maya
4. Hotel La Posada
5. Hotel Los Gemelos
6. Hotel Los Jaguares
7. Hotel Marina Copán (R)
8. Hotel Posada de Anne
9. Hotel Yaragua
10. Iguana Azul
11. La Casa de Café

(R) Establishment with restaurant (see description)

RESTAURANTS

1. Café Cinema Vamos a Ver
2. Carnitas Mia Lola
3. Pizza Rica
4. Restaurant El Zaguán
5. Restaurant Izabel
6. Restaurant Llama del Bosque
7. Restaurant Los Gauchos
8. Típicos El Rancho

Copán Ruinas
The Town

©ULYSSES

human figures depicting 16 former rulers, was moved here from the West Court of the Acropolis. Like the rest of the museum's contents, alas, it is off limits to visitors.

Copán Ruinas is set amid lush, mountainous countryside. There are **hot springs** nearby, and **horseback rides** can be arranged through forests and coffee plantations (see p 60 for names of tour companies). **Santa Rita**, 9km away on the road to La Entrada, is a picturesque village with some fine colonial architecture.

Other attractions in the area include the **Rubi** waterfalls, a 45min hike from Santa Rita, as well as several **caves** within easy reach of Copán.

The countryside around Copán is inhabited by **Chorti** Indians, and visits can be arranged to their villages.

Visiting the Ruins

The ruins are a 10min walk from the centre of Copán Ruinas and are open every day from 8am to 4pm. Admission to the site is $10. Admission to the Museo de Esculptura de Copán is $5. Visitors wishing to see the Rosalila tunnel must pay a further $14, a highly effective means of crowd control. Thus, a complete visit costs $29, a real budget-breaker for some travellers but not

Exploring 103

a huge amount when weighed against the magnificence of the experience. Near the entrance are snack counters, gift shops, and a visitors' centre with exhibits and a model of the site.

The ruins are situated within an archaeological park that also includes a 1km-long nature trail with many species of trees. The main group of ruins lies about 400m beyond the visitors' centre. For $10 to $20, guides may be hired at the entrance for a 2 to 3hr tour of the ruins. Alternatively, there are books for sale that provide a more detailed description of the ruins than what follows here. The site is administered by the Instituto Nacional de Antropología e Historia de Honduras.

The site lies on the northern bank of the Río Copán, whose course was diverted to help preserve certain monuments. It comprises patios, courts, stelae, pyramids, temples and a structure known as the Acropolis. Apart from the structures that have been excavated and restored, there are many others that remain buried beneath the jungle, for now at least.

Toward the end of the preclassical period (from 300BC to 100AD)

the Maya world experienced a period of profound social change, with the establishment of the first Maya royal dynasties and the erection of the first monumental structures that came to characterize this grandiose civilization. The Copán valley was populated only by small, relatively self-sufficient communities of farmers.

Mayan King, Palenque

During the second to fourth centuries AD, the Copán region was transformed by a sustained demographic growth leading to the founding of the city-kingdom of Copán. The area flourished between the first and ninth centuries, when it was governed by a series of dynamic rulers. Most of the visible monuments date from this period. Soon afterward, however, Copán went into decline, weakened by war and famine, according to some historians. Maintenance of physical structures was neglected, and the jungle began to take over

again, enveloping the city completely by about AD 1200.

Today, as in the past, nobody visiting Copán can fail to be overwhelmed by the majestic beauty and mystique of the ruins, just as Diego García de Palacio related in a letter to the king of Spain in 1576:

"[In the province called Copán] . . . are ruins and vestiges of a great civilization as well as magnificent buildings, such that it is difficult to imagine how a spirit as primitive as that shown by this region's inhabitants could once have conceived a site as artistic and sumptuous."

Following the era of the first Spanish explorers, the site was visited in the 19th century by a series of American and British travellers and archeologists who began the excavations that have uncovered what we see today and that will doubtless continue in the years and decades to come.

The dynamism of the searches carried out up to now at Copán make it the most studied site in the entire Maya area. The passion of archeologists and art historians for these ruins rests upon several factors, especially the fact that Copán contains more hieroglyphic inscriptions and sculptures than any other site in the New World. For laypeople and specialists alike, Copán's splendour lies not necessarily in the quantity but in the exceptional quality of the sculpted stone works. The artists and craftspeople of Copán managed to attain a level of perfection and dexterity without equal in the Americas.

They succeeded in sculpting high reliefs of a precision and depth that make the human silhouettes appear to be detached from the rock.

What happened early on in this lush Central American forest for small groups of farmers to join together in the Copán valley and build an illustrious city over the centuries whose splendid temples and monuments still admired today?

Population growth created by a demographic boom resulted in uneven access to the valley's limited resources. Accumulated surpluses of food and wealth accruing to certain segments of the population created serious inequalities in what had been a relatively egalitarian community. Society had to undertake major changes in efforts to abate the social tensions that, sooner or later, might have threatened the survival of this new human establishment.

The creation of large, complex societies usually involves the elites inventing mechanisms of social and political control to establish a social order justifying and entrenching their privileged position. At Copán, as throughout the Maya cultural area, the strategy of the elite was to develop a religious ideology directly at the service of its political power. By giving themselves the status of semi-deities, they could legitimize and perpetuate the social structure over which they would have complete authority.

The pyramids, temples, hieroglyphics, icons, stelae, altars, ball courts, sculptures – all these manifestations of a great civilization – represent ways of conveying Copán's religious ideology. These works were created under the supervision of various kings to consolidate their religious and political authority.

The ubiquity of Maya hieroglyphic characters (a complex writing form combining a phonetic and pictographic logic) on all of Copán's artistic and architectural works enables us increasingly to reconstitute the highlights of this city's royal history.

The year AD 426 marks the foundation of the royal dynasty known as Yax-Kuk-Mo and the development of Copán as a powerful Maya political and economic centre. Upon taking power, each of his 16 heirs took great care to commemorate him as a reminder of their descent from this founding father and their relationship to a divine order.

The reigns of Yax-Kuk-Mo and his 11 first successors remain relatively obscure, nonetheless, since archeologists have as of yet found few vestiges of this period. This is not at all surprising since Maya leaders, upon taking power, followed the ritual of destroying their predecessors' monuments and building their own palaces on top.

Only starting in 628, when Smoke-Imix rose to the throne as the 12th sovereign of the dynasty, does the history of Copán really start to become clear. The 67-year reign of one of the most powerful and dynamic kings of Copán was marked

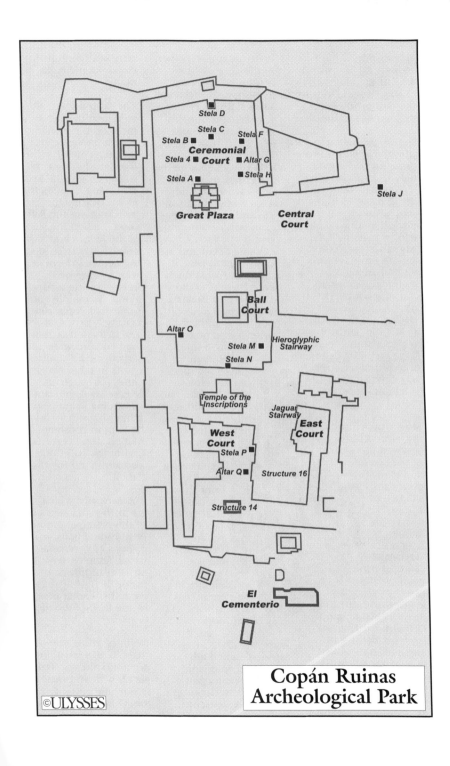

Stela D

Stela C

Stela B ■

Stela F ■

Ceremonial Court

Stela 4 ■ ■ Altar G

Stela A ■ ■ Stela H

Stela J ■

Great Plaza

Central Court

Ball Court

Altar O

Stela M ■

Hieroglyphic Stairway

Stela N

Temple of the Inscriptions

Jaguar Stairway

East Court

West Court

Stela P ■

Altar Q ■

Structure 16

Structure 14

El Cementerio

Copán Ruinas Archeological Park

©ULYSSES

by prosperity, hegemony, and an extension of the kingdom of Copán's boundaries to the detriment of its neighbours and rivals.

In 695 "18-Rabbit" took power. While his predecessor had contributed to extending the kingdom's boundaries, the dynasty's 13th monarch would leave his mark in a remarkable transformation of the city of Copán. Exhorting the most accomplished architects, sculptors, scribes and craftsmen of his era to surpass themselves, "18-Rabbit" raised the artistic standards of Copán and the entire Maya area to a degree of technical and esthetic refinement that would never be surpassed.

Most works from this period have survived the wear of the centuries, and their splendour can still be admired today. "18-Rabbit" built the **Ceremonial Court**, or main court, which stretches along an elegant avenue near the northern entrance to the ruins. This is a large quadrangular amphitheatre flanked by majestic stairways on three sides. At the edge of the northeastern entrance is **Stela J**, the first monument of his reign, built to cele-brate his rise to power. At the centre of the court are "18-Rabbit"'s masterpieces, **Stelae and Altars A, B, C, D, F, H** and **4**, which are Copán's most beautiful high reliefs.

Stela A is sculpted in the shape of a masculine figure whose headdress bears a mask of a sun god and is regarded as a symbol of authority. Stela A and **Stela B** have very fine detail and are considered to be among the most finely crafted works in the Mayan world. **Stela C** has human figures on both sides, and lay buried for many centuries, assuring a fine state of preservation. Some of the original red colouring is still visible. On **Stela D** a series of numerals is represented by full human figures. A large circular stone in front shows a series of grotesque faces representing Chac, the rain god. Another sculpture in the Ceremonial Court labelled **Altar G** displays a double-headed serpent with its jaws wide open and a human head emerging. **Stela H**, forming part of a rectangle with Stelae F, B and A, presents a female figure and is the only sculpture in Copán depicting a queen.

The **Central Court**, situated near the Ceremonial Court, is home to several more stelae, including **Stela J**, whose four facades are carved with hieroglyphic texts displaying a geometric motif. Beyond the Central Court lies the **Ball Court**, built in the shape of the letter *I* and surrounded by large sloping benches decorated with hieroglyphic inscriptions in a band along the middle and stone sculptures with macaw heads above. The ball court is 28m long and 7m wide and served, as did similar courts in other Mayan cities, for rough and religiously significant games involving heavy rubber balls that had to be kept in constant motion. Final construction of the Ball Court is also attributed to "18-Rabbit."

The **Acropolis**, which forms the southern side of the principal group of ruins and consists of a series of pyramidal bases, temples, terraces, platforms and patios. Part of it was eroded in earlier times by the flow of the Río Copán.

North of this is one of "Rabbit-18"'s most important buildings, **Temple 22**, with an ornate facade and several rooms inside. The door leading to the sanctuary is framed by voluminous skull-shaped sculptures, a symbol of death and the nourishing earth, while the seated personalities illustrate the lives of gods and humans. Recent studies suggest that this temple may symbolize a sacred mountain and that its main door may represent the entrance to a grotto sheltering Maya ancestors. Within the sacred building, "18-Rabbit" and his successors may have held rituals of self-mutilation aiming at communicating with the supernatural world.

"Rabbit-18"'s brilliant 43-year reign ended tragically on May 3, 738, when he was captured and apparently sacri-   ficed by the Quirigua dynasty. This humiliating rout at the hands of a small satellite kingdom seriously shook Copán's confidence. The defeat and the weakening of the elites' prestige is reflected in the absence of grandiose structures in honour of the 14th sovereign, "Smoke-Monkey," who seems not to have rallied sufficient political support to consolidate his authority during the nine years of his reign.

In 749, his successor, "Smoke-Shell," inherited a kingdom that was crossing one of the darkest periods of its history. Despite his brief reign (14 years), he managed to revive the glory of the royal

dynasty. Soon after taking power, he undertook major architectural projects. The spectacular result of his efforts, the **Temple of Hieroglyphic Stairways** located south of the ball court, represents one of the finest masterpieces of pre-Hispanic architecture. The thousands of hiero-glyphs carved on its 63 steps relate the triumphal saga of the royal dynasty of Copán and constitute the longest-known pre-Hispanic text. The six statues adorning the central passage at regular intervals represent some of the previous sovereigns in war dress. At the foot of the temple, to its southwest, are **Stelae M** and **N**, showing "Smoke-Shell" in all his magnificence. Copán's 15th sovereign may have used this temple in efforts to revive the people's faith in the royal dynasty through the glorification of its past.

The 16th and final king, Yax Pac, ascended the throne in 763. Like his father, he undertook ambitious projects commemorating the grandeur of the kingdom. Most of the visible structures in the Acropolis date from his reign. These include the final versions of two of the site's most imposing buildings, the **Temple of Inscriptions** (Structure 11) and **Temple 16.**

Located north of the western court of the Acropolis, the Temple of Inscriptions has four entrances adorned with hieroglyphic panels, one for each cardinal point. Five stairways are linked to the base of this temple and form the spectators' stands facing a symbolic ball court. According to some researchers, this may have been the site of human sacrifices in which the victim's head was used as a ball. Temple 16 is located right in the heart of the Acropolis. This massive pyramid sports several war-like sculptures with the effigy of the Mexican god Tlaloc. At its base is **Stela P**, representing Copán's seventh leader, and **Altar Q**, which portrays and acclaims the 16 sovereigns of the dynasty. Some archeologists consider this the most important artistic work on the site because of its rich historical detail. In erecting this altar, Yax Pac may have sought to legitimize himself in this glorious regal clan and to position himself as the messenger of the gods, in charge of assuring the kingdom's well-being.

The exaltation of Copán's brilliant past by its élites was not enough to do away with the growing problems faced by the valley's inhabitants. Sustained demographic growth over the centuries began to show detrimental consequences. Overexploited farmland no longer met demand for food. Famines, revolts and wars became the daily fate of the people. One of history's most fascinating civilizations was dying, finally disappearing in 805, the last date carved by the scribes of Copán.

The **Rosalila tunnel**, opened to visitors in 1999 (an additional charge applies), enables the traveller to penetrate deep beneath the temples and other monuments. This is a dark, labyrinthine netherworld, and you can almost feel the spirits that inhabited this zone in an earlier millennium. At the end of the tunnel is an exciting view of the splendid **Rosalila Temple**, an architectural masterpiece that remains mostly intact.

Santa Rosa de Copán

This pleasant old town, founded shortly before independence from Spain, is set at an altitude of 1,100m amid delightful mountain scenery with farming country nearby. Santa Rosa has a colonial air, with cobbled streets and many traditional red-tile-roofed buildings. The **parque central** is perched on a hill and faces an old church. While not worth a long detour, the town does make for an agreeable stopover. There are several hotels and restaurants here and a lakeside park 5km away **Parque Natural La Montañita** (see p 110).

At **La Flor de Copán Cigar Factory**, near the Hotel Elvir, visitors may watch workers roll cigars by hand in time-honoured fashion. Countless workers sit at long tables in a scene out of another century *(Mon to Fri, 7:30am to noon and 2pm to 5pm, and Sat, 7:30am to noon).*

Gracias

This sleepy but picturesque town was founded in 1536 and served briefly as a centre of Spanish military and administrative activity, though it soon lost much of its importance. Gracias, whose original name was Gracias a Dios (Thanks to God), continued to enjoy a modest prosperity in the intervening centuries but never really thrived, and was connected to the outside world by paved highway only recently. This relative isolation has helped lend the town a timeless air that visitors can enjoy today.

Set near the **Celaque** mountains and the national park of the same name (see p 110), Gracias is filled with traditional low-slung buildings and has three colonial churches, **San Sebastián**, **San Marcos** and **Las Mercedes**. The **Fortaleza San Cristóbal**, a restored Spanish fort with fine cannons, is perched on a hillside at the edge of town. There are thermal pools 6km away at **Balnerio Aguas Thermales** (see p 111).

La Esperanza

La Esperanza lies at the heart of mountainous Intibucá department and exudes an off-the-beaten-track sort of atmosphere. A district of the town with a significant indigenous population also bears the name Intibucá. This town lies along the shortest (though not the fastest) route between Tegucigalpa and the Copán district, leaving the main highway near Siguatepeque. In fact, getting from La Esperanza to the town of Gracias further west can seem like something of an adventure, crossing 83km (it seems longer) of wild, mountainous and sparsely populated terrain along an unpaved road.

La Esperanza, set at an altitude of about 1,600m, is a typical Central American backwater town with low-slung buildings and dusty streets, which turn muddy in wet weather. There is a scruffy central plaza bordered by military barracks and a large but simple **church** with a distinctive clock tower. Being the administrative centre of the district, the town offers banking and other services, including a small selection of lodgings and restaurants. Much of the surrounding countryside is inhabited by Lenca Indians.

The most important attraction in La Esperanza is the lively **Sunday market**, which fills the market area and spills into neighbouring streets. Lenca women can be seen wearing their colourful headscarves, but most of the merchandise on offer consists of food and run-of-the-mill industrial goods. There is little by way of handicrafts, although some local textiles can be found. Things start winding down by early afternoon.

Nueva Ocotepeque

This is the first real town that many travellers arriving overland from El Salvador or Guatemala are likely to see or, conversely, the last Honduran town that departing visitors will see apart from the border villages. Most travellers will have little reason to linger here unless they seek a place to stay overnight or need to visit the Salvadoran consulate (☎663-3357). Despite its appealing mountain setting and clusters of traditional-style buildings, the town is not very attractive and looks rather spooky at night, although it is reasonably safe until about 10pm. There are suitable places to eat and sleep.

The Salvadoran border at **El Poy** lies 9km south. The highway (and hourly buses) continue south to San Salvador. Another 9km south of the border is the mountain village of **La Palma** in El Salvador, noted for its many handicraft workshops. This makes a worthwhile excursion for those who are willing to tolerate border formalities (and, for visitors of some nationalities, extra visas). The Guatemalan border near **Agua Caliente** is 22km west of Nueva Ocotepeque. A short way beyond lies **Esquipulas** (in Guatemala), an important centre of religious pilgrimage, with its impressive basilica and famous statue of a black Chirst.

Both borders are open from 6am to 6pm. Travellers arriving later would be wise to stay overnight in Nueva Ocotepeque.

Parks

★★

Parque Nacional Cusuco

Just 20km west of San Pedro lies Parque Nacional Cusuco (*entrance fee $10, payable at the visitors' centre in the village of Buenos Aires*), which contains some of the finest cloud forest in Central America. The nucleus of the park covers 1,000ha and comprises the highest portion of Cerro Jilinco, the highest peak in the area at 2,242m. The remaining 8,900ha of park territory form a buffer zone where some economic activity is permitted. There are plans to expand the boundaries of the park, which forms the top of the watershed providing 80% of San Pedro Sula's drinking water. About 1,500ha of park territory consist of virgin forest. Within its boundaries, however, are 45 villages with a population of about 60,000 people. The climate is cool and rainy, with up to 3m of annual rainfall. The area feeds the basins of the Río Motagua and the Río Chamelecón.

Despite its proximity to the city, Cusuco is hard to reach because of primitive road conditions. A four-wheel-drive vehicle or high truck is required, and the trip takes close to 2hrs each way. A dirt road runs north from the town of Cofradía and through the village of Buenos Aires, where a visitors' centre is situated. Simple lodgings are available in the village for about $5 per person. There is a campground west of the park entrance part way up Cerro Jilinco. Full-day organized tours (expensive) are available from agencies in San Pedro Sula (see "Outdoors" chapter p 60).

Many types of birds can be observed, including toucans and, occasionally, quetzals, and the park is also home to monkeys and a variety of reptiles. There is an extensive variety of vegetation, including very tall pine trees and cloud forest at higher elevations. Hiking is possible (see p 111).

Parque Nacional Santa Bárbara

Situated near the town of Santa Bárbara, this park encompasses the mountain peak of the same name, the second highest in Honduras, at 2,744m. It also contains two abandoned mines, which visitors may enter, at sites known as El Mochito and Las Vegas. The park offers hiking trails but no services or facilities of any sort.

No permit is required. Information is available at the government forestry service (COHDEFOR) office in Santa Bárbara (☎643-2519).

Balneario La Torre

This popular bathing and entertainment spot is situated at the edge of Santa Bárbara, where a river has been channeled to form a series of pools. Entry is $1, or $3 when musicians are performing on the weekend. Food and drinks are available.

Parque Natural La Montañita

Situated 5km east of Santa Rosa de Copán, with the final kilometre along a very bad dirt road, this park is centred on a tree-fringed lagoon with boating and fishing.

Parque Nacional Celaque

Reaching 2,849m above sea level, Monte Celaque is the highest peak in Honduras. Its steep slopes are now protected as part of the Parque Nacional Celaque. Vegetation in the park includes many types of pine and, at higher altitudes, one of the largest areas of cloud forest in Central America. Birdlife is abundant during the dry season from November to April, and quetzals can be occasionally spotted. Rare species of mammals include pumas, jaguars, ocelots and peccaries.

The park entrance lies 8km from the town of Gracias; the last several kilometres are only suitable for four-wheel-drive vehicles or high trucks. There is a $1 admission charge to the park and no fixed schedule for entry. Simple lodgings and kitchen facilities are available at the visitors' centre, which is situated at an altitude of about 1,400m, and there are two campsites further up, with water available. Warm clothing is recommended.

Balneario Aguas Termales

A group of thermal pools, with temperatures in the dry season ranging from 37° to 40°C (a degree or two lower in the rainy season) is set amid lovely tropical forest in this spot 6km from Gracias on a side road off the highway to La Esperanza. The site is hard to reach without a private vehicle, but it is sometimes possible to find lifts from Gracias. Admission is $1, and opening hours are 6am to 8pm, or later by prior arrangement. The area is illuminated, and camping is allowed. Drinks and light meals are available, and towels and hammocks can be rented.

Outdoor Activities

Hiking

Four trails run through **Parque Nacional Cusuco**. The shortest one takes just 30m, the longest up to two days. Some stretches of trail run along high ridges, providing superb views of surrounding countryside.

For further information, contact:

Fundación Ecologista Hector Rodrigo Pastor Fasquelle
Edificio Pastor
1ª Avenida at 7ª Avenida
San Pedro Sula
☎ *552-1014 or 557-6598*

The climb from the **Parque Nacional Celaque** visitors' centre to the summit takes about 6hrs. There are clear trails up to an altitude of 2,050m. Coloured notches in trees indicate the rest of the way, which lies mostly through cloud forest. Further information is available from the COHDEFOR office just off the central plaza in Gracias.

Accommodations

San Pedro Sula

San Pedro Sula has seen a recent boom in the construction of high-end hotels, far exceeding any apparent increase in demand (and raising questions about the provenance of the funds used to build them). The city also has a reasonable selection of middle-range hotels, but the budget category presents a real problem. In some places in Honduras, it is possible to find cheaper hotels whose charm makes up for what they may lack in comfort, but such is not the case in San Pedro Sula. Search as we might, we did not come across any budget hotels we can truly recommend. Those indicated below are some of the less dismal choices and carry the proviso that surrounding streets tend to be gritty and not very safe at night.

Hotel Palmira
$9 with ⊗
$15 with ≡
⊗, *tv*
7ª Avenida between 4ª and 5ª Calles S.O.
☎*550-2363*
This is one of the better budget choices. Rooms are simple but adequate.

Western Honduras

Hotel Manhattan
$10 with sb
$14 with pb, ⊗
$21 with pb, ≡
7ª Avenida between 3ª and 4ª
Calles S.O.
☎550-2316
The 29 rooms here are
clean, bright and sim-
ple. The entrance is
above street level.

Hotel Ambassador
$12 with ⊗
$18 with ≡
7ª Calle at 5ª Avenida S.O.
☎557-6824
⇌557-5860
The 32 rooms here are
spacious but rather
plain and unappealing.
The entrance is up-
stairs.

Hotel Acropolis
$14 with ⊗
$19 with ≡
3ª Calle between 2ª and 3ª
Avenidas S.E.
☎557-2091
This 30-room hotel
offers simple, fresh
lodgings. It is situated
just east of the city
centre and has an up-
stairs entrance.

Hotel Terraza
$14 with ⊗
$20 with ≡
ℜ
6ª Avenida between 4ª and 5ª
Calles S.O.
☎550-0798
This is one of the better
choices in its price
range. Its 40 rooms are
simple but bright and
reasonably pleasant.
Rear rooms are quieter,
some facing a small
wooded area.

Hotel Colombia
$14 with ⊗
$20 with ≡
tv, ☎
3ª Calle between 5ª and 6ª
Avenidas S.O.
☎553-3118
⇌557-5345
This 27-room hotel
remains adequate but
has seen better days.
Rooms vary enor-
mously; some are quite
dark.

Hotel Bolívar
$34
≡, ℜ, ≈, ☎, tv, bar
2ª Calle at 2ª Avenida N.O.
☎553-3224 or 553-1811
⇌5534823
This well-situated 70-
room hotel has a grand
lobby, a decent restau-
rant and a pleasant
pool area, but rooms
are quite dilapidated
for lack of upkeep.
Those facing inside are
considerably quieter
than those facing the
street.

Hotel Ejecutivo
$38-$46 bkfst incl.
≡, ☎, tv
2ª Calle at 10ª Avenida S.O.
☎552-4289
☎552-4361
⇌552-5868
This 52-room hotel is
housed in two nonde-
script modern buildings
across the street from
one another. Rooms in
the higher-priced
newer building are
smaller but more pleas-
antly furnished.
Friendly service.

Hotel El Almendral
$61
≡, K, ☎, tv, P
16ªB Avenida at 12ªB Calle,
Colonia Trejo S.O.
☎556-8008 or 556-8989
Situated on a quiet
suburban street, this
single-storey, 25-room
hotel offers a homey
atmosphere and clean,
simple, pleasant rooms.
It is well suited to
longer-staying guests;
special rates are avail-
able.

Hotel Suites Los Andes
$65
≡, ℜ, K, ⊛, ≈, tv, bar
Avenida Circunvalación at 17ª
Avenida N.O.
☎553-4425 or 553-2526
⇌557-1945
Each of the 40 rooms at
this suburban spot has
a small sleeping area
plus a separate area
with kitchenette, table
and sofa. Decor is non-
descript, and service
can be somewhat slow.
Common areas are
pleasant, centred
around a big wooden
terrace with lounge
chairs facing a pool
and garden.

Apart-Hotel Suites Delvalle
$68
≡, tv, ☎
6ª Avenida between 11 and 12
Calles N.O.
☎552-0134
⇌552-0737
fcastro@globalnet.hn
Situated in a quiet area
1.5km from the city
centre, this spot offers
13 big, attractively fur-
nished rooms with lofty
wooden ceilings but
poor views.

Plaza Cristal Suites
$81
$\Re, K, \equiv, tv,$ ☎
10^a Avenida between 1^a and 2^a
Calles N.E.
☎ *550-8973*
☎ *550-9772*
⇌ *550-9822*
Situated a few blocks
from the *parque central*,
this spot has 19 suites
of various sizes. Most
have separate sittings
areas; all have kitchen-
ettes. Decor is comfort-
able but rather plain,
and some rooms are
dark.

Hotel Honduras Plaza
$92 bkfst incl.
$\Re, bar, \approx, tv,$ ☎
6^a Calle at 4^a Avenida N.O.
☎ *553-2424*
⇌ *553-2140*
Located at the edge of
the city centre, this spot
offers 40 bright, com-
fortable, modern
rooms. Service is
friendly, but prices
seem a bit high.

🏨Gran Hotel Sula
$167
$\Re, \approx,$ ☎, ☉, tv, bar, P
1^a Calle facing parque central
☎ *550-9900*
U.S. reservations:
☎ *800-223-6767*
⇌ *552-1170*
This 125-room land-
mark hotel has the best
location in town and
comfortable, appeal-
ingly furnished rooms.
Many rooms were reno-
vated in 1998. The ho-
tel, a Best Western affiliate, caters to business
travellers with an exec-
utive centre open long
hours, providing secre-
tarial service, fax, pho-
tocopies, computers
and courier pick-up.

There are two good
restaurants on site, as
well as a gift shop, tour
agency and car-rental
counter. The pool area
is pleasant.

Hotel Princess
$157
$\approx, ☉, \Re, bar, \equiv, tv,$ ☎
Avenida Cincunvalación at 10^a
Avenida S.O.
☎ *556-9600*
☎ *556-9590*
⇌ *556-9595*
hotelprincess@globalnet.hn
The 128 rooms here are
elegantly and comfort-
ably furnished. They
include work desks
with telephones. The
hotel also offers the
services of a business
centre with Internet
links. The small, circu-
lar lobby is appealing.

Copantl Hotel y Club
$166 executive floors
$171-$182
$\equiv, \approx, \Re, ☉,$ ☎, tv, bar, P
Boulevard del Sur, salida a
Chamelecón, 3km from the city
centre
☎ *556-7108 or 556-9461*
copantl3@copantl.hn
Guests at this 200-room
hotel are greeted by a
vast, three-storey lobby
elegantly decorated
with hanging baskets.
Other features include
glassed-in elevators, a
big pool, six tennis
courts, a bank and
shops with good selec-
tions of U.S. magazines
and local handicrafts.
Rooms are smallish but
very comfortably fur-
nished and decorated
in pale tones, with a
small sofa in each room
and work tables on the
executive floors. There
are three restaurants,

including a 24hr café
with a buffet.

Camino Real
Inter-Continental
$280
$\approx, ☉, \Re, bar, \equiv, tv,$ ☎
Multiplaza Mall,
Boulevard del Sur
☎ *553-0000*
⇌ *550-6255*
caminoreal@caminoreal.h
This is the top business
hotel in Honduras. Al-
though opened only
recently, it has devel-
oped a good reputation
for service. Its 150
rooms (there are also
seven bigger suites) are
smallish but bright and
cheerful, and comfort-
ably furnished, includ-
ing work desks. The
hotel includes a busi-
ness centre.

Santa Bárbara

Gran Hotel Colonial
$7 with pb and $\otimes$;
$10 with pb and $\equiv$
½ block from market
☎ *643-2665*
This friendly spot has
32 small, whitewashed
rooms set on two lev-
els, plus a handicraft
shop in the lobby.

La Entrada

There are several small
and inexpensive
*hospedaje*s and *hotelitos*
in La Entrada, but only
one hotel offering
reasonable levels of
comfort.

Hotel San Carlos
$11 with ⊗
$22 with ≡
tv, ℜ, ☎
at the crossroads
☎*661-2187*
The 46 rooms here are fresh and modern but a bit dark. The air-conditioned rooms are bigger, each with two beds. The new wing is better and very friendly.

Copán Ruinas

Hotel La Posada
$4 sb
$14 pb
near the plaza
☎*651-4070*
The rooms with private bath are simple but adequate and face a small garden courtyard. The others are very scruffy. All 20 rooms have fans. The lobby is dismal.

Iguana Azul
$5/ person for bunks
$11/ couple for private rooms
next to La Casa de Café
☎*651-4620*
www.todomundo.com/iguanazul
This is not your ordinary hostel. Situated at the edge of town facing a picturesque valley, it offers three private rooms plus two four-bed dormitories, all with shared bath. Rooms are spacious, with lofty wooden ceilings, and there is a pleasant outdoor terrace. Superb value.

Hotel Los Gemelos
$7
sb, ⊗
near the plaza
☎*651-4077*
⇝*651-4315*
This friendly spot has 13 rudimentary rooms facing a bright but unkempt garden.

Hotel California
$7
sb, ⊗
near the plaza
Right across from Los Gemelos, this is the spot to "go native." Four simple rooms are set on grounds decorated with wood, bamboo and palm leaves. Facing them are hammocks and a big, wild garden.

Hotel Posada de Anne
$11
⊗
near the bus zone
☎*651-4536*
The four rooms here are simple and reasonably comfortable.

Café Via-Via
$13
two blocks from the plaza
☎*651-4652*
Four simple rooms with private bath are tucked behind this café, which bills itself as a traveller's rendezvous.

Hotel Yaragua
$18
⊗
half-block from the plaza
☎*651-4464*
⇝*651-4050*
With 15 clean, simple rooms on two floors set around an attractive garden, this friendly spot offers excellent value.

Hotel Los Jaguares
$41
≡, *tv*
near the plaza
☎*651-4451*
⇝*651-4075*
The 10 rooms here face a shaded terrace with Mayan decorative touches. They are spacious but nondescript.

La Casa de Café
$44 bkfst incl.
☎*651-4620*
⇝*651-4623*
www.todomundo.com/casadecafe
Situated a few blocks from the plaza near the edge of town facing a picturesque valley, this spot offers five rooms with fan, high ceilings and simple, attractive decor. Run by Howard Rosenzweig, a Honduran-tourism writer and former New York schoolteacher, this establishment has a broad terrace with hammocks and superb views of the valley and the surrounding hills. Hospitality includes the use of a living room with TV and a library.

Hotel Camino Maya
$52
≡, *tv, ☎*
facing the plaza
☎*651-4518*
☎*651-4646*
⇝*651-4517*
This spot has 23 big, comfortable rooms set on two floors around a narrow garden courtyard. The decor is somehow a bit off.

Hotel Marina Copán
$98
≈, ℜ, *bar*, ≡, *tv*, ☎
facing the plaza
☎*651-4070*
☎*651-4071*
⇝*651-4477*
www.netsys.hn/~hmarinac/
Set in a series of
colonial-style buildings,
the 40 rooms here are
spacious, comfortable
and well appointed.
Decor is a blend of
modern and colonial.
Most rooms face one of
three lush garden
courtyards. The pool
areas is pleasant. Ame-
nities include a reading
room and gift shop.

Santa Rosa de Copán

Hotel Copán
$6-$10
sb / pb⊗
1ª Calle two blocks east of the
plaza
☎*662-0265*
Rooms are clean and
rather basic. The
higher-priced rooms
have private bath.

Hotel Elvir
$27
⊗, *tv*, ☎
Calle Real Centenario, two west
of the plaza
☎*662-0103*
☎*662-0805*
This centrally located
spot has 43 rooms,
many of them facing an
attractive central court-
yard. Rooms have been
renovated recently and
are pleasantly deco-
rated.

Hotel Mayaland
$29
ℜ, *bar*, ⊗, *tv*, ☎
along the highway near the bus
station
☎*662-0233*
⇝*662-0147*
This hotel offers 24
clean, modern, nonde-
script rooms.

Gracias

Hotel Erick
$9
tv, ⊗
near the plaza
☎*656-1066*
The 25 rooms here are
somewhat dingy but
reasonably comfortable
for the price.

Hotel Fernando's
$13
ℜ, ⊗, *tv*
three blocks from the plaza
☎*656-1231*
Seven reasonably com-
fortable rooms with
high wooden ceilings
are set in a row facing
a tree-shaded area.

Posada del Rosario
ℜ, ⊗, *tv*
four blocks from the plaza
☎*656-1219*
⇝*656-1234*
The nine rooms here,
set in a whitewashed
building 1.5 blocks
from the castle, are
bright, simple and
attractive. Set at different levels, they face a
garden.

Aparthotel Patricia
$21
⊗, ℜ
four blocks from the plaza
☎*656-1281*
⇝*656-1175*
This establishment
offers five pleasant,

modern rooms facing a
wooded area. The de-
cor has rustic touches.
Each room has a sepa-
rate sitting area.

La Esperanza

Hotel Solis
$10
ℜ, *bar*
near the market
☎*998-2080*
The 10 rooms here are
simple but reasonably
comfortable, with pri-
vate bath and hot
water.

Nueva Ocotepeque

Hotel Sandoval
$19
⊗, *tv*, ℜ
on a side street two blocks from
the bus terminal
☎*653-3098*
This 21-room hotel
provides very good
value. Small but pleas-
antly furnished rooms
are situated in a mod-
ern three-storey build-
ing.

Restaurants

San Pedro Sula

Although the city centre
offers a reasonable
variety of restaurants,
most of the more ele-
gant and comfortable
spots are situated along
or near Avenida
Circunvalación a short
taxi ride away.

Western Honduras

Fast-food spots can be found here and there throughout the city. Those yearning for something American-style in the city centre will find Wendy's, Burger King, Little Caesar's Pizza and Pizza Hut clustered near the corner of 4ª Avenida and 3ª Calle S.O., at the end of the pedestrian-only zone. Pollo Campero, a Central American chain offering U.S.-style fried chicken, has a large outlet nearby on 3ª Avenida.

Restaurant Shanghai
$
every day 10am to 9pm
4ª Avenida
in the pedestrian zone
☎ *550-1033*
Formerly called Super Paso, this popular spot offers a wide choice of economical Chinese and western dishes in an air-conditioned dining room.

China Town
$
10:30am to 9pm
7ª Calle at 5ª Avenida S.O.
China Town is close to some of the cheaper hotels and bus terminals. It offers a selection of Chinese and Western dishes in a pleasant, air-conditioned dining room.

Skandia
$-$$
open 24hrs
in the Gran Hotel Sula facing the parque central
☎ *552-9999*
Skandia is a throwback to the traditional U.S. hotel coffee shop, with a 1950s menu and de-cor to match. A broad range of dishes, with an emphasis on sandwiches and other light items, is served in a bright, air-conditioned dining room. The daily specials provide especially good value, and many American-style desserts are available. This is a fine spot to escape the daytime heat or to indulge in a late-night snack.

Pamplona
$-$$
Mon to Sat
7:30am to 8pm
Sun 8am to 8pm
across the *parque central*
from the Gran Hotel Sula
☎ *550-2639*
Pamplona offers a full menu, including some Spanish items and very good soups, in an air-conditioned dining room with undistinguished decor.

Vicente
$-$$
Mon to Fri 10am to
2:30pm and 5:30pm to
10pm
Sat and Sun 10am to
10pm
7ª Avenida between 1ª and 2ª Calles N.O.
☎ *552-1335*
Vicente is an authentic Italian restaurant and one of the few places in Honduras where pasta items are not overcooked. Opening dishes include *zuppa pavesa* and *antipasto*. Pastas include spaghetti with garlic and anchovies, spaghetti with shrimp, and *cannelloni bolognes*. A variety of rice, meat and seafood dishes round out the menu. The air-conditioned dining room is pleasant but nondescript, and service can be slow.

Restaurant Almanarah
$$
every day 11am to 9pm
4ª Calle between 15 and 16 Avenidas S.O.
☎ *557-4593*
This spot serves a variety of Lebanese dishes, including grilled meats and appetizers such as hummus and kibbeh, in a small, air-conditioned dining room.

Ternera
$$
every day 11am to 3pm
and 5pm to 10pm
Avenida Circunvalación at 8ª Calle N.O.
☎ *552-4498*
Ternera specializes in grilled meats, including Argentine-style mixed grills. A variety of lighter dishes are available for under $3. The restaurant has an air-conditioned dining room with rustic decor and an outdoor terrace.

La Espuela
$$
11am to 2pm and
4pm to 11pm; until 1am
on weekends
Avenida Circunvalación at 17ª Avenida N.O.
☎ *557-4221*
This establishment specializes in grilled meats, including Argentine-style mixed grills. Some lighter items are also available. Most seating is on an outdoor terrace with some road noise.

Sim Kon

$$

Mon to Fri 11am to 2pm and 5:30pm to 10pm, Sat and Sun 11am to 10pm

Avenida Circunvalación at 17ª Avenida

☎*557-6370*

Sim Kon has one of the most interesting Chinese menus in Honduras and a comfortable air-conditioned dining room with subdued decor. Specialties include seaweed soup with dried shrimp, smoked duck, fish roll with Chinese sausage, fish with bacon and mushroom, and beef with ginger root.

Café Latte

$$-$$$

Mon to Sat 6:30am to 10:30pm, Sun 8am to 2pm

Avenida Circunvalación at 16 Avenida N.O.

behind Hotel Los Andes

☎*553-2526*

The specialty of the house is *paella valenciana*. The menu also includes a variety of salads, pasta, meat and shrimp dishes, as well as breakfasts, desserts and coffees. The dining room is bright and pleasant.

Restaurant La Tejana

$$-$$$

every day 10am to 11pm later on weekends

16 Avenida at 9ª Calle S.O.

☎*557-5276*

With spacious indoor and outdoor dining areas, this spot offers an interesting selection of meat and seafood dishes.

Restaurant Las Tejas

$$-$$$

every day 10am to 11pm

17 Avenida at 9ª Calle S.O.

☎*552-2705*

This restaurant serves grilled meats and a variety of fish and seafood dishes, including seafood soups, in a simple, open-air dining area.

The Italian Grill

$$-$$$

Mon to Sat 10am to 11pm

8ª Calle at 16 Avenida S.O.

☎*552-1770*

The menu here is broad, ranging from soups, salads and pastas to steaks, fish and shrimp. The dining room is modern, air-conditioned and comfortable.

Italia y Mas

$$-$$$

Tue to Sun 11:30am to 11pm

1ª Calle at 8ª Avenida N.O.

☎*550-1837*

This delightful spot, with an outdoor terrace set around a garden courtyard and an indoor air-conditioned dining room, offers interesting and authentic varieties of antipasti, pasta and pizza, as well as grilled meats, fish and shrimp. Desserts include home-made ice creams.

Granada

$$$

11:30am to 2:30pm 6pm to 11:30pm

upstairs in the Gran Hotel Sula facing the parque central

☎*552-9999*

Granada is an elegant, comfortable spot in the city centre offering a big salad bar and, something even rarer in Honduras, an interesting choice of vegetables with main courses and a selection of breads, including a wonderful corn bread. Specialties include sea bass, snapper, pepper steak, filet mignon, and shrimp tempura. There is a wide choice of desserts for under $2.

Don Udo's

$$$

Mon to Fri noon to 2 pm and 6pm to 11pm, Sat 6pm to 11pm Sun 11:30am to 2:30pm

Boulevard Los Próceres at 20ª Avenida just beyond Avenida Circunvalación

☎*553-3106*

Don Udo's is a delightful outdoor café with a variety of soups, ceviche and seafood cocktails as openers and some light dishes including quiches, croquettes and steak sandwiches. Main items include the usual steak, chicken, fish and shrimp as well as rabbit and fondue bourguignonne. There is a good variety of desserts.

Pat's Steak House

$$$

every day 11:30am to 3pm and 6pm to 11pm

Avenida Circunvalación at 17ª Avenida and 5ª Calle S.O.

☎*553-0939*

Pat's Steak House specializes in grilled steaks, with ribs, chicken, fish and shrimp rounding out the menu. The decor is reminiscent of an

American steakhouse, with several small air-conditioned dining rooms.

South of San Pedro Sula

Oasi Italiana
$$-$$$
open 24hrs (30% surcharge from 11pm to 7am)
Km 58 on the highway to Tegucigalpa, near Lago de Yojóa
☎*991-1195*
An open-air restaurant set on peaceful, tree-shaded grounds offers a great variety of pasta, including lasagne and gnocchi, as well as polenta, meat and fresh fish dishes, seafood, and salads. Elegant (but expensive) breakfasts are also available.

La Entrada

San Carlos
$-$$
in the Hotel San Carlos, at the crossroads
San Carlos offers a broad menu with good food at remarkably cheap prices (e.g. filet mignon for $5). The dining room is comfortable and air-conditioned but rather dark.

Copán Ruinas

All restaurants shown here are located within two or three blocks of the central plaza. Exact locations are shown on the map on page 102.

Típicos El Rancho
$
every day 8am to 10pm
This open-air spot, shaded by a big thatched *champa*, offers simple meat dishes plus tacos, enchiladas and pupusas.

Restaurant El Zaguán
$
every day 10am to 8pm
☎*651-4592*
This spot offers simple, low-priced meat dishes, as well as spaghetti, in a simple, slightly funky dining room.

Restaurant Izabel
$
every day 6:30am to 9pm
This very humble spot offers good but simple food, including eggs, spaghetti, and fruit plates.

Café Via-Via
$
every day 7am to 10pm
☎*651-4652*
This popular hangout for budget travellers, run by an elderly Belgian couple, offers a varied menu in casual surroundings. Items include meats, vegetarian dishes, spaghetti, and waffles.

Pizza Rica
$-$$
every day 11am to 11pm
☎*651-4016*
The name says it all. Pizza is served in a small dining room with hanging baskets.

Carnitas Mía Lola
$-$$
every day 10am to 10pm
☎*651-4196*
This interestingly decorated spot offers a selection of simple Mexican and Honduran dishes, including *carnitas* and *pollo al pastor*.

Café Cinema Vamos a Ver
$-$$
every day 6am to 10pm
This very casual open-air spot (the service can be downright slow) offers a variety of eggs, salads, pasta, tea and coffee. Specialties include quiche and ginger chicken.

Restaurant Llama del Bosque
$$
every day 6:30am to 10pm
☎*651-4431*
With a big, attractive, high-ceilinged dining room decorated with colourful handicrafts, this spot offers a variety of breakfast dishes, soups, salads, pasta, meats and rice dishes.

Restaurant Los Gauchos
$$$
every day 6pm to 10pm
☎*651-4221*
This Uruguayan-style steakhouse serves a variety of grilled meats in a big, air-conditioned dining room. Shrimp is also on the menu.

Restaurant Glifos
$$$
every day 6am to 10pm
in the Hotel Marina Copán,
facing the plaza
☎*651-4070*
This comfortable, air-
conditioned restaurant,
set on two levels, offers
a selection of Hondu-
ran and so-called inter-
national dishes, includ-
ing chicken with
poppyseed and steak
flambé.

Santa Rosa de Copán

A diminutive restaurant
row, along Calle
Centenario two blocks
south of the central
plaza, accounts for
some of Santa Rosa's
better dining opportu-
nities.

El Rodeo
$-$$
*Mon to Sat 10am to
midnight*
Calle Centenario
☎*662-0697*
This spot offers meats
and lighter items in a
Wild West decor, with
wooden benches and
tables.

Flamingos
$-$$
*10am to 10pm, closed
Tue*
Calle Centenario
☎*662-0654*
A varied menu includ-
ing meat, fish and
seafood dishes as well
as pasta and pizza, is
offered in a pleasant,
breezy dining room
and on an outdoor
terrace in back.

Gracias

Restaurant Típicos La Galera
$
every day 8am to 10pm
one block west of the plaza
☎*656-1080*
Breakfasts and a variety
of dinner items, includ-
ing grilled meats,
fajitas, burritos, smoked
pork chops and pizza,
are served at tables set
around a garden court-
yard.

Restaurant Juancascos
$-$$
every day 7am to 10pm
at Posada del Rosario, four
blocks from the plaza
☎*656-1219*
A variety of Honduran-
style dishes are offered
on a breezy terrace
overlooking the town.

Nueva Ocotepeque

Comedor Tomasita
$
everyday 7am to 9pm one
block from the main street near
the central plaza
Comedor Tomasita is
popular with local
families and offers a
selection of snacks and
full meat-based meals,
including daily specials,
at very reasonable
prices. A typical special
is steak with egg,
cheese and beans for
under $2.

Sandoval
$-$$
7am to 9pm
in the Hotel Sandoval
Sandoval offers a vari-
ety of snacks, sand-
wiches, meats and sea-
food dishes in a bright
dining room.

Entertainment

San Pedro Sula

There are several **cine-
mas** in San Pedro Sula,
including the Cine
Presidente and the Cine
Tropicana a couple of
blocks apart on 2ª Calle
between 7ª and 9ª
Avenidas S.O. in the
city centre. Listings
appear in the daily
newspapers. As else-
where in Honduras,
soccer (*fútbol*) is very
popular. The stadium is
situated on 1ª Calle just
a few blocks west of
the city centre. Almost
anyone, including taxi
drivers and hotel clerks,
will be pleased to tell
you when their favour-
ite teams are playing.
Occasional **plays** or
recitals are staged in the
auditorium of the
Museo de Antropología,
3ª Calle at 3ª Avenida
N.O. Check at the
museum for details.

For later at night, there
is a small **casino** in the
Copantl Hotel (*8pm to
4am, proof of foreign
nationality required*),
and several **dance clubs**,
including Shadows on
Avenida Circunvalación
at 15ª Avenida N.O.

Copán Ruinas

This is an early-to-bed, early-to-rise sort of place, but certain restaurant-bars offer lively evening scenes, particularly in the area to the south and west of the plaza. **Café Cinema Vamos a Ver** has film showings most nights at 7pm.

Shopping

San Pedro Sula

Mercado Guamilito, bounded by 8ª and 9ª Avenidas and 6ª and 7ª Calles N.O. is a good spot to shop for handicrafts. Most of the market is devoted to food and cheap industrial items, but at one end are several rows of stalls offering a wide range of Honduran items as well as some objects from Guatemala and El Salvador.

Items include wood carvings, ceramics, leather goods, hand-painted wooden objects, textiles, basketry and imitation Mayan carvings. Although most prices are marked, a little haggling can reduce the bill. In the heart of the city, the pedestrian-only portion of 4ª Avenida and the adjacent portion of the *parque central* are lined with shops and stalls offering a wide range of handicrafts. Although prices may be slightly higher in the shops, they tend to offer a more careful selection of items than the street or market stalls.

Santa Bárbara

Several stalls at the public market offer selections of hats and other items woven with *junco*, a straw-like fibre. The gift shop at the nearby Gran Hotel Colonial has colourful basketery items as well as many hats and some ceramic items.Copán Ruinas

The centre of town is dotted liberally with shops offering an interesting variety of Central American handicrafts. There are also a couple of shops near the entrance to the ruins. Some shops stock books in several languages on Copán and Mayan history in general.

The Caribbean Coast ★★

Most people,

even in Honduras itself, tend to think of the country as being almost entirely Central American in character.

This notion is reinforced by Honduras's geographic position right smack in the middle of the Central American isthmus. It is also suggested by the language, culture and origins of the great majority of its population.

But Honduras is also a Caribbean country, with wonderful sparkling beaches and cultural influences that harken well beyond the Amerindian and Spanish heritage that has shaped most of Central America. The Caribbean influence is most evident on Islas de la Bahía (see p 143), with their largely English-speaking, West Indian population, but the northern coastal regions of the mainland have also been permeated to some degree. The coast is washed by azure Caribbean waters, peopled partly by the

dark-skinned Garífuna, and dotted with ancient forts built to ward off pirate attacks. These days, it swings to the rhythms of salsa, meremgue, *punta* and reggae. More than in other Central American countries (with the obvious exception of Belize), Honduras's economy, which is a combination of the old fruit-based economy and the newer light manufacturing and tourism industries, favours the Caribbean rather than the Pacific side.

The Caribbean coast stretches from Omoa and its fort near the Guatemalan border, to the busy banana port of Puerto Cortés, to the beaches and nature reserves of Tela. It continues eastward to La Ceiba, with its port facilities and nature treks, and onward to the beach-rimmed colonial city of Trujillo. From there, the coast extends still farther on into the wild, sparsely populated Mosquitia region, which continues beyond even the distant Nicaraguan border.

Tela and Trujillo, with their broad sheltered bays and palm-fringed beaches, both have tremendous tourism potential. Tela's tourism sector has grown at a gentle pace, whereas the number of visitors to Trujillo has declined in recent years, for reasons that are mentioned later in this chapter. There are also fine beaches close to La Ceiba and Puerto Cortés with good accommodations nearby. For nature lovers, spectacular seaside wildlife reserves beckon near Tela and La Ceiba, there are good mountain hiking and whitewater rafting opportunities near La Ceiba, and a little of each near Trujillo. There are interesting colonial forts at Omoa and Trujillo. In short, there is a little something for just about everyone along Honduras's Caribbean coast.

Finding Your Way Around

By Car

A four-lane highway runs eastward from **San Pedro Sula** to La Lima and El Progreso, narrowing to two lanes and turning northeast to **Tela**. From there the highway continues eastward, running inland much of the way, to **La Ceiba** and on to **Trujillo**. The distance from San Pedro Sula to Tela is 90km, 188km to La Ceiba and 440km to Trujillo. The paved highway ends at Puerto castilla, just east of Trujillo. Farther east, a dirt road runs to the village of Limón, where it peters out and turns into little more than a track.

Another four-lane highway runs 58km north from San Pedro Sula to **Puerto Cortés**. From there, a paved highway runs west to **Omoa**, continuing to Cuyamel and ending just short of the Guatemalan border. There is no official border crossing there, although local people sometimes cross the river that forms the boundary.

On the Guatemalan side, a newly paved road runs from **Puerto Barrios** to the Honduran border, and plans call

for a full-scale international link once Honduras comes up with the money to build a bridge across the Río Matagua at Cuyamelito. This will provide the missing road link between Puerto Barrios and Puerto Cortés, two of Central America's busiest commercial seaports. From Puerto Cortés to points east, it is necessary to detour via San Pedro Sula.

From **Tegucigalpa** to Tela or La Ceiba, the best is the main highway to San Pedro Sula, taking the Santa Rita cutoff about midway between Lago de Yojoa and San Pedro Sula. This leads to El Progreso and the junction with the main coastal highway.

From Tegucigalpa to Trujillo, the shortest route runs northeast from the capital along the highway to Juticalpa, making a left turn about 40km before Juticalpa at the tiny crossroads village of Los Limones. From there, a wide gravel road runs north past the town of La Unión, near Parque Nacional La Muralla, eventually meeting a paved highway just east of Olanchito. This highway goes east to Savá (sometimes spelled Sabá) and the junction with the coastal highway (which at this point runs quite far inland). A rougher alternate route from Tegucigalpa to Trujillo

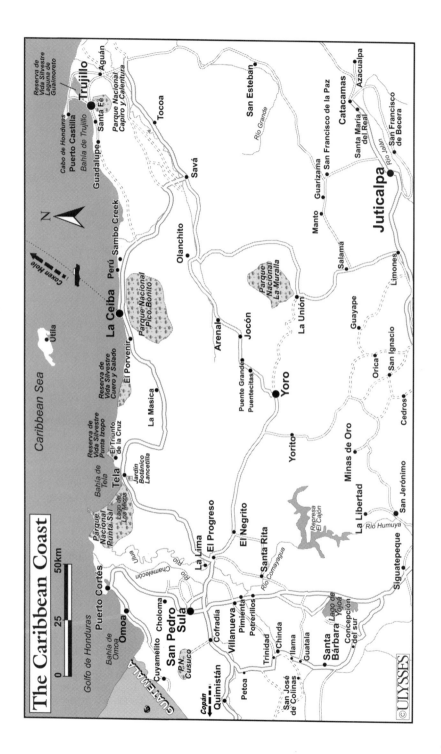

The Caribbean Coast

0   25   50km

Caribbean Sea

Golfo de Honduras

Bahía de Omoa

GUATEMALA

Coxen Hole

Útila

Reserva de Vida Silvestre Laguna de Guaimoreto

Trujillo
Aguán
Santa Fe
Cabo de Honduras
Puerto Castilla
Bahía de Trujillo
Parque Nacional Capiro y Calentura
Guadalupe
Tocoa
Savá
San Esteban
Río Grande
San Francisco de la Paz
Azacualpa
Catacamas
Santa María del Real
San Francisco de Becerra
Río Jalán
Juticalpa
Guarizama
Manto
Salamá
Limones
Guayape
San Ignacio
Orica
Cedros
San Jerónimo
Río Humuya
La Libertad
Minas de Oro
Siguatepeque
Represa El Cajón
Río Comayagua
Santa Rita
El Negrito
El Progreso
Yorito
Yoro
Puentecitas
Puente Grande
Jocón
Arenal
La Unión
Parque Nacional La Muralla
Olanchito
Sambo Creek
Perú
La Ceiba
Parque Nacional Pico Bonito
El Porvenir
Reserva de Vida Silvestre Cuero y Salado
La Masica
El Triunfo de la Cruz
Jardín Botánico Lancetilla
Tela
Bahía de Tela
Lago de Los Micos
Parque Nacional Punta Sal
Reserva de Vida Silvestre Punta Izopo
La Lima
La Lima
Río Chamelecón
Río Ulúa
Puerto Cortés
Omoa
Cuyamelito
Choloma
San Pedro Sula
P.N. Cusuco
Cofradía
Villanueva
Pimienta
Potrerillos
Trinidad
Chinda
Ilama
Guatala
Santa Bárbara
Concepción del Sur
Lago de Yojoa
Petoa
San José de Colinas
Quimistán
Copán

N

© ULYSSES

runs via Juticalpa and San Esteban.

The highway from La Ceiba to Trujillo runs quite far inland over most of its length, and the scenery tends to be rather tedious. This routing was chosen, in part, to serve the palm-oil plantations near Savá. Long-range plans call for a true coastal highway running parallel to the existing road. There are many fine beaches along the coast here but, except for those nearest La Ceiba, they are very difficult to reach (and bereft of amenities) because of the absence of road links.

Car Rentals

Puerto Cortés
Maya
3ª Avenida between 2ª and 3ª Calle Este
☎ *665-0064*

La Ceiba
Budget
Colonia Miraflores
☎ *441-1105*

Dino's
Hotel Partenon Beach, 1a Avenida
☎ *443-0434*

Maya
Hotel La Quinta
☎ *443-3071*

Molinari
Gran Hotel Paris
☎ *443-0055*

By Bus

Bus services on the Caribbean coast, as elsewhere in Honduras, vary enormously in speed and comfort. Fast, comfortable service is available on routes linking San Pedro Sula, Tela, La Ceiba and Trujillo, although in certain instances, notably at Tela, this involves the chancy business of flagging buses along the highway near the edge of town. Passengers can travel in comfort on the Tegucigalpa – Tela – La Ceiba and Tegucigalpa – Trujillo routes. Service between San Pedro Sula and Puerto Cortés is fast and very frequent but not very comfortable. Elsewhere, passengers have to put up with cramped conditions, slow service and numerous stops. This is true also of the Tela – San Pedro Sula and Tela – La Ceiba local services.

From Puerto Cortés

Three companies, Impala, Citul and Expresos del Atlántico, provide service several times an hour on the 50min journey between Puerto Cortés and **San Pedro Sula**. Buses leave from points near the *parque central* and make several stops in town before heading out. Look for buses marked "Directo" or "Expreso." Otherwise, the trip is much slower. All have very cramped seating. Buses to **Omoa** and **Cuyamel** run twice an hour from a terminal at 6a Avenida and 4a Calle, almost across from the Impala and Citul terminal. Journeys from Puerto Cortés to most parts of Honduras involve connections at San Pedro Sula. An exception is the air-conditioned express service (less than 4hrs) to **Tegucigalpa** provided by Maya Express (☎ *665-6404*), with a single early-morning departure from Puerto Cortés and an afternoon return from Tegucigalpa.

From Tela

Plenty of fast, comfortable buses go past Tela about twice an hour en route between **San Pedro Sula** *(1.5hrs, $2)* and **La Ceiba** *(1hr 15min, $2)*. These buses can be flagged at a point near an open-air restaurant called Merendero Tío Jaime, but since they originate elsewhere it can be tricky to pinpoint departure times, and finding seats is not a sure bet. The alternative is to use the slow, crowded local services, leaving two or three times an hour until 6pm in either direction from a terminal facing the public market two blocks from Tela's *parque central*. It becomes something of a tradeoff: you either spend time standing at the edge of the highway waiting for a comfortable express bus, or you subject yourself to a slow journey in cramped conditions on the multi-stop local service. If you are travelling to Tela from either San Pedro Sula or La Ceiba, the clear choice is the express service, even if it costs slightly more. Taxis are readily available at the highway drop in Tela. The above applies also to service to or from **Trujillo**, running four times a day. To **Tegucigalpa** *(5.5hrs, $5)*, Etrusca *(☎448-1328)* and Cristina *(☎441-2028)* both run fast, comfortable buses several times a day, stopping in Tela en route from La Ceiba. Etrusca has a small terminal about 100m east of Merendero Tío Jaime.

From La Ceiba

La Ceiba is just about the only place in Honduras with a well organized (if somewhat drab) central bus terminal, from which nearly all long-distance services operate. (One notable exception is the Viana luxury service to Tegucigalpa, which runs from the Esso gas station about a block-and-a-half away.) The main terminal is located about 2km from the city centre. To **Tela** *(1hr 15min, $2)* and **San Pedro Sula** *(2.5hrs, $2)*, Catisa, Tucsa and City run a coordinated service with departures every 30 to 60min from

5:30am to 6pm. Local service to Tela *($1, 2hrs)* goes at half-hour intervals. To **Trujillo** *(3.5hrs, $2)*, slow, uncomfortable buses run several times daily, with departures at irregular intervals. Alternately, buses head to Tocoa every half-hour, with connections there for Trujillo every 15min until late afternoon. A more attractive but trickier alternative is the comfortable San Pedro Sula – Trujillo express service run four times daily by Cotraipbal *(☎557-8470 in San Pedro Sula, ☎434-4932 in Trujillo)*, which stops in La Ceiba near Hotel La Quinta. To **Tegucigalpa**, *(6.5hrs, $6)*, **Etrusca** *(☎441-0340)* and **Cristina** *(☎441-2028)* each provide comfortable service a few times daily, with departure times from 3am to 3:30pm. **Viana** *(☎441-2330)* runs an air-conditioned luxury service *(6hrs, $17)* twice daily with drinks and snacks served aboard.

From Trujillo

Most buses leave from the side streets just off the *parque central*. To **La Ceiba** *(2.5hrs, $3)*, **Tela** *(3.5hrs, $4)* and **San Pedro Sula** *(5hrs, $5)*, Cotraipbal runs fast, comfortable buses with four daily departures, most early in the morning. Cotuc runs slow uncomfortable buses to **La Ceiba** *(3.5hrs, $2)* several times daily, with departure times

from 2am to 1:30pm. Another option is the bus that runs several times an hour to **Tocoa**, with connections there to **La Ceiba**. To **Tegucigalpa** *(8hrs, $7)*, Cotraipbal runs twice daily, with very early departures. These buses pass through La Unión, the nearest town to Parque Nacional La Muralla.

By Train

Honduras's only regular intercity passenger train runs between **Tela** and **Purto Cortés**, observing a very leisurely 4hr schedule through seemingly endless banana plantations and other agricultural establishments. Trains operate on Friday and Sunday only, with a 7am departure from Puerto Cortés and a 1:45pm return from Tela. Schedules may change, so it is essential to check ahead. The train is more a scenic adventure than a comfortable means of conveyance. Noise and dust levels are high, and seating is rudimentary. Fares are minimal, however.

Service from San Pedro Sula to Tela was suspended after a bridge was destroyed by Hurricane Mitch in 1998. Baracoa is the stop nearest to San Pedro Sula.

In **La Ceiba**, an urban train with open carriages runs twice hourly on a short loop between the centre of town and the Puente Cangrejal. For most visitors, this will be more a curiosity than a practical means of transport. The beach excursion trains that once ran east from La Ceiba have been discontinued because of hurricane damage to the rail line.

By Taxi

Taxis are available in all the larger towns mentioned in this chapter. Local fares in La Ceiba and Tela are especially cheap, although passengers may have to share a taxi with others who are headed in the same general direction. In Trujillo, taxis are very scarce at night. Those who expect to be out late should arrange beforehand to be picked up at a particular time and place. Bus passengers leaving La Ceiba in the late afternoon bound for Trujillo may find that the bus goes only as far as Tocoa. Taxis are available for the final 61km stretch.

By Bicycle

Bicycles are a popular form of local transportation in most towns along the Caribbean coast. In Puerto Cortés, busy reserved bicycle lanes run parallel to the main road leading to the centre of town; bicycle use is also heavy in La Ceiba. Bicycles are used much less commonly for travel between towns. **Rentals** are available in **Tela** at Mike's Bikes, near the Luces del Norte restaurant, and at the Hotel Villas Telamar, and in **La Ceiba** at Renta Bicicletas, 13ª Calle between Avenida San Isidro and Avenida 14 de Julio.

By Ferry

Ferry service provides an interesting alternative to air service for travel between La Ceiba and Islas de la Bahía. The *Galaxy*, a modern 350-passenger vessel with an air-conditioned main deck and an open-air upper deck, operates daily between La Ceiba and Roatán *(1hr 45min, $10)* and between La Ceiba and Utila *(1hr, $9)*. Approximate schedules are as follows:

dep. Roatán 7:00am
arr. La Ceiba 8:45am

dep. La Ceiba 9:30am
arr. Utila 10:30am

dep. Utila 11:00am
arr. La Ceiba noon

dep. La Ceiba 3:00pm
arr. Roatán 4:45pm

The *Galaxy* is operated by Safeway Transportation Company *(☎445-1695 in Roatán, ☎425-3161 in Utila, no phone in La Ceiba)*. The ferry terminal in Roatán is located in the town of Coxen Hole. In Utila, the ferry docks at the centrally located municipal pier. Arriving passengers step right into the swing of things. In La Ceiba, however, the terminal is situated in a remote spot about 10km by road from the centre of town. Taxis *($3.50 per passenger)* are just about the only way of getting there.

By Air

La Ceiba is the main hub for domestic air travel in Honduras, with flights radiating to San Pedro Sula, Tegucigalpa, Islas de la Bahía of Roatán, Guanaja and Utila, as well as Trujillo, and several points in the Mosquitia. Three companies, all based in La Ceiba, compete on most of these routes. The three are **Isleña Airlines** (now part of Grupo Taca), **Aerolíneas Sosa** and **Rollins Air**. Fares are mostly quite cheap (e.g., $19 to Utila). Nearly all flights operate during daylight hours. Service is less frequent on Sundays. All three companies connect La Ceiba with San Pedro Sula, Tegucigalpa, Roatán and Guanaja. Sosa and Isleña fly to Utila, with three daily flights, while only Rollins goes to Trujillo, with one daily flight. The Trujillo flight continues on to Palacios, in the Mosquitia. As flight schedules and routes are subject to change, call ahead to confirm.

Very few international flights arrive at La Ceiba, apart from a couple of flights a week from Grand Cayman and a leg of the daily flight from Belize to Roatán. Most international passengers have to go via San Pedro Sula or Tegucigalpa. La Ceiba is the main connection point for Islas de la Bahía.

Information on airports and ticket offices is found in "Practical Information," below.

Practical Information

Tourist Information

There are no formal tourist information offices in the towns covered in this chapter. Hotel clerks and taxi drivers are the most reliable sources of local information, and tour company offices can also be helpful, although visitors should remember that they are in business to sell tours.

Airports

Golosón airport is situated 10km west of **La Ceiba** and has a restaurant, a bar and gift shops. Special airport taxis waiting just outside the terminal build-

ing charge about $6 per passenger for trips into town. Regular city taxis often wait just outside the gate past the parking area and charge $3 to $4 per passenger. The airstrip in **Trujillo** (there is no terminal building) is located about 2km from the centre of town near the beach, with several hotels and restaurants close by. Taxis meet each incoming flight.

Airline Reservations

International reservations in Honduras must be reconfirmed at least 72 hours in advance. Domestic reservations should be reconfirmed at the latest the day before, earliest if possible. Passengers with return tickets but without confirmed reservations for the return portion should book at the airport or at a city ticket office. Following are addresses and phone numbers in **La Ceiba**:

Aerolíneas Sosa
Avenida San Isidro, facing the *parque central*
☎*443-1399 or 443-1894*
airport
☎*441-2512*

Grupo Taca
Avenida San Isidro, facing the *parque central*
☎*443-3720 or 443- 1915*
airport
☎*441-2534 or 441-2536*

Isleña
Avenida San Isidro, facing the *parque central*
☎*443-0179*
airport
☎*441- 2521 or 441-2522*

Rollins Air
at the Hotel Príncipe, 7ª Calle between Avenida Atlántida and Avenida 14 de Julio
airport
☎*441-0641 or 443-4181*

In **Trujillo**, the Rollins Air office is located in the centre of town just off the *parque central*.

Money Exchange

Nearly all banks in the towns mentioned in this chapter exchange U.S. dollars in cash, and most also exchange travellers' cheques. Rates tend to be slightly lower in Trujillo than elsewhere.

Long-Distance Telephone and Fax

Hondutel offices are located in the central areas of each of the towns mentioned in this chapter. Hours of operation vary, but most are open until at least 9pm. In La Ceiba, the Hondutel office is on Avenida Ramón Rosa at 6ª Calle two blocks from the *Parque Central* and is open 24hrs.

Language Schools

Centro Internacional de Idiomas in La Ceiba
☎440-0547
www.worldwide.edu/hondur as/cici/

Centro Internacional de Idiomas in La Ceiba offers one-on-one instruction of Spanish and English, with courses available at various levels. Courses run 4hrs a day, five days a week. Tuition is $135 per week. Tuition plus lodging with a local family is $200 per week.

Exploring

Puerto Cortés

Puerto Cortés has the most extensive port installations in Honduras, stretching several kilometres along a bay near the mouth of the Río Chamelcón, but generally this bustling commercial town is of little interest to most visitors.

Nearby, however, are fine stretches of beach (see p 134) with comfortable lodgings, and a few kilometres to the east lie the Garífuna villages of Travesía and Bajamar. A short distance west is Omoa, with its ancient Spanish fort. The central plaza in Puerto Cortés is a lively spot, sheltered by large, mature trees.

Travesía is reached by a dirt road running east from Puerto Cortés. The village still has a few of the traditional Garífuna cane and thatch dwellings, although it is less picturesque than **Bajamar**, which lies just a little further east. Buses run to both towns several times a day. These two towns seem to stretch forever in a narrow line along the beach, and it is hard to tell where one ends and the other begins. There are several stalls where fried fish and Garífuna specialties such as *pan* de coco (coconut bread) are available. The beach, dotted with fishing boats, is rather narrow and offers little shade.

The best stretches of beach lie between the two towns. An annual festival is held in August.

Omoa

The port of Omoa, 13km west of Puerto Cortés, was founded in 1752 near the mouth of the Río Motagua to handle trade and shipments for both Guatemala and Honduras. It also served as a fortress to protect against further encroachment by the British, who already had protectorates in Belize and Islas de la Bahía and were looking to control the entire coast.

The **Castillo de San Fernando** ★★ was built between 1759 and 1775 with heavy loss of human life. It was captured briefly a few years later by English-led forces. This vast fortress which, despite its name, is not really a castle, has been restored and is now open to visitors *($2; Mon to Fri 8am to 4pm, Sat, Sun, and holidays 9am to 5pm)*. It is set well back from the sea just beyond the edge of town. At the entrance is a visitors' centre with a gift shop and a small museum containing historical information and a few ancient objects such as a cannon, anchors, bottles and vases. The fortress has high, thick walls,

Castillo de San Fernando

The town of Copán Ruinas is set amid lush, mountainous countryside.
- *Claude Hervé-Bazin*

Roatán offers an enchanting setting that promotes relaxation and discovery, as do all of the Islas de la Bahía (Bay Islands).
- *Claude Hervé-Bazin*

Copán is characterized by, among other things,
the unusual high relief etched onto green volcanic stone. - *Claude Hervé-Bazin*

with a broad perimeter along the top that provides expansive views of the sea on one side and mountains on the other. The walls, pocketed by dark interior chambers, surround a large grassy area.

The town of Omoa has a small, somewhat scruffy beach area with several little restaurants and and a growing selection of lodgings. For several years, Omoa has been carving itself a place on the backpackers' circuit. Lodging improvements in town are beginning to attract other categories of tourists as well. There are waterfalls about a 45 min walk south of town. Visitors may enquire at local hotels or restaurants for precise directions.. A more lavish hotel is situated a few kilometres east.

Tela

These days, Tela is a sleepy tropical port city surrounded by beaches and nature reserves, but it once thrived as a big banana port and railhead. Ironically, the main Honduran operating subsidiary of Chiquita Brands (formerly the United Fruit Company) is still called the Tela Railroad Company, though the company ended its connection with the now government-owned railway long ago. These days all bananas are shipped to port by truck.

The banana industry has lost much of its importance in the area, and Tela is beginning to reinvent itself as a tourist town. The selection of comfortable lodgings is currently limited, but the hotel scene has gradually been improving. There was talk some years ago of major developments just west of town, and an environmental review panel was convened to examine possible effects. For the moment, most of these plans appear to be on hold.

Tela has a somewhat dumpy but not unpleasant appearance, with zinc-roofed buildings and beaches stretching in long, sandy crescents both east and west of town. It is possible to walk a considerable distance before running out of beach.(please see "Security in Tela and Trujillo," p 141) The central plaza lies two blocks inland from the beach, and there are many shops and services nearby as well as a lively public market.

The area just west of the centre of town is connected by bridges and is known as **Nueva Tela** (New Tela). It includes the Hotel Villas Telamar, a vast, fenced-in enclave that practically formed a city within the city to house American managers of the United Fruit Company and their families. The managers are long gone, and their villas now house tourists in simple splendour (see p 142).

Tela has two main attractions apart from its beaches. These are the **Jardin Botánico Lancetilla**, set well inland with a vast variety of tropical trees and plants, and the **Parque Nacional Punta Sal** along the coast a little to the west of Tela. Both are presented in more detail on p 135 and 134.

There are several Garífuna villages near Tela. Heading west along a dirt road, the nearest village is **San Juan**, accessible by bus several times daily. At low tide or during drier periods, a sand bar in San Juan provides a road connection to **Tornabé** (at other times, motor launches provide passenger connections). Tornabé is a bigger town and has fewer remaining traditional Garífuna dwellings. It can also be reached by a new road connecting it to the main highway west of Tela.

From Tornabé, a narrow, sandy road suitable only for four-whee-drive vehicles after heavy rains, runs 12km west to the traditional fishing village of **Miami**. The road skirts palm-fringed ocean beach on one side and, for a certain distance, runs along what seems to be a narrow isthmus with a large lagoon on the other side. This is one arm of Laguna de los Micos, a favoured spot for bird-watchers. Unfortunately, some of the palms in this area have been afflicted by disease, and replanting did not get under way soon enough. Miami has no hotels or restaurants, and the ocean waves are rougher than at Tornabé. For those without private vehicles or boats, passenger-carrying trucks pass on an irregular basis. Beyond Miami, and clearly visible from the village, is the Parque Nacional Punta Sal.

About 7km east of Tela lies the Garífuna village of **El Triunfo de la Cruz**, accessible on foot along the beach or by bus. It was once the site of an ancient Spanish settlement, and today a couple of restaurants and at least one hotel can be found along the beach.

★★

La Ceiba

La Ceiba is the third largest city in Honduras and the site of a bustling port. The port's biggest customer is Standard Fruit, whose bananas, pineapples and other produce are sold abroad under the Dole label. La Ceiba and Standard Fruit grew up together, but fruit no longer dominates the local economy the way it once did. Food processing, garment manufacturing and other industries have sprung up around La Ceiba. The city now has a university campus known as CURLA (Centro Universitario Regional del Litoral del Atlántico) on the western outskirts, with important agriculture and forestry faculties.

La Ceiba is also seeing growth in tourism-related activities. The city's cheerful tropical disposition makes it suitable for tourism even if attractions within the city itself are rather limited.There is also a small but growing resident expatriate population, and new beachfront hotel developments near villages east of La Ceiba have been begun drawing larger numbers of tourists.

Golosón airport, 10km to the west, is the main hub for domestic air travel in Honduras, and La Ceiba has long been the main jumping-off point for Islas de la Bahía. It is also quickly becoming a base for nature tourists and hikers bound for the Cuero y Salado and Pico Bonito national parks (see p 136, 137).

The city has a compact central area with streets laid out mostly in a rectangular grid pattern. Avenues have names rather than numbers and run north and south. The most important is Avenida San Isidro, which runs through the heart of the city past the Parque Central. Streets run east and west and are numbered, with their numbers rising with increasing distance from the waterfront. The area just west of the centre is called Barrio Mazapán. To the east is a short but picturesque *estero* (inlet) along whose western bank is anchored the immense, ancient ceiba tree that gave the city its name. The soccer stadium lies at the southern end of this inlet. Barrio La Isla and Barrio La Barra, further east, include broad, sandy stretches of ocean beach. The eastern suburbs are separated from the city by the Río Cangrejal.

A new attraction is town is the **Museo de la Mariposa** ★, or butterfly museum (*$1, Mon to Sat 8am to noon and 2pm to 5pm; Colonia El Sauce, Segunda Etapa, Casa G-12, ☎442-2874*). This is a private museum, located on a quiet residential street (most taxi drivers know how to get there) in a small

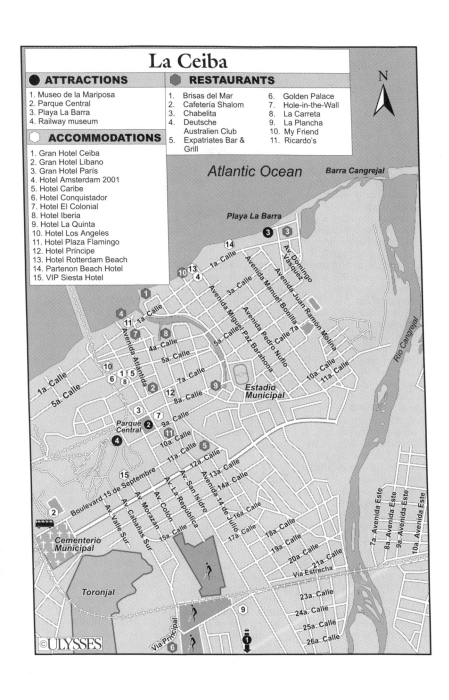

La Ceiba

● ATTRACTIONS

1. Museo de la Mariposa
2. Parque Central
3. Playa La Barra
4. Railway museum

⬡ ACCOMMODATIONS

1. Gran Hotel Ceiba
2. Gran Hotel Líbano
3. Gran Hotel París
4. Hotel Amsterdam 2001
5. Hotel Caribe
6. Hotel Conquistador
7. Hotel El Colonial
8. Hotel Iberia
9. Hotel La Quinta
10. Hotel Los Angeles
11. Hotel Plaza Flamingo
12. Hotel Príncipe
13. Hotel Rotterdam Beach
14. Partenon Beach Hotel
15. VIP Siesta Hotel

⬣ RESTAURANTS

1. Brisas del Mar
2. Cafetería Shalom
3. Chabelita
4. Deutsche Australien Club
5. Expatriates Bar & Grill
6. Golden Palace
7. Hole-in-the-Wall
8. La Carreta
9. La Plancha
10. My Friend
11. Ricardo's

N

Atlantic Ocean

Barra Cangrejal

Playa La Barra

Av. Domingo Vásquez

Avenida Juan Ramón Molina

Avenida Manuel Bonilla

Avenida Miguel Paz Barahona

Avenida Pedro Nufio

Calle 7a

1a. Calle

3a. Calle

5a. Calles

4a. Calle

5a. Calle

7a. Calle

8a. Calle

10a. Calle

11a. Calle

Estadio Municipal

9a. Calle

10a. Calle

11a. Calle

12a. Calle

Avenida 13a. Calle

Avenida 14a. Calle

Av. San Isidro

Av. La República

Avenida 14 de Julio

16a. Calle

17a. Calle

18a. Calle

19a. Calle

20a. Calle

21a. Calle

Vía Estrecha

23a. Calle

24a. Calle

25a. Calle

26a. Calle

7a. Avenida Este

8a. Avenida Este

9a. Avenida Este

10a. Avenida Este

Río Cangrejal

Avenida Atlántida

1a. Calle

1a. Calle

4a. Calle

5a. Calle

1a. Calle

5a. Calle

Parque Central

Boulevard 15 de Septiembre

Av. Morazán

Av. Colón

Av. Cabañas Sur

Av. Valle Sur

15a. Calle

Cementerio Municipal

Toronjal

Vía Principal

©ULYSSES

building behind the home of the American owner and curator, Robert Lehman, who has collected butterflies for more than 25 years. Display cases in the museum exhibit more than 5,000 butterflies, many of them brilliantly coloured and most native to Honduras. Many other insects are also on display. Staff can provide information in Spanish or English. Another butterfly museum, with live specimens flying freely in a vast enclosure, operated briefly at Pico Bonito national park and is supposed to reopen at a new, but still undecided, location in the park.

La Ceiba has several curiosities that will appeal to **railway** buffs. An urban train, with open carriages, makes a twice-hourly circuit from 6am to 6pm between the city centre and the Puente Cangrejal to the east. A tiny remaining portion of an old railway line provides the main access to **Parque Nacional Cuero y Salado** (see p 136, 137). A small open-air **railway museum** in an attractively landscaped park one block west of the Parque Central exhibits distinctive items of railway rolling stock, including a 1915 locomotive.

East of La Ceiba are several Garífuna vil-

lages, notably **Corozal**, 12km from La Ceiba, and **Sambo Creek**, 18km away. They are served by bus twice an hour, and both places have restaurants. Some traditional dwellings made of cane stalks, mud and thatch can still be seen, although these have largely been replaced by modern concrete and adobe structures. Fishing boats dot the beaches.

Trujillo

Trujillo is one of the oldest European settlements in the New World, founded in 1525 and briefly the capital of Honduras and seat of the bishop of Honduras. At one time it lay along an important gold-shipping route and drew many pirate attacks. A fort built to repel these attacks is one of the few surviving reminders of Trujil-

lo's early history. As Honduras's population and economy became centred further west and south, Trujillo languished as an isolated outpost on the way to forgotten Mosquitia.

A brief flurry of activity occurred in 1860, when William Walker, an American adventurer who had captured and then lost power in Nicaragua, tried his luck in Honduras using Trujillo as a base. British forces, posted to ensure that port revenues were used in the repayment of Honduran debts to British banks, induced Walker to surrender by offering him safe conduct; they then promptly turned him over to Honduran authorities, who did not hesitate to shoot him. There is a small plaque on his tomb in the *cementerio viejo* (old cemetery), up the hill from the centre of town on the way to the museum.

In the 20th century, Trujillo became part of the U.S.-financed fruit economy, although in agricultural importance it has now been eclipsed by the town of Tocoa, 61km west. It has also been eclipsed in port activity by Puerto Castilla, situated on an isthmus 20km east of Trujillo. The centre of Trujillo is hilly and has a friendly, relaxed atmosphere, with many wooden, zinc-roofed buildings in the Caribbean style. It is perched on a bluff with a beach below, and there is a broad lookout a block from the *parque central* facing the sea. Besides beaches and cultural attractions, **Parque Nacional Capiro-Calentura** boasts waterfalls and hiking trails (see p 137), while the **Refugio de Vida Silvestre Laguna** Guaymoreto is a great spot for birdwatching (see p 138). Both are nearby.

With its fine sheltered bay and idyllic beaches, Trujillo seemed destined to attract growing numbers of tourists, but somehow this just hasn't happened. If anything, visitor numbers appear to have declined in the late 1990s. This is partly because of Trujillo's relative inaccessibility. Getting there by air usually requires an overnight layover in La Ceiba and a pre-dawn wakeup call. The highways from the west and south can seem long and dreary, and for a few months after Hurricane Mitch hit in 1998, they were in very rough shape. The biggest resort hotel has suffered from indifferent management, unable to draw steady group traffic. Added to this, there have been some concerns about crime (see page 141). These developments have sapped energy from the local scene. Still, the town has a certain appeal that can

overcome these drawbacks.

Fortaleza Santa Bárbara ★ (*$0.20; every day 8am to noon, 1 pm to 4 pm; one block from the Parque Central*) is a Spanish castle and fort built to repel attacks by English pirates. Construction began in 1599. Ancient stone walls surround a grassy area, and a small former prison within the walls houses temporary exhibits. Ten cannons are perched on a bluff overlooking the beach. Beyond the walls of the mostly destroyed castle is a modern hospital and a second tomb for William Walker. The large, austere **Iglesia y Catedral San Juan Bautista**, dating from 1832, faces the Parque Central.

Museo y Piscina Riberas del Pedregal ★★ (*$1; no fixed hours, can usually be visited any time between 7am and 6pm; about a 10min walk from the centre of town*) is a private museum with a fascinating collection of bric-a-brac and archaeological objects. The owners, Doña Margarita and Don Rufino Galán, founded the museum in 1954. Their heteroclite collection includes more than 20,000 pre-Hispanic pieces, only a small portion of which are on display. These

include carved heads, pottery and utensils, mostly of Mayan origin.

The wreckage of a U.S. military aircraft that crashed nearby in 1985 lies on the grounds. Firearms, antique office machinery, bottles, sewing machines, coins, stamps, musical instruments and pottery are among items exhibited in the museum's cavernous interior. There is also a small library.

But this is more than a museum: it is also a bathing resort! On the slope below is a series of pools filled by the Río Cristales (the water may be murky with sediment after heavy rains). These pools are surrounded by an enchanting stand of tropical forest, including clusters of bamboo. There are also wooden and rope bridges over the river, picnic areas and changing rooms.

Most residents of the **Barrio Cristales** neighbourhood, facing the beach on the western side of town, are Garífuna. The area is noted for its beachfront restaurants, discotheques and musical groups (see p 150).

There are **hot springs** just off the main highway, 7km from Trujillo and 2km west of the Puerto Castillo junction, where the Hotel Agua Caliente used to operate. The hotel later closed its doors, although access was still provided to the springs on a not-always-reliable basis. It is best to enquire locally. Four pools with sulphurous waters, said to have curative powers, vary in temperature from 20° C to 40° C and are covered by shelters.

West of Trujillo, along a coast-hugging dirt road, are three Garífuna villages. **Santa Fe**, 12km west of Trujillo, **San Antonio**, 15km west, and **Guadalupe**, 18km west, lie along a series of palm-fringed beaches. Buses run four times daily, with the first outbound trip from Trujillo at 9am, and the last return in early afternoon. In Santa Fe, the biggest of the three villages, there are restaurants and a couple of very humble hotels. Guadalupe is the smallest and prettiest of the three, with many traditional dwellings of mud and thatch. Elsewhere, these old-style houses have mostly been displaced by modern concrete block structures. Other villages lie beyond Guadalupe, but they are accessible only by boat. The area is quiet most of the year but receives many visitors during Holy Week preceding Easter and during the local festivals in June.

Santa Rosa de Aguán, about 40km east of Trujillo at the mouth of the Río Aguán, is a Garífuna village that was noted for its traditional-style dwellings and pleasantly isolated atmosphere. Most buildings in the village were severely damaged by Hurricane Mitch in 1998, and there was heavy loss of life. New post-Mitch construction is less aesthetically pleasing. The road (served by several daily buses) does not reach the village: it is necessary to take a boat across the river.

Parks and Beaches

Near Puerto Cortés

Playa Coca-Cola (yes, it really is known by that name) lies just west of Puerto Cortés, although getting there from the centre of town involves a long detour around the port facilities and oil refinery. The beach is about 2km long, with several small restaurants along its eastern end. There is dancing on weekend nights, but the beach area is generally unsafe after dark.

A better bet in the immediate area are the **Playas de Cienaguita** ★★, further west on the way to Omoa. There are several hotels along this attractive group of beaches, which have white sand and gentle waves. The port installations of Puerto Cortés are visible in the distance.

Ankla's Restaurant (☎665-2331) near the Hotel Playa arranges diving and fishing trips and rents mountain bikes.

Near Tela

There are fine beaches in Tela extending for many kilometres in either direction. (please see "Security in Tela and Trujillo," p 141). Some of the most beautiful palm-fringed beaches in the area are located west of the town of Tornabé. Some of these palms were afflicted by disease, and replanting is under way. In some places the salt water of the ocean and the fresh water of the Laguna de los Micos are separated only by a narrow isthmus of land.

Parque Nacional Punta Sal ★★, situated along the coast about 22km west of Tela, is a pristine marine and forest reserve with a little something for everyone. It can be reached by boat from Tela in about one hour or by foot from the Garífuna village of Miami in 4 to 5hrs along the beach and then a forest path. Organized boat tours leave from Tela nearly every day, returning a few hours later. Camping is possible along the beach. Entry to the park is free of charge, and hours are unrestricted.

Punta Sal offers picture-postcard beaches fringed with palms, crystalline waters, a variety of ecosystems, and a great wealth of flora and fauna. Ecosystems include coastal reefs, freshwater coastal lakes, wet savannah, mangroves, tropical forest, rivers, and both sandy and rocky beaches. Fauna include dolphins, manatees, tigers, several species of monkeys, lizards, parrots, toucans, ducks and eagles.

Laguna de los Micos

(*mico* means monkey), near the village of Miami, is lined partly by sandy beach, partly by mangrove. It is home to a rich variety of birds.

Refugio de Vida Silvestre Punta Izopo,

9km east of Tela, encompasses lagoons along the Río Plátano and Río Hicaque and also offers great biological diversity. Organized tours are available to both spots, including those operated by Garífuna Tours in Tela. Visitors travel by road and canoe.

Jardín Botánico Lancetilla ★★

(*$5; gates open 7:30am to 2:30pm, visitors may stay until 4pm*) covers a vast area and harbours thousands of species of trees and plants, including one of the world's leading collections of Asian fruit plants. There is a particularly impressive bamboo archway near the entrance. The botanical garden was established by the United Fruit Company in 1926 as an experimental station to develop new types of bananas and other crops; it was turned over to the Honduran government in 1975. The Wilson Popenoe arboretum, named for Lancetilla's long-time director, contains numerous fruit trees and plants as well as orchids, palms, bamboo, precious woods such as mahogany, ornamental plants and medicinal plants. It is divided into plots with collections of citrus, coffee, cacao, mango, nutmeg, teak and various other sorts of trees and plants, all clearly marked. Adjacent to the garden is a vast biological reserve, tree nursery and research laboratory.

Toucan

The main gate is situated along the highway just 1km west of town, but it is 4km from the gate to the actual park and there are no regular buses. Taxis provide the most convenient option for those without private transport, but anyone planning a long stay should arrange a pick-up time or reach a firm understanding about the charge for waiting time. Free guided tours are offered at 30min intervals. Leaflets outlining self-guided tours are available at the entrance, as are lists of the many bird species that have been drawn to the gardens. There is a small restaurant near the entrance.

Near La Ceiba

There are acceptable beaches in the eastern part of town, notably **Playa La Barra** between the *estero* (inlet) and the Río Cangrejal, but the best beaches in the area lie well outside town. **Perú ★★**, 9km east of La Ceiba, has a gorgeous palm-shaded white-sand beach and good facilities for day-trippers, with sheltered picnic tables, cooking grills, toilets and a snack bar that is open weekends throughout the year and all week long during the peak season.

There are fine palm-fringed beaches a little further east near the Garífuna villages of **Corozal** and **Sambo Creek**. At Corozal, pigs roam along the beach in town; there are better stretches of beach just to the east. Balneario Playas de Zambrano offers facilities to day visitors for a small admission charge. At Sambo Creek there is a freshwater inlet where a small river reaches the sea; local people sometimes do their laundry there.

Parque Nacional Cuero y Salado ★★ is situated 41km west of La Ceiba between the Cuero and Salado rivers and has the particularity of being easily accessible only by railway. There is no road access, and there is nowhere to anchor boats, although canoes and light skiffs can be brought onto the beach. In land from the coast, a network of canals links various lagoons and estuaries. The park offers marine and terrestrial ecosystems, with 12km of beaches and areas of mangrove with a rich variety of birds. Nearly 200 species of tropical birds are found here, representing close to 30% of all bird species in Honduras. Other parts of the park are covered by tropical forest, with many animal species, including monkeys, manatees and jaguars.

Howler Monkey

Howler monkeys are especially active in the morning, and the resounding call of the male as he swings among tree branches has become a firmly ingrained part of tropical myth and reality. A variety of fish are also abundant in the refuge, as are reptiles including crocodiles, iguanas, turtles and several types of snakes.

Despite serious efforts to protect this fragile ecosystem, economic activity in some of the surrounding lands is having harmful effects. Deforestation to make way for cattle ranching and agriculture has led to increased sedimentation. Plantations that grow fruit, African palm or cacao have allowed pesticides and fertilizers to seep into the soil and the waterways. Clandestine fishing has also been a problem.

Several tour companies (see p 59) organize visits to Cuero y Salado, arranging both land and water transport. It is also possible for enterprising tourists to visit on their own. The Fundación Cuero y Salado (FUCSA) is the private foundation responsible for administering the park. Its office in La Ceiba (*Mon to Fri, 8am to 11:30am, 1:30pm to 4:30pm,* ☎*443-0329*) is located

in Zona Mazapán two-and-a-half blocks west of the *parque central* behind the Standard Fruit offices. Prior reservations must be made in person or by telephone, and there is a $10 entrance fee to the park.

To reach the park, buses run hourly on the half-hour, starting at 6:30am, from La Ceiba to the village of La Unión 33km west, a slow 60min journey. From there, a 9km stretch of railway once used for hauling coconuts runs to the park. Two types of vehicle use this railway. One is the motor-powered *motocarro* run by the Standard Fruit Company. It operates according to demand and the trip takes 30 to 40min. The fare is $4 per person for groups of up to 16 passengers. Advance requests must be made by phone to Standard Fruit, (☎*443-0511, extension 2171 or 2184*). There are also the human-powered *burras*, with a journey time of about 60min. These provide work for local people and are available without reservations. The rate varies from $7 for a single passenger to $1.50 per person for a group of eight. Inside the park, a motorboat and guide can be hired for about $20 for 2hrs for an entire group of up to 10 people. Canoes are also available for hire.

There are washrooms and a small convenience store near the park entrance, but visitors should bring their own food and drinking water. Camping is allowed along the beach. Some local tour companies organize visits to Cuero y Salado. People living within park boundaries make their livings mostly from fishing and coconut harvesting.

Parque Nacional Pico Bonito ★ is one of the biggest national parks in Honduras. It shelters spider monkeys, howler monkeys, jaguars, ocelots, eagles, iguanas and quetzals. There are many streams and waterfalls deep inside its heavily forested slopes, but the trail system remains in a very rudimentary state. There is a 3 to 4hr hike along a trail departing from a study base established by CURLA, the local university. This base is situated near the village of Armenia Bonito (served by local bus number 1). Pico Bonito itself soars 2,433m and takes several days to climb. The tropical rain forest near the base changes to cloud forest at higher elevations

The park's extensive buffer zone offers some of the main attractions, including visits to Bejuco falls involving a 30min trip by four-wheel-drive vehicle and 1.5hrs of hard climbing.

There is white-river rafting along the Río Cangrejal just outside park boundaries. Various tour companies organize excursions in the park. A waterfall along the Río Zacate inside the park can be reached by taking the Tela highway to the bridge crossing the river (buses to Tela allow passengers to disembark there) and then going 2km south along a dirt road through the pineapple fields.

A butterfly museum, with live specimens flying freely in a vast enclosure, operated briefly and was set to reopen at a new but still undecided location in the park ☎*442-2874*.

Jaguar

Several tour companies offer excursions to the Parque Nacional Pico Bonito. The park is administered by the Fundación Parque Nacional Pico Bonito (FUPNAPIB), a private foundation. Its office in La Ceiba is located upstairs in the Plaza del Caribe building on Boulevard 15 de Septiembre, two blocks

south of the *parque central* (*Mon to Fri 7am to 5pm, Sat 7am to 11am,* ☎*443-3824*). An entry permit, (*$6*), available at this office, is required for visits to the park. There are two entrances to the park, both open daily from 7am to 4pm. The Río Cangrejal entrance lies just 2km out of town and includes a visitors' centre. The Río Zacate entrance lies 16km from town along a dirt road. Free camping is available near the Río Cangrejal.

Near Trujillo

There are several fine beaches in the area around Trujillo. A broad expanse of beach lies directly beneath a bluff in the centre of town, with many beachfront restaurants. This is also a gorgeous palm-fringed beach 2km away near the airstrip, with several hotels and restaurants close by. Farther afield, there are long and remote stretches of beach around the point beyond Puerto Castilla. This would be all the more idyllic were it not for security concerns (see p 141).

Parque Nacional Capiro-Calentura ★ encompasses an area of mountains and rivers with hiking trails, waterfalls and swimming holes. There is also plenty of wildlife, including howler monkeys which can often be heard in the early morning and late afternoon, and a variety of parrots and toucans. There are two peaks within the park, Capiro, reaching 625m above sea level, and Calentura, 1,250m high. Both can be climbed along trails that in earlier times were used almost exclusively by local peasants and are now also used by tourists, although they are not well marked.

Besides the mountains, there are portions of three rivers within the park, the Río Negro, Río Grande and Río Cristales. There are waterfalls and swimming holes along each of these rivers. Plans call for building a catwalk bridge over the Río Negro for a view of the waterfalls.

A 1.5km circular trail near the entrance includes some steep climbs but provides superb views over Trujillo and its bay.

This park and the Laguna Guaymoreto wildlife reserve (please see below) are administered by the Fundación Calentura y Guaymoreto (FUCAGUA), a private foundation. Its offices (*Mon to Fri 7:30am to noon and 1:30pm to 5pm, Sat 7:30am to noon;* ☎*434-4294*) are located in Trujillo on Calle 18

de Mayo, up the hill from the *parque central*, past the Hotel O'Glynn and around the corner. The park entrance is open 7:30am to noon and 1:30pm to 5pm daily except Sunday (they are considering adding Sunday visits). There is a $4 entrance fee, payable at the FUCAGUA offices or at the park entrance. FUCAGUA recommends hiring a guide for trail hikes. They can also arrange a motorboat for visits to Laguna Guaymoreto with one day's advance notice.

Refugio de Vida Silvestre Laguna Guaymoreto lies 8km from Trujillo. Much of it is lined with mangrove, and it has been declared a nature reserve. Those interested in bird-watching or fishing can rent kayaks near the old bridge (*puente viejo*) crossing the lagoon. A rich variety of birds and also some monkeys can be seen, but the lagoon is under siege from ranchers and peasant farmers who have misappropriated some neighbouring land. For the moment, the authorities seem unwilling to dislodge them.

Accommodations

Puerto Cortés

Most hotels within the city are rather dismal, with one or two exceptions. Better hotels are situated along the beach outside town.

Hotel y Restaurante Fronteras del Caribe
$14
⊗, ℜ
Barrio Camaguey facing the beach just east of town
☎*665-5001*
This modest, seven-room beach-front hotel and seafood restaurant is very good for the price. It is situated just outside town and can be reached by local bus number 2. Rooms are big and bright but rather austere, and there is a broad wooden terrace facing the sea. The beach is wide and sandy, interspersed with tufts of grass and a few palms and thatched shelters. Waves are often rough.

Mister Ggeer Hotel
$27
≡, *tv*, ☎
2ª Calle at 9ª Avenida
☎*665-0444* or *665-0422*
⇆665-0750
This centrally located 30-room hotel has friendly service. Rooms are big but rather dark and are furnished in bargain-basement style.

Hotel Palmeras Beach
$45
tv, ≡, ℜ, bar, ≈
Playa Cienguita Carretera a
Omoa
☎*665-3891*
Facing the beach a few
kilometres west of
Puerto Cortés, Hotel
Palmeras has eight big
rooms with a somewhat
appealing decor and
hammocks. The beach
area is attractive.

🌴Hotel Playa
$56
tv, ≡, ℜ, bar, ≈
Playa Cienguita Carretera a
Omoa
☎*665- 0453* or *665-1105*
⇄*665-2287*
Hotel Playa offers a
livelier scene than the
other hotels in the area.
Located along the
beach a few kilometres
west of Puerto Cortés,
it has 22 attractive
rooms spread over a
central pavilion and a
row of bungalows at
the edge of the
grounds. Rooms have
wooden floors and
walls and comfortable
armchairs. The beach
area is clean and attrac-
tive, with shaded
lounge chairs and ta-
bles.

Hotel Villa Capri
$57/person
tv, ≡, bar
1a Avenida at 2a Calle
☎*665-6136* or *665-0860*
⇄*665-6139*
Hotel Villa Capri is a
new hotel at the edge
of the city centre. Its
nine big, bright rooms
have high wooden
ceilings and vibrant
colours. Unusually, its
rates are set per per-

son, making it poor
value for couples. A
light breakfast is in-
cluded in room rates.

Omoa

Several hotels lie be-
tween the highway and
the beach, some of
which are quite scruffy;
there are at least two,
however, that are wor-
thy of mention.

Roli's & Bernie's Place
$8
sb
200m from the beach
☎*658-9082*
R&B@yaxpactours.com
Roli's & Bernie's Place
has four simple rooms
and a spacious porch
with armchairs. The
Swiss owners are good
sources of travel infor-
mation and can arrange
tours. Bicycle, kayak
and windsurfer rentals
are available.

Hotel Bahía de Omoa
$25
≡, ℜ, bar
☎*658-9076*
Hotel Bahía de Omoa
is a small but comfort-
able and friendly
beachfront hotel with
cozy, attractive rooms.

Acantilados del Caribe,
also known as **Caribbean
Cliffs Marine Club**
$59
$67 for up to four persons
$81 for two-bedroom cabin
**$137 for large family cabin
for up to eight persons**
≡, ℝ, tv, ☎, ℜ, bar;
5km east of Omoa
☎*665-1403*
U.S. reservations
☎*1-800-327-4149*
This small but lavish
resort hotel and confer-
ence centre has 10 bun-
galows, five big
cabañas and three
apartments spread over
a sprawling hillside
overlooking both the
sea and a big stand of
tropical forest. The
attractive wood or
adobe structures are
comfortably furnished
and face a long but not
especially appealing
stretch of beach a short
hike away. The real
attraction is the 300ha
forest reserve immedi-
ately behind, with hik-
ing and nature trails.
The hotel offers good
service, including water
sports and fishing, and
has a bar, discotheque
and two restaurants.

Tela

All hotels shown here
are located near the
city centre unless indi-
cated otherwise. Street
names are not used
much in Tela, and the
addresses shown below
take account of this.

For visitors who need
to be near the Jardín
Botánico Lancetilla, a
small *hospedaje* near the
entrance offers 13

simple, fan-cooled rooms. Information is available at the visitor's centre.

Hotel Marazul
$8

⊗
along the main road one block from the beach
☎*448-2313*
The 14 rather basic rooms here face a tree-shaded courtyard.

Hotel Bertha's
$13 with ⊗
$24 with ≡
one block behind the bus termi-nal, three blocks from the beach
no telephone
This family-run spot has 15 bright, simple rooms with adequate furnishings. The air-conditioned rooms are bigger and more attrac-tive. All face a tatty courtyard.

Hotel Tela
$15
⊗, ℜ
along the main street midway between the parque central and the old bridge
☎*448-2150*
This 15-room time-warp hotel, run by two elderly women, has been open since the 1950s but feels older. Rooms are simply but comfortably furnished in very old-fashioned style and are rather dowdy. The entrance is above street level.

Hotel Bahía Azul
$13 with ⊗
$25 with ≡
ℜ, *bar*
facing the sea next to the new bridge
☎*448-2381*
The 18 rooms here are bright, simple and a little faded but quite acceptable. Rooms do not have sea views, but the hotel's restaurant, set on a terrace facing the beach, does.

Hotel Bellavista
$16 with fan
$24 with ≡ *and tv*
one block west of the parque central
☎*448-1064*
Hotel Bellavista offers 18 plain, reason-ably comfortable rooms in a four-storey build-ing without an elevator, one block from the beach. Rooms with kitchenette are avail-able.

Hotel Vista Maya
$17-$31
fan, ℜ, *bar*
on a hilltop four blocks east of the parque central
☎*448-1497*
Hotel Vista Maya is a very friendly spot run by a couple from Qué-bec, Canada. The six guest rooms are set in a high concrete building perched on a hilltop with panoramic views of the sea a few blocks away. Rooms vary in size. All are simple, bright and comfortable, and good natural venti-lation. Some have paintings by local art-ists. There are two en-trances, one by the road, the other by a long stairway.

Posada de Don Carlos
$24
tv, ≡
half-block from the parque central
☎*448- 1820*
Posada de Don Carlos offers seven pleasant, simple, high-ceilinged rooms in a horse-shoe-shaped building.

Hotel César Mariscos
$31
tv, ≡, ℜ, *bar*
facing the beach
☎*448-1934*
⇢*448- 2083*
Hotel César Mariscos offers 11 simple, pleas-antly furnished rooms, some with balconies facing the sea.

Ejecutivo Apart-Hotel
$32
⊗, ≡, *K, tv*
four blocks from the beach, half-block from the Hondutel office
☎*448-1076*
The eight white-and-pale-orange rooms in this striking, white-washed building offer very good value for those looking for large beds, a big sitting area, and a full kitchen. Weekly and monthly rates are available.

Caribbean Coral Inn
$41
tv, ⊗, ℜ, *bar*
Triunfo de la Cruz
no on-site telephone
☎*669-0224 for messages*
⇢*448-2942*
www.globalnet.bn/caribcoralinn
Caribbean Coral Inn faces the beach in the Garífuna village of Triunfo de la Cruz, about 7km east of Tela. This idyllic inn, opened

Security in Tela and Trujillo

In the late 1990s, growing numbers of visitors in Tela and in Trujillo reported assaults on their person and property. Most often these assaults were committed by armed gangs of youths, usually operating under cover of darkness or along remote stretches of beach, although in a few cases the thieves were more daring. Money, passports and expensive watches are favourite items, but designer clothing and footwear are also attractive. Authorities in Tela began fighting back by visibly augmenting police patrols, whereas their counterparts in Trujillo, perhaps less aware of the damage being inflicted on Honduras's image abroad (and on individual visitors), appeared more reluctant to act.

That said, visitors can take a few simple precautions that will greatly reduce the likelihood of falling victim to any unpleasant act:

• Take advantage of facilities offered by most hotels for the safe storage of valuable items, and avoid carrying large quantities of money, jewelry, and so on.

• As tempting as it may be to take solitary strolls along remote stretches of idyllic tropical beach, remember that there is safety in numbers. Thieves are less likely to act when other people are around. If you do want to go for a long walk along the beach outside settled areas, do so in a group rather than alone. There is a secluded stretch of beach just east of Tela that has become unofficially recognized as a nude beach and has been popular with foreigners, but because of a string of attacks there it should be considered off limits for the moment.

• If you are going to be out late at night, make sure you have a safe way of getting back to your lodgings. In Trujillo, few taxis operate after 10pm. Several interesting restaurants line the waterfront down the hill from the parque central, but there have been numerous assaults in that area. When going there at night, arrange beforehand to have a taxi pick you up at a fixed hour.

Once again, Honduras is not a particularly dangerous country, and Tela and Trujillo are not especially violent spots, but it is wise to be aware of potential hazards and to act accordingly.

in 1999, has six thatch-roofed, stucco-walled *cabañas*, that are simply but comfortably furnished. Each accommodates up to four people (the rate shown above is for two). The open-air lounge and dining area is breezy and pleasant. Bicycles, surfboards and snorkelling gear are available. Rates include a light breakfast. All-inclusive packages can also be arranged.

Hotel Sherwood
$42, reduced rates for longer stays
≡, ℜ, *tv, bar*
facing the beach near the centre of town
☎ *448-2416*
⊷ *448-2294*
The 14 rooms here are bright, fresh and comfortably furnished, with terraces facing the sea. The rooms upstairs are somewhat more attractive.

The Last Resort
$42 with ⊗
$52 with ≡
ℜ, *bar*
in Tornabé, 7km west of Tela
☎ *448-2545*
New owners have been resuscitating this hotel and its nine rooms, all set in big wooden bungalows with rustic decor, some with sea views, and all close to the beach. Wood-plank pathways, stone patios and a big, palm-shaded wooden terrace with lounge chairs add to the comfortable atmosphere. The open-air, thatch-roofed restaurant is surrounded by trees

with a lagoon on one side.

Hotel Villas Telamar
$64 double
$96 for suite with K
$116 to $231 for villas with 2 to 4 bedrooms $212 to $353 for beach-front villas with 3 to 5 bedrooms
≡, ☎, *tv*, ℜ, *bar*
1km west of the centre of town
☎ *448-2196*
⊷ *448-2984*
U.S. reservations
800-742-4276
This city within a city contains 97 lodgings set in villas spread over a sprawling site with a large beachfront area. To call them lodgings is perhaps an understatement, for many of them are simple but magnificent wooden houses with high ceilings, bright, airy interiors, polished hardwood floors, comfortable armchairs and sofas, separate bedrooms, big dining areas, and many of the general comforts of home. Some of the villas are divided into several guest rooms, and these obviously are smaller and more humble but still quite pleasant.

This spot used to house American managers of the United Fruit Company and their families, and the layout of this fenced-in site suggests a tropical version of a small U.S. town. The landscaping is undistinguished, facilities are adequate though not luxurious, and there are occasional lapses in service, but this is still a very interesting place.

Facilities include shops, meeting rooms, water sports, four tennis courts, a 9-hole golf course, fishing, horseback riding and child-care services.

La Ceiba

Hotel rates are quite economical in La Ceiba, and there is a good selection in the budget and intermediate ranges. A new beach-front resort hotel east of the city is starting to fill demand at the higher end. Plans call for a luxury hotel as part of a new mixed-use development near the edge of town. Hotels here are shown in two sections: the first section covers the area in or near the city centre, while the the second section covers hotels in rural areas to the east of the city.

Central Area

Hotel Los Angeles
$3/person sb
$4 pb
Avenida La República
near 5ª Calle
☎ *443-0723*
Delightfully seedy or drab and fetid: you can take your pick. This rambling old wooden building has big, dark, austere rooms, a few of them facing a broad balcony.

Hotel Amsterdam 2001
$7
sb
Barrio La Isla near the beach,
1km from the city centre
☎*442-1133*
Hotel Amsterdam 2001
has four simple rooms
plus an eight-bed dor-
mitory for $3/person.

Hotel Rotterdam Beach
$5
⊗, ℜ
Barrio La Isla near the beach,
1km from the city centre
☎*440-0321*
Eight pleasant, simple
rooms are set on a
quiet street near the
beach. In front is a
grassy area with palms
and hammocks. Very
good value.

Hotel Caribe
$9 double
⊗
5ª Calle between Avenida San
Isidro and Avenida Atlántida
☎*443-1857*
The 18 rooms here are
bright and airy but
rather shabbily fur-
nished. The lobby is
one floor above street
level.

Hotel Príncipe
$19
≡, *tv*, ℜ
7ª Calle between Avenida 14 de
Julio and Avenida San Isidro
☎*443-0516*
↝*443-2720*
The 52 rooms at this
modest city-centre
hotel are simple but
adequate.

Gran Hotel Líbano
$20
≡, *tv*, ℜ
directly behind the bus terminal, 2 km from the city centre
☎ *443-4102*
This 29-room, three-
storey hotel offers good
value and is better than
it looks from the out-
side, with simple but
fairly pleasant rooms.

Hotel Conquistador
$13 with ⊗
$19 with ≡
tv, ☎
Avenida La República at 5ª Calle
☎*443-3670*
The 23 rooms in the
city-centre hotel are
clean, fresh and de-
cently furnished. Air-
conditioned rooms
have outside windows,
while rooms with fan
face an interior pass-
age. There is no eleva-
tor and only a narrow
stairway in this four-
storey building.

Hotel Iberia
$21
≡, ☎, *tv*
Avenida San Isidro between 5ª
and 6ª Calles
☎*443-0401*
↝*443-0100*
The 44 rooms in this
very centrally located
hotel are plain but rea-
sonably comfortable
and are set
around a
broad
courtyard
with a foun-
tain. Those on
the street side
are noisy.

Gran Hotel Ceiba
$24
≡, ☎, *tv*, ℜ, *bar*
Avenida San Isidro at 5ª Calle
☎*443-2737*
↝*443-2747*
Corridors are dingy and
the sole elevator in this
six-storey building is
tiny, but the 40 rooms
here are adequately
furnished and service is
friendly. Rooms on the
street side are noisy.

Partenon Beach Hotel
$18 old wing
$50 new wing
≡, ☎, *tv*, ℜ, *bar*
facing Playa La Barra 2km from
the city centre
☎*443-0464*
↝*443-0434*
The new wing has
bright, pleasant rooms
with white tile floors
and balconies facing
the sea. Rooms in the
old wing are smaller
and darker and a bit
run down; some have
sea views. There are
110 rooms in all.

Hotel El Colonial
$24
≡, ☎, *tv*, ℜ, ⊛, △
Avenida 14 de Julio
between 6ª and 7ª Calles
☎*443-1953* or *443-1954*
↝*443-1955*
This friendly 40-room
hotel is pleasant de-
spite the absence of an
elevator to serve its five
floors and the absence
of windows in some
rooms. Special atten-
tion is paid to decor,
with Guatemalan-
influenced fabrics,
wooden furniture and
painted tiles.

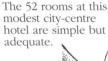

Hotel Plaza Flamingo Beach
$33
tv, ≡, ☎
1a Calle at Avenida San Isidro
☎*443-3149*

Hotel Plaza Flamingo Beach located one block from the sea, offers 19 big, nondescript rooms in a modern three-storey building. Some rooms face the sea.

Gran Hotel Paris
$35
tv, ≡, ☎, ≈, ℜ, bar
facing the *parque central*
☎*443-2391*
⇌*443-1614*

Right smack in the city centre, Gran Hotel Paris is looking decidedly better following renovations in 1997. The 63 rooms in this three-storey, horseshoe-shaped building are comfortable if nondescript. All face the palm-shaded pool area.

VIP Siesta Hotel
$44
tv, ≡, ⌣, ℜ, bar
Boulevard 15 de Septiembre
☎*443-0968* or *443-0969*
⇌*443-0970*

Located just beyond the city centre, VIP Siesta Hotel offers 23 smallish rooms with pleasant decor. Some rooms have only tiny windows facing a narrow courtyard.

Hotel La Quinta
$41
≡, ☎, tv, ℜ, bar, ≈
2km from the city centre on the highway to Tela
☎*443-0223* or *443-0225*
⇌*443-0226*

The 113 rooms here are ordinary but comfortable and are set around a series of small gardens and terraces. This modern hotel provides very good value for money, and service is efficient. Prices at the restaurant are high by local standards, but the food is good.

East of La Ceiba

Hôtel Canadien
$21
≈
just east of Sambo Creek 17km east of La Ceiba
no local phone reservations
☎*1-450-658-5015*

Run by a couple from Québec, Canada, Hôtel Canadien offers 22 simple, comfortable, whitewashed rooms in an *L*-shaped two-storey building facing the beach. Each room has separate sleeping and sitting areas as well as a refrigerator. One room is designed for visitors with disabilities. A beachfront restaurant is located next door. Road access is via a small side road a few hundred metres east of the main cutoff for Sambo Creek.

Villa Rhina
$43 rooms
$68 cabañas
ℜ, bar
highway to Trujillo 14km east of La Ceiba
☎*443-1222* or *443-1434*
⇌*443-3558*
www.honduras.com/villarhina

Villa Rhina is located in a wooded area next to a mountain stream with natural river pools and views over the ocean in the distance. Rooms (smaller) and *cabañas* (bigger, with high ceilings) are located up long flights of stairs, with wooden exteriors and somewhat nondescript interior decor. Hiking tours, mountain bikes and horseback riding are available.

Caribbean Sands Resort
regular room $81
suites higher
tv, ≡, ⌣, ≈, ℜ, bar
22km east of La Ceiba 4km west of Jutiapa
☎*443-0035*
⇌*443-1026*
www.caribbeansands.com

Caribbean Sands Resort is a modern beachfront resort hotel, opened in 1999, with a lavish reception area and 42 big, comfortable, high-ceilinged rooms set in four buildings on sprawling grounds. Amenities include a three-hole golf course, volleyball, tennis, an artificial lagoon, and a natural river nearby suitable for bathing.

Trujillo

Trujillo offers a selection of lower- and middle-priced hotels, and one fancy resort hotel. Some of the more interesting spots are situated away from the centre of town. Camping is possible in the Capiro-Calentura national park (see p 137).

Hotel Plaza Centro
$5
⊗
Calle Conventillo, near the central market
☎434- 4651
Hotel Plaza Centro offers 12 (soon to be 22) small, quiet, very plain rooms set on two storeys around a courtyard.

Hotel Mar del Plata
$7 sb
$11 pb
four blocks uphill from the *parque central*
☎ 434-4458
This spot offers friendly service and 11 clean, simple rooms.

Hotel Emperador
$9
⊗
three blocks from the *parque central*
☎434-4446
The 14 rooms here are small but reasonably attractive. Some face a small concrete terrace. There is a small gift shop here.

Villa Brinkley Hotel
$22 with ⊗
$31 with ≡
tv, ℜ, bar, ≈
2km uphill from the *parque central*
☎434-4444
Set high on a hillside with magnificent sweeping views of Trujillo bay, this 20-room inn is built of stone and wood. Rooms are big, bright and very nicely decorated, all with terraces facing the sea. The restaurant, also with panoramic views, offers a full menu in the evening but only sandwiches for lunch. The road leading to the hotel is in bad shape.

Hotel Colonial
$23
≡, *tv, ℜ*
near the parque central opposite the church
☎434-4011
The 20 rooms here are simply but attractively furnished, most with tile floors and all with wooden ceilings. The upstairs rooms are preferable; most have mountain or sea views. The corridors are decorated with naive paintings.

Hotel O'Glynn
$26
≡, *tv*
three blocks from the *parque central*
☎434-4592
The 22 rooms here are brightly furnished, and most have balconies. The hotel offers a comfortable lobby and attentive service.

Cabañas Campamento
$28-$42
⊗, ℜ
on the road to Santa Fe 5km west of Trujillo
no telephone on site
☎434-4200
Facing an idyllic stretch of palm-fringed beach, this cluster of five thatch-roofed, concrete-floored *cabañas*, spread over a broad grassy area, offers simple but attractive accommodations. Price varies according to the size of the *cabaña*. The restaurant is open long hours and specializes in fresh fish.

Trujillo Bay Hotel
$43
≡, *tv, ℜ*
2km from the centre of town next to the airstrip
☎434-4732
Situated 3min by foot from one of the better beaches, this friendly spot has 25 big, quiet, pleasantly furnished rooms all situated on a single level.

Christopher Columbus Beach Resort
$62
≡, *tv, ☎, ℜ, bar, ≈*
along the beach 2km from the centre of town
☎434-4966
≈434-4971
This is one of the most lavish resort hotels on the Honduran mainland. Its 70 rooms are situated in two low-slung, green-and-white buildings facing the beach with the local airstrip directly on the other side. Rooms have tile floors, colourful bedspreads and drapes and private balconies.

Each room has a sea view; some also have a view of the mountains. Services and facilities include a waterslide, tennis courts, video games, fishing and a private pier.

Restaurants

Puerto Cortés

Fronteras del Caribe
$$
every day 7am to 7pm
Barrio Camagüey facing the beach, just east of town
☎665-5001
With a beachfront open-air dining area, this spot offers a variety of fish and seafood dishes, especially conch, as well as rice dishes and chicken.

Restaurant Candiles
$$
every day 11am to 11pm
2a Avenida bewteen 7a and 8a Calles
☎665-0765
Set beneath a high thatch roof, this establishment specializes in meat dishes, including *pinchos* (brochettes).

Restaurant Matt's
$$-$$$
Mon and Tue 11am to 9pm, Wed to Sun 11am to 11pm
2a Avenida between 6a and 7a Calles
This restaurant specializes in seafood dishes, including seafood cocktails and *ceviche*. Several shrimp and conch dishes are on the menu, along with meats and sandwiches. The dining area is air conditioned, with non-descript decor.

Restaurant Delfín
$$-$$$
every day 8am to 11pm
facing Laguna Alvarado toward the southern end of town
☎665-1409
This restaurant was rebuilt following hurricane damage and is more elegant than before. This is a pleasant and comfortable open-air seafood restaurant facing a lake. Suggested dishes include *sopa marinera* (mixed seafood soup), *caracol al coco* (conch in coconut sauce) and *camarón al ajillo* (garlic shrimp).

Tela

Several restaurants, most specializing in seafood, are clustered along a three-block stretch of beachfront near the centre of town. East of town along the beach is a row of rough and noisy bars.

Los Angeles
$
10am to 2:30pm, 5pm to 10pm
along the main street one block east of the old bridge
Los Angeles serves an assortment of Chinese and western dishes in a gloomy air-conditioned dining room.

Luces del Norte
$
7am to 10pm
one block from the beach next to the Gran Hotel Puerto Rico
Luces del Norte is something of a backpackers' hangout although prices are not notably cheaper than elsewhere. This rambling, open-air restaurant, painted green and white, has a funky atmosphere and a sandwiches-to-seafood menu. It is a good spot for breakfast.

Pizzería El Bambino
$
every day 9:30am to 10pm
one block west of the parque central, one block from the beach
This spot offers a variety of pizzas served at a simple outdoor terrace.

Rancho Gably
$
every day 8am to 9pm
facing Villas Telamar
Rancho Gambly serves simple Honduran dishes such as pork chops, sausages and burgers beneath a high, thatch shelter.

Restaurant Garibaldi
$
every day 7am to 3am
one block west of the plaza
☎448-1909
This establishment offers an enticing variety of Mexican dishes on a big outdoor terrace. The menu includes specialties such as barbecued beef, tongue Veracruz-style, and *mole poblano*. Breakfasts are also available.

Casa Azul
$
4pm to midnight
closed Tue
midway between the *parque
central* and the beach
☎*448-1443*
Casa Azul has an Italian
menu with a variety of
pasta, sandwiches, sal-
ads and specialties such
as *pollo cacciatore*. This
charming spot has a
small dining room, a
quiet bar and an art
gallery in back, as well
as an espresso ma-
chine, a local rarity.

Restaurant La Red
$-$$
every day 7am to 11pm
in the Hotel Bahía Azul, facing
the sea next to the bridge
☎*448-2381*
This restaurant special-
izes in seafood casse-
roles and soups. Meats,
pasta and sandwiches
are also available,
served at an indoor
dining room and an
outdoor terrace.

Restaurant Vista Maya
$$
every day 9am to 9pm
on a hilltop four blocks east of
the parque central
☎*448-1497*
Run by a couple from
Québec, Canada this
spot offers a menu
featuring spaghetti,
shrimps, fish and
chicken. Specialties
include garlic spaghetti
with shrimp and home-
made tropical fruit pies.
The dining area is a
breezy terrace over-
looking the sea.

Restaurant César Mariscos
$$
every day 7am to 10pm
facing the beach just west of the
parque central
☎*448-1934*
This is a breezy, com-
fortable beachfront
restaurant specializing
in fish and seafood.

Restaurant La Estación Victoria
$$
Wed to Mon 9am to 9pm
facing Villas Telamar
☎*448-2154*
This restaurant has a
handsome formal din-
ing room and a small
rear terrace. Specialties
include seafood soups.
Salads, fish, steak and
chicken are also avail-
able.

La Ceiba

La Ceiba has a lively
dining scene. Seafood
lovers and night owls
will be happier than in
most other parts of
Honduras. Things tend
to stay open a little
later here. Restaurants
are scattered across the
city centre, in the *zona
viva* just to the east,
and in the outskirts.
Among restaurants
open 24hrs is **La
Cumbre**, an open-air
spot specializing in
roast chicken, situated
2km from the city
centre along the high-
way to Tela. Outside La
Ceiba, **Esquina Ethel** in
Corozal and **La Champa**
in Sambo Creek are
open-air, straw-roofed
restaurants offering
fresh fish and seafood
dishes at moderate
prices.

Cafetería Shalom
$
every day 7am to 8pm
in Plaza Panayotti, 7a Calle
between Avenida 14 de Julio and
Avenida San Isidro
Cafetería Shalom is a
little hole-in-the-wall
restaurant in an indoor
mall offering hummus,
felafel, shawarma and
other Middle Eastern
specialties. Very good
for vegetarians and
meat-eaters alike.

Hole-in-the-Wall
$
Mon to Sat noon to 3am, Sun
4pm to 3am
14 de Julio at 1a Calle
Formerly Bar El
Canadiense, now under
U.S. ownership, this is
a bar and restaurant
offering Tex-Mex spe-
cialties and other items
including steak sand-
wiches.

Deutsche Australien Club, also known as Dieter's
$-$$
every day 8am to midnight,
kitchen open until 9pm
facing the beach near Avenida
14 de Julio
Deutsche Australien
Club is an open-air bar
and restaurant, run by
an Australian-born Ger-
man, offering a variety
of German and Hondu-
ran dishes in a casual
atmosphere.

Restaurant Brisas del Mar, also known as Marvin's
$-$$
*Tue to Sun 8am to 10pm
or later*
facing the beach east of the
estero near Disco Arenas
This is a two-storey,
open-air spot set be-
neath a high thatch
shelter. Run by a U.S.

expatriate, it features items such as fried fish and country fried steak. Friendly.

La Carreta
$$
10:30am to 11:30pm
Calle La Barra at Avenida 14 de Julio near Hondutel
☎*443-0111*
La Carreta specializes in grilled meats, including a variety of steaks and *pinchos*, but it also offers seafood soups and *ceviche*. The decor in this open-air spot is attractive, with wooden tables, hanging baskets and pottery, and plants and shrubs everywhere.

Chabelita
$$
10am to 10pm
Chabelita Barrio La Barra near the end of 1ª Calle, 2km from the city centre
☎*440-0027*
Chabelita has developed a reputation for its fish and seafood dishes, including various seafood soups and fried or grilled fish. Meat dishes are also available. The restaurant has a simple dining room with wooden tables and friendly service.

Restaurant My Friend
$$
every day 10am to 2am
facing the sea three blocks east of the estero
☎*443-2859*
This is a simple, open-air seafront restaurant specializing in fish and shrimp dishes. Meat, soup and pasta also appear on the menu.

Expatriates Bar & Grill
$$
Thu to Mon 4pm to midnight
Barrio El Imán, at the end of 12a Calle
☎*443-2272*
Located a couple of blocks beyond the city centre, this is a friendly spot popular with North Americans. Run by a Canadian, it specializes in grilled meats and fish. Vegetarian dishes are also available. It is reached by a flight of stairs and is sheltered by a high, thatch roof.

La Plancha
$$-$$$
10am to 2pm
5pm to 11pm
Calle Lempira, Barrio El Imán near the soccer stadium
☎*443-0223*
La Plancha offers a broad menu including a variety of steaks, *pinchos* and seafood soups. The air-conditioned dining room here is pleasant but ordinary.

Golden Palace
$$
11am to 3pm
5pm to 11pm
on the highway to Tela 2.5km from the city centre
☎*443-0243*
Golden Palace offers both Chinese and Western preparations of a variety of meat and seafood. For instance, duck is available *à l'orange* or Peking-style. Honduran touches include seafood soups and, for dessert, coconut flan. The big air-conditioned dining room is comfortable but nondescript.

Ricardo's
$$$
11am to 1:30pm
5:30pm to 10pm
closed Sun
Avenida 14 de Julio at 10ª Calle
☎*443-0468*
Ricardo's has a gorgeous garden terrace and an air-conditioned dining room. The menu includes varied meat dishes as well as shrimp, squid and fish. Specialties include shrimp thermidor, fish with a jalapeño cream sauce and blackened fish. Vegetarian dishes and pasta are also available.

East of La Ceiba

Restaurant Mi Rancho
$$
every day 8am to 11pm
in Sambo Creek facing the beach near the eastern end of the village
Restaurant Mi Rancho is a small, pleasant open-air restaurant with quiet music and a wide variety of fish and seafood preparations, some seasoned with curry or coconut. A special dish is casava with fish, accompanied by coconut-scented rice and beans. Salads and meat are also available.

Helen's Restaurant
$$
every day 10am to 6pm or later
just east of Sambo Creek, road access a few hundred metres past the main Sambo Creek cutoff

Run by a couple from Québec, Canada, this is an idyllic open-air beachfront restaurant with a broad menu including fish, shrimp, *ceviche*, seafood soups, and fresh juices.

Villa Rhina
$$-$$$
every day 7am to 1am
highway to Trujillo 14km east of La Ceiba
☎*443-1222 or 443-1434*
Villa Rhina is a hotel and restaurant with a big open-air dining room offering views of the sea and the forest. Some tables are set next to natural pools formed by a mountain stream. The menu centres around meat and seafood dishes. Sandwiches and a full breakfast menu are also available.

Trujillo

The restaurant scene in Trujillo cannot be described as exciting, but lovers of simple seafood dishes will not be disappointed. On the beach directly below the centre of town is a row of humble seafront restaurants offering fresh fish and seafood at moderate prices. Some of them stay open well into the evening, but please note the security warning on p. 141. In Barrio Cristales to the west, traditional Garífuna fare is offered by several seafront restaurants. Dishes include fish or conch soup with coconut, fried fish, and

varied preparations of plantain and yuca. Dining elsewhere around Trujillo leans to the more conventional. There are a couple of very economical spots directly facing the parque central.

Perla del Caribe
$
8:30am to 10:30pm
along the beach below the lookout
Perla del Caribe is one of a row of beachfront restaurants near the centre of town and is said by some local people to be among the best. It offers tasty seafood soups and grilled fish, conch, shrimp and lobster at very reasonable prices.

Pantry
$
7am to 10pm
closed Tue
two blocks from the parque central
Pantry offers pizza plus a regular Honduran menu and good pancakes for breakfast. The Dutch owners have ambitious plans. The restaurant is air-conditioned.

Café Oasis
$-$$
every day 7am to 10pm or later
half-block from the parque central
☎*434-4828*
This place offers an interesting variety of Honduran and Cuban dishes in a simple, pleasant dining room. The broad menu includes seafood soups,

salads, tacos and sandwiches. One delicious item is *sopa de capirotadas*, a soup made of cornmeal, white cheese and vegetables. A variety of breakfasts are available.

Gringo's Restaurant and Bar
$-$$
Tue to Sun 7am to 10pm
adjacent to the airstrip, facing the beach
☎*434-4277*
Gringo's is a popular American-run spot set beneath a high thatch roof facing the sea, with wooden tables and benches. Meats, fish, seafood and sandwiches fill most of the menu. Weekend barbecues centre around chicken and ribs.

Restaurant Pirulos
$-$$
every day 10am to 11pm, later on weekends
along the beach below the parque central
This is a simple, open-air beachfront restaurant offering seafood soups along with fresh fish, conch, shrimp and lobster.

Bar Bahía
$-$$
7am to 10pm
along the beach 2km from the centre of town near the Christopher Columbus Beach Resort
Bar Bahía is an open-air beachfront bar and restaurant with thatch shades and a casual atmosphere. It is a popular hangout for the resident foreign population. The selection includes sandwiches, vegetarian platters, and

a variety of meat, fish and shrimp dishes.

Comedor Caballero
$$
8am to 6pm
open evenings during holiday periods only
in Santa Fe, 12km west of Trujillo

Comedor Caballero is set in an ordinary house next to a church in the Garífuna town of Santa Fe. Fresh fish and seafood, including grilled red snapper and conch stew, are served in plentiful quantities and accompanied by salad. The owner is a former cruiseship chef.

Entertainment

In most towns in this chapter, restaurants and bars provide the focus of evening activity. In **Tela**, the **Restaurant Casa Azul** *(midway between the parque central and the beach)* is also a popular drinking spot. In La Ceiba, an area known as the *zona viva*, with several restaurants, bars and discotheques occupying a four-block stretch of 1a Calle running east from Avenida 14 de Julio, tends to be lively (and fairly safe) at night. A dance club called **Cherrie's** just east of Avenida 14 de Julio is considered the most popular. The rooftop bar at **Hotel El Colonial** *(Avenida 14 de Julio between 6a and 7a Calles)* is pleasant and conge-

nial, with panoramic aerial views of the city. La Ceiba's annual **festival**, with street dances and various other festivities, begins May 11 and culminates with a bang on May 21.
In **Trujillo**, traditional **Garífuna dances** and **punta**, an original tropical rhythm, are presented Friday and Saturday evenings in Barrio Cristales, a predominantly Garífuna neighbourhood facing the beach in the western part of town. One place to look is the **Sede Afro-Garífuna**, right on the beach, where the best known of the local groups, Grupo Menudo, performs with as many as 20 musicians and dancers. Other folkloric groups perform in nearby venues. There are also several **dance clubs**, including Black & White, Kenya and Mountain View. There have been reports of night-time muggings in Barrio Cristales, so it is better not to wander through poorly lit areas.

Shopping

In **Tela**, the Hotel Villas Telamar has a small shopping centre including a gift shop with a selection of handicrafts. The public market in the centre of town is lively but offers few handicrafts.

In **La Ceiba**, selections of Honduran and other Central American handicrafts may be found at **Artesa**, near the city centre on Avenida Colón near Avenida San Isidro, and also at the gift shop at the **Hotel La Quinta**, and also at **The Rain Forest** *(Calle La Julia, just off 9a Calle four blocks east of the parque central, ☎443-2917).* The latter offers a book exchange and a selection of Honduran cigars as well. **Virgie Gallery of Caribbean Art** *(1a Calle near Avenida San Isidro, ☎440-0666)* presents works by the gallery owner, Virgie Castillo, and by other local artists. *(Further information at ☎441-2733.)*

In **Trujillo**, the gift shop at the Hotel Emperador, three blocks from the *parque central*, offers a selection of local handicrafts, including Garífuna drums.

Islas de la Bahía ★ ★ ★

Imagine, for a moment, a group of small Caribbean islands with fabulous diving, sandy beaches, swaying palms, lush mountain vegetation, a broad range of hotels and restaurants and, miracle of miracles, moderate prices.

This is a pretty good description of the Islas de la Bahía (Bay Islands), which offer the flavour of the Caribbean and some of the world's finest diving at prices well below the usual Caribbean levels. Granted, it is quite possible to drop a bundle at some of the luxury resorts in Roatán or Guanaja, but there are plenty of cheaper places to stay, and even some of the more expensive spots offer good value compared to what can be found in much of the Caribbean. Prices do, however, tend to be somewhat higher here than on the Honduran mainland.

Tourism developed earlier on Islas de la Bahía than in most other parts of Honduras. This has much to do with the series of coral reefs extending all the way from Belize, the second longest reef structure in the world after Australia's Great Barrier Reef. The exceptional diving possibilities began attracting visitors decades ago, particularly to Roatán, and to this day Islas de la Bahía account for more foreign tourist dollars than the rest of Honduras combined. Tourism and fishing are the main local industries.

Arriving on any of Islas de la Bahía, it is difficult to believe they form part of a country that is predominantly Spanish-speaking and *mestizo*. Although thousands of mainlanders have settled on the islands in recent years to take advantage of their relatively strong economic opportunities, the majority of the island population is black and English-speaking. Most are descendants of escaped slaves from the Cayman Islands and elsewhere in the Caribbean. Because schools and officialdom operate mostly in Spanish, most people are bilingual. Otherwise, Bay Islanders bear a close resemblance to many Belizeans in matters ranging from cuisine and musical tastes to the style of spoken English.

Islas de la Bahía consist of three main islands and many smaller cays, all situated between 35km and 60km from the coast. **Roatán** is by far the biggest and most varied. The island is long and narrow, more than 40km long but only 2km to 4km wide, and its population is approaching 20,000. Roatán has the greatest choice of accommodations on Islas de la Bahía and some fine beaches. The village of West End, near the western tip of the island as its name suggests, is popular with budget and mid-range travellers,while adjacent West Bay, more recently developed, runs on average a couple of notches higher. Resorts on several parts of the island cater to the well heeled, although spots for the mid-range traveller are never far away. Coxen Hole is the main town on the island and boasts several moderately priced hotels. Most tourists, however, choose lodgings elsewhere and visit the town for money exchange and other practical matters.

Guanaja and Utila, both with smaller populations than Roatán, sit almost at opposite poles in terms of the visitors they draw. **Guanaja**, about 18km long and 6km wide at its widest point, is lush and mountainous, with several top-end resort hotels scattered around different parts of the island, most accessible only by boat. The intriguing town of Bonacca lies on a tiny island of its own and is crisscrossed by canals. Its narrow streets are open to pedestrians only.

Utila, about 14km long and 5km wide, is a haven for travellers with limited funds. Most visitors stay in the island's single town, where nearly everything lies within walking distance. Though it may seem difficult to reconcile scuba diving with low spending, many seem to manage it. Of course, not all visitors go diving – the place has a certain charm that makes mere repose a pleasure. It is the sort of spot where people arrive planning to spend a couple of days and end up staying many weeks.

But not all hotels and restaurants on Utila cater to the impecunious – several fancier spots have cropped up. Conversely, it is possible to see Guanaja without spending an arm and a leg. Visitors to either island should bring a good supply of insect repellent. The sandflies on Utila in particular can be quite vicious, especially during the rainy season.

Many visitors to Honduras spend all their time on Islas de la Bahía. While it may seem a pity to neglect some of Honduras's other attractions, the idyllic surroundings in parts of the islands can make it difficult to tear one's self away. This is especially true of divers, for whom Islas de la Bahía are a veritable paradise. And although the beaches are not as enticing as some of those on the mainland, many a traveller has considerable overstayed a planned visit.

Finding Your Way Around

By Plane

Frequent daily flights operate between La Ceiba and Roatán. There are many flights also connecting La Ceiba with Guanaja and several to Utila. Fares are surprisly cheap. Service is less frequent on Sundays. Isleña Airlines, Aerolíneas Sosa and Rollins Air all fly to Roatán and Guanaja, while at the time of writing Sosa is the only airline with service to Utila. Nearly all flights operate during daylight hours only, although there is at least one early-evening flight from Roatán to La Ceiba. During busy periods, extra flights are sometimes added to accommodate as many passengers as possible.

No scheduled flights run between islands – it is usually necessary to make connections at La Ceiba. The same applies to travel to or

from San Pedro Sula or Tegucigalpa, although on some occasions, especially where group travel is involved, non-stop flights are added between San Pedro Sula and Roatán or between San Pedro Sula and Guanaja.

Roatán receives some limited international traffic, including direct jet flights on weekends, from Miami and Houston with Grupo Taca. The same company provides daily turbo-prop service between Roatán and Belize, where connections are available to and from Miami and Houston. Some charter flights also call on Roatán, including a year-round service from Milan, operated once a week. There are no international flights to Guanaja or Utila.

Airports

Roatán

The airport in Roatán is situated 1km east of Coxen Hole. A sparkling new terminal building opened in 1995. Its Spanish designers seem to have had an aversion to windows. Arriving passengers who are bound for parts of the island other than Coxen Hole may find it cheaper to take a taxi into Coxen Hole and a collective taxi or minibus from there.

Guanaja

The airstrip in Guanaja is situated by the water's edge on the main island a short hop by boat from Bonacca. The fare is $2. Small boats meet all incoming flights and depart from town about 20min before each outgoing flight. There is a refreshment stall by the airstrip but no terminal building. The luxury resorts usually send boats to meet their guests' flights. If not, it is necessary to hire a water taxi, and this can be expensive, at $20 or more.

Utila

The airstrip in Utila is perched at the edge of town within easy walking distance for those without heavy baggage. A pickup truck meets incoming flights and provides taxi service.

By Ferry

Ferry service provides an interesting alternative to air service for travel between La Ceiba and Islas de la Bahía. The *Galaxy*, a modern 350-passenger vessel with an air-conditioned main deck and an open-air upper deck, operates daily between La Ceiba and Roatán *(1hr 45min, $10)* and between La Ceiba and Utila *(1hr, $9)*. Approximate schedules are as follows (and are subject to change):

Islas de la Bahía

Departure Roatán
7am
Arrival La Ceiba
8:45am

Departure La Ceiba
9:30am
Arrival Utila
10:30am

Departure Utila
11am
Arrival La Ceiba
noon

Departure La Ceiba
3pm
Arrival Roatán
4:45pm

The *Galaxy* is operated by Safeway Transportation Company (☎445-1695 *in Roatán,* ☎425-3161 *in Utila, no phone in La Ceiba*). The ferry terminal in Roatán is located in the town of Coxen Hole, near the Cay View Hotel. In Utila, the ferry docks at the centrally located municipal pier. Arriving passengers step right into the swing of things. In La Ceiba, however, the terminal is situated in a remote spot about 10km by road from the centre of town. Taxis *($3.50 per passenger)* are just about the only way of getting there.

By Road

There are no roads in Guanaja; boats (and footpaths in Bonacca town) provide the main forms of transport. Utila has only a tiny road network with scarcely any motor vehicles. Most traffic there moves by bicycle or on foot. A good paved highway runs almost the entire length of Roatán, passing through or near all the main towns, with spurs running to other spots. From Coxen Hole and the adjacent airport, the road runs east near the southern shore of the island to Brick Bay and French Harbour, and then turns inland farther east with a spur to Oak Ridge, following a hilly, twisting route with the sea visible on both sides. Heading west from Coxen Hole, the road crosses to the north side of the island and then passes by Sandy Bay and West End.

Minibuses and collective taxis run several times an hour until early evening from Coxen Hole west to Sandy Bay and West End, and less frequently from Coxen Hole east to French Harbour and Oak Ridge. Minibus fares are about $1 to West End and about $2 to Oak Ridge. Collective taxis charge slightly more.

Practical Information

Currency Exchange

Banks in Coxen Hole, Bonacca and Utila change U.S. dollars or U.S. travellers' cheques at the official exchange rate, which is usually better than the rates offered by hotels. The morning is generally the best time to go. Some banks are not open in the afternoon. In all cases, visitors should be prepared for a long wait. Coxen Hole is the only place in Roatán with banking services.

Airline Reservations

Roatán

Grupo Taca
☎445-1387 or *445 1918*
Isleña
☎445-1550
Rollins
☎445-1967

Guanaja

Isleña
☎453-4208
Rollins
☎453-4202
Sosa
☎453-4349

Utila

Sosa
☎425-3368
Isleña
☎425-3368

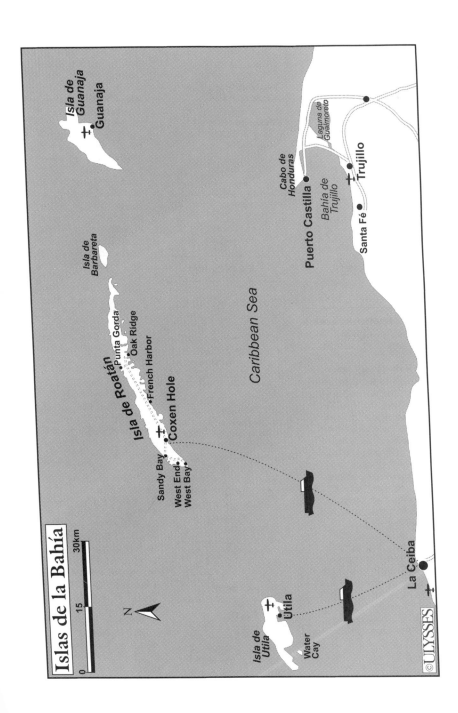

Islas de la Bahía

0 15 30km

N

Isla de
Guanaja
+ Guanaja

Isla de
Barbareta

Isla de Roatán
Punta Gorda
Oak Ridge
French Harbor
+ Coxen Hole
Sandy Bay
West End
West Bay

Caribbean Sea

Cabo de
Honduras

Puerto Castilla

Bahía de
Trujillo

Laguna de
Guaimoreto

+ Trujillo

Santa Fé

Isla de
Utila
+ Utila

Water
Cay

La Ceiba +

© ULYSSES

Car Rentals

Rental cars are available in Roatán but not on the other islands.

Avis
airport
☎445-1568

Sandy Bay Rent a Car
airport
☎445-1741

Sandy Bay Rent a Car
Sandy Bay
☎445-1710

Toyota Rent a Car
airport
☎445-1729

Telephone and Internet

Hondutel has offices in Coxen Hole (Roatán), Bonacca (Guanaja), and Utila, where local and international calls may be placed. Elsewhere, visitors may have to rely on hotels (with their often high surcharges) for phone service until public phones and prepaid phone cards are available.

Internet cafés (the "café" part is usually an afterthought) have been springing up like mushrooms since the late 1990s in Roatán and Utila. A shakeout seemed almost inevitable.

Here are some of the establishments in operation:

Coxen Hole (Roatán)
Hotel Cay View

West End (Roatán)
Foster's Restaurant

Utila
Internet Café

Howell's Internet and E-mail Service

Exploring

The pleasures of Islas de la Bahía centre largely around their offshore reef formations and palm-shaded beaches, but there are other attractions as well.

Islas de la Bahía are an archipelago consisting of three bigger islands (Utila to the west, Guanaja to the east, and Roatán in between) as well as several smaller, mostly uninhabited islands, the most noteworthy of which is Cayo Cochinos. Each island has its own special character.

★★★

Roatán

Roatán, the biggest of the islands, offers the most variety. The town of **Coxen Hole,** on the south coast of the island toward the west, is where most visitors get their first glimpse of Roatán. This is the main commercial centre, the place to change money, take care of groceries, buy air or ferry tickets, renew immigration documents and look after various other practical odds and ends. Islas de la Bahía Conservation Authority has offices here, in the Cooper building, with maps, pamphlets, and information of special interest to naturalists. The town itself offers little of real interest, although it may still be worth taking a stroll along the main street and over to the public market two blocks behind.

Several villages lie to the east, including **French Harbour** and **Oak Ridge**, the two towns that are home to most of Roatán's fishing fleet. Both are also home to tourist resorts. Oak Ridge is perhaps the most picturesque of Roatán's villages, with a strong Caribbean flavour and a harbour that bustles with small fishing and passenger vessels. Not far away, on the north side of the island, is the Garífuna village of **Punta Gorda**, which was hit hard by Hurricane Mitch in 1998. Houses and other buildings stretch in a thin line along the beachfront, in typical Garífuna fashion. East of here, the island is

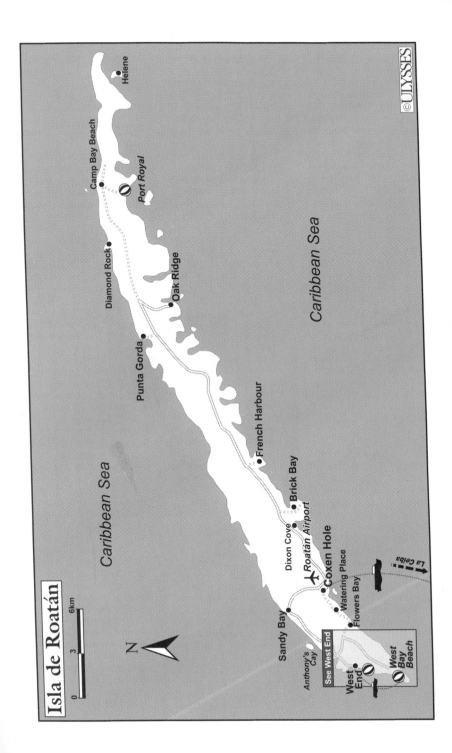

very sparsely populated.

It is to the west of Coxen Hole that most recent development has taken place. **Sandy Bay** is home to several of the top resort hotels, and further west are the laid-back environs of **West End**, with its long sandy shore and broad choice of low-to-medium-priced accommodations. South of West End, reached by a newly built road that swings inland behind the coastal hills, is **West Bay**, with its especially beautiful beach and its dynamic tourism scene. New hotels have been built but at any given moment, visitors still number in the hundreds and not yet in the thousands, and that is likely to remain the case for several years to come.

The **Tabayana Beach Resort** in West Bay is not a hotel, regardless of what its name may suggest, but rather a beach and picnic area intended mainly for cruise ship passengers and also for guests of Anthony's Key Resort, which administers it. This expansive area of beach and forest includes a restaurant, several shops, diving facilities and several rustic buildings, although from time to time the only human presence here is its caretakers.

The **Carambola Botanical Gardens** *(free admission, small charge for guide; every day 7am to 5pm; in Sandy Bay near Anthony's Key Resort, ☎445-1117)* are home to a wide variety of exotic trees and plants. Walkways lead visitors through areas of flowering plants, orchids, ferns, spices, fruit trees, and hardwood trees, including Honduran mahogany. The summit of Carambola Mountain can be reached in an easy 20min hike. Along the way are breeding grounds for iguanas and parrots. There are fine views from the top of the mountain, including an interesting perspective on the reef formations.

The **Roatán Museum** and **Institute for Marine Sciences** *($4; Thu to Tue 8:30am to 5pm; Anthony's Key Resort, Sandy Bay)* contains a small air-conditioned museum with a few pre-Hispanic pieces as well as artefacts and dioramas illustrating the colonial period. But most people come to see the dolphin shows *(every day except Wed, 10am and 4pm, with extra shows at 1pm on Sat and Sun)* It is possible to go swimming with the dolphins at specific hours for $75 per person or to go diving

with them for $100 per person.

Guanaja

The main attractions here are the reefs and beaches ringing the main island and the town of **Bonacca**, which has been dubbed, perhaps exaggeratedly, the Venice of the Caribbean. True, it is situated on a small, separate island, crisscrossed by canals, but the resemblance ends there. Bonacca is a thoroughly West Indian place, with clapboard dwellings and a real sense of being by the sea. The absence of wheeled motor vehicles, and its maze of narrow streets and wood-planked passageways makes it a delight. There is little of special interest, but there is certainly plenty of atmosphere.

Guanaja was hit especially hard by Hurricane Mitch in 1998, with the shore swept by high winds and waves towering 20m high. Hundreds of houses and various other buildings were destroyed. The island's handful of hotels was not spared either, and while most got back on their feet within a matter of months, one or two of them may never

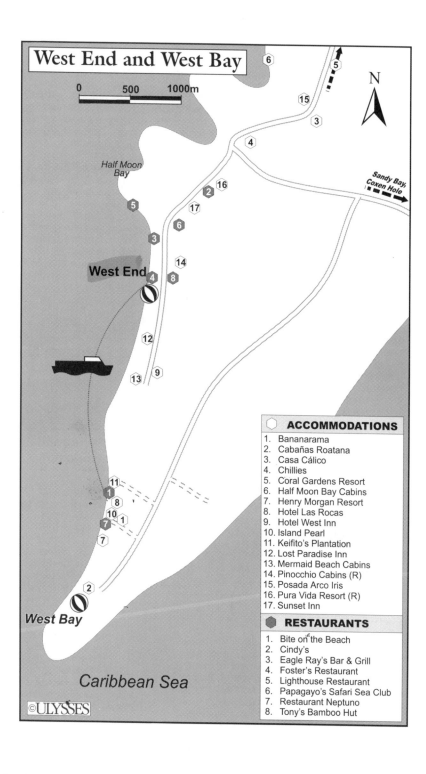

reopen. The hurricane also took a toll on the island's vegetation, felling thousands of trees. Although Guanaja may look very lush and tropical to first-time visitors, it may be several years before the tree cover has returned to what it was before.

Utila

The smallest of the three main Islas de la Bahía, Utila is the flattest and least scenic, but its low prices and relaxed atmosphere draw many repeat visitors. Nearly everyone stays in the island's single town with its long and lively main street, which has very few motor vehicles. As elsewhere in Islas de la Bahía, diving, snorkelling and swimming are among the attractions. Travellers should bring a good supply of insect repellent: the sand flies are vicious.

Beaches

Roatán

West Bay Beach, a short distance beyond West End, is a long, broad, white-sand, palm-shaded beach, justifiably one of the most popular on the islands. It can be reached by a

footpath along the shore but is easier to get to by boat. Boats leave regularly from the pier at Foster's Restaurant from 9am to 9pm, with service about every hour; the 10min trip costs $1.50. West Bay can also be reached by a new road that runs inland behind the coastal hills. The snorkelling is good at the far end of the beach and swimming is great everywhere.

On the eastern part of the island, there is a good beach at **Half Point Bay** near Oak Ridge. Farther east is **Port Royal**, which has the remains of a fort and a beautiful, almost deserted beach, with some nude bathing.

Guanaja

Michael Rock and **Diana Beach** are two of the gorgeous, secluded beaches along the north side of the island. The east side of the island boasts 5km of almost uninterrupted beach. There are smaller beaches near each of the resort hotels.

Utila

One of the finest beaches around Utila is not on the main island but on an islet called **Water Cay** just to the southwest. From town, Water Cay can be reached by dory in

about 30min at a cost of about $5 per person once a group has been assembled. The beach is nearly deserted, camping is allowed, and there is good snorkelling nearby.

Pumpkin Hill Bay, on the north side of the island of Utila itself, can be reached on foot in about a half-hour. The beach is sandy, and nude bathing seems to be accepted. Nearby are several caves reputed to have been used by pirates.

Outdoor Activities

Diving and Snorkelling

Diving is the main outdoor activity on Islas de la Bahía, which lie amidst one of the world's great coral reefs. Many divers return year after year to enjoy some of the most fabulous sites available. In addition to experienced divers, Islas de la Bahía also attract many people who are just learning to dive, and instruction is available at many spots. Those without much experience should familiarize themselves with the very important safety precautions associated

This reconstruction of Temple 16, a shrine to the Mayan sun god, is part of Honduras's rich archeological heritage. - *Claude Hervé-Bazin*

This lovely palm tree-lined beach is located near West End on Roatán, the country's largest island.
- *Claude Hervé-Bazin*

Diving sites around Roatán have plenty of caves and reefs that guarantee interesting discoveries.
- *John Haught*

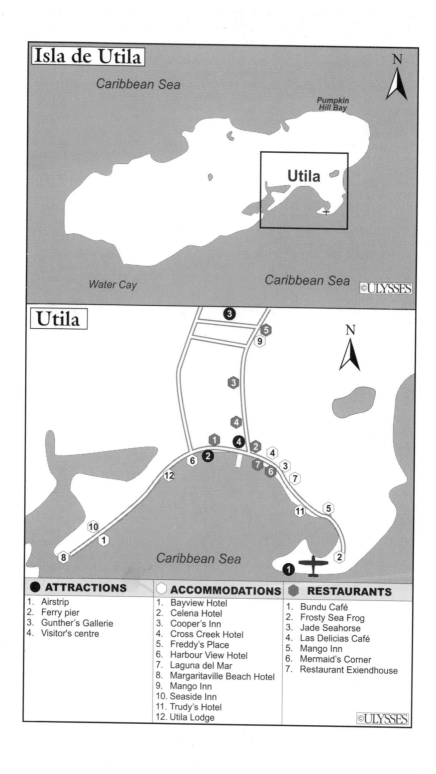

Isla de Utila

Caribbean Sea

Pumpkin Hill Bay

Utila

N

Caribbean Sea

Water Cay

Caribbean Sea

©ULYSSES

Utila

N

3

5

9

3

4

1

4

2

6

2

4

7

6

3

7

12

11

5

10

1

8

Caribbean Sea

1

2

● ATTRACTIONS	⬡ ACCOMMODATIONS	⬢ RESTAURANTS
1. Airstrip 2. Ferry pier 3. Gunther's Gallerie 4. Visitor's centre	1. Bayview Hotel 2. Celena Hotel 3. Cooper's Inn 4. Cross Creek Hotel 5. Freddy's Place 6. Harbour View Hotel 7. Laguna del Mar 8. Margaritaville Beach Hotel 9. Mango Inn 10. Seaside Inn 11. Trudy's Hotel 12. Utila Lodge	1. Bundu Café 2. Frosty Sea Frog 3. Jade Seahorse 4. Las Delicias Café 5. Mango Inn 6. Mermaid's Corner 7. Restaurant Exiendhouse

©ULYSSES

with diving. Good instruction is utterly essential. A moment's carelessness can be deadly. There were fears that Hurricane Mitch with the vicious waves it created, would damage the coral, but this did not occur. In fact, some divers say conditions are better than they were before since some detritus was actually swept away.

Equipment rental, instruction, boats and guides can be arranged at any of the numerous dive shops and resort hotels that dot the islands. At press-time, the going rate for four days of instruction leading to certification is about $160, which represents excellent value when compared to prices in many other parts of the world. Beware that diving industry in Honduras is largely unregulated. Do not be afraid to ask some pointed questions before signing up for a course or heading out on a dive. Instruction is generally available in English or Spanish and, occasionally, in French or German.

The largest concentrations of dive shops is found at West End in Roatán and in Utila. Most of these cater to people who are staying at more modest hotels that do not provide dive packages – the majority of the more

lavish resort hotels have their own dive shops. Each dive shop manager, guide and instructor has some favourite sites. For those who want detailed information on the various dive sites, we can recommend *Diving and Snorkelling Roatán and Honduras Islas de la Bahía* by Sharon Collins, published by Pisces Books in Houston and sold for $15 at Librería Casi Todo in West End, among other places.

Where reefs lie close to the surface of the water, snorkelling may be just as popular as diving. Anyone who can swim can also snorkel. The only equipment required are fins and a tightly fitting mask and pipe. These can be rented from most dive shops for a few dollars a day. After that, you just swim out a short distance, float on the surface of the water, breathe through the

snorkel, and peer at the reef below you. Scuba diving is a far more elaborate exercise and requires tanks with pressurized air. It is also a more expensive undertaking. Again, diving can be dangerous if you do not know what you are doing.

Roatán

There is a good variety of dive sites around Roatán, with walls, drifts, caves, canyons and both deep and shallow reefs. There are also some wrecks near **French Harbour**. Most dives sites are only a short boat trip away.

Some of the best diving is found off the area around **Oak Ridge** in the eastern part of the island. One of the more spectacular dive sites, **Calvin's Crack**, has a hole in the reef full of lobster, king crab, pufferfish, sharks, spotted eels and green moray eels.

Near **West End**, a dive site called **La Punta** consists of a long platform with a current strong enough for drift diving. The coral is in good shape, and there is a wide variety of fish. **West End Wall** extends from a depth of 15m to 45m and features a variety of sharks which, it is said, have an abundance of food and do not concern themselves with divers. **Pablo's Place** has beautiful coral walls and an abundance of barrel sponge at depths below 25m.

Guanaja

The island is surrounded by coral, and visitors are never very far from good dive sites. Some of the more interesting sites go by the names **Yellow Trader** and **Black Rock**. Dive masters at the resort hotels have plenty of other suggestions.

Utila

Diving sites on the south side of the island are shallower, easier to reach and more popular than those on the north. One of the more popular sites is the **Labyrinth**, with sheets, caves and beautiful coral. Reef formations on the north side run deeper and are preferred by some advanced divers. There are deep walls with big coral gardens, several small caves, sea moun-

tains and many fish 2km from the island. Boats take 20 to 40min to reach these sites from town.

There is good snorkelling by the reef near the airstrip and also at Water Cay (see page 160).

Islas de la Bahía

Entering the 21st Century After Missing the 20th

In the history of communications, it is a commonly accepted fact that telephones came into common use long before the inception of the Internet. In parts of Honduras, especially on the Bay Islands, this is not always so evident. Hondutel, the state-owned telephone monopoly and one of the least respected public institutions in a country that rarely holds its public institutions in high esteem, has been slow to extend service to some areas. This was true, for instance, of West Bay, a burgeoning

resort zone near the southwestern corner of Roatán. The biggest resort hotel in Honduras opened there in 1999 without telephone links to the outside world (apart from a very expensive satellite link) because Hondutel hesitated to extend its land lines by a mere 4km, an investment that would easily have paid for itself within weeks from long-distance revenues alone. And this is not the only example. It is not unusual here to come across hotels that have E-mail addresses and Web sites but no pho-

nes. Hotel personnel go each day to a spot with phone and Internet access to collect their messages and send replies. The inadequacy of phone service (and sky-high international rates) have created an enthusiasm for Internet use that would not normally be expected in a country at Honduras's stage of economic development. This, after all, is a place where visitors may find themselves rediscovering rotary dial telephones years after forgetting they ever existed.

Accommodations

Roatán

Lodgings on the island of Roatán cover a wide gamut and can be divided roughly into two categories: those that cater mostly to divers and those that draw a more varied group of guests. These are not hard-and-fast categories: some people stay at ordinary hotels and make separate arrangements for diving, while some non-divers may choose to stay at dive-oriented hotels and forego diving packages. In general, divers' hotels aim at an affluent clientele and tend to be more lavish, more comfortable and more expensive than the other sort, but several are quite modest and make a point of offering diving packages that are accessible to people on tighter budgets. No resort hotel, no matter how many divers may be staying there, will turn away guests who are not interested in diving.

The best selections of lower- to middle-priced lodgings are found in West End and Coxen Hole. Medium- and upper-priced accommodations are scattered across the island.

Coxen Hole

Hotel Allen
$8
⊗, *tv*
Barrio El Ticket near the edge of town
☎445-1247
This rustic, tree-shaded spot has 11 small, basic rooms with shared bath and double bed.

Hotelito Ronnie
$10
⊗
Barrio El Ticket near the edge of town
The 10 rooms here are tiny but pleasant in a simple sort of way. Some have shared bath, others have private bath.

Hotel El Paso
$12
⊗, ℜ, *bar*
in the centre of town
☎445-1059
The six clean rooms here have shared bath and are basic and a bit dark.

Hotel Cay View
$30
≡, *tv*, ℜ, *bar*
in the centre of town
☎445-1202
Rooms are bright, breezy and simple, with new furniture, and the service is friendly.

Hotel Bella Vista
$30
⊗, ℜ, *bar*
☎445-1036
Watering Place, away from the centre
This friendly spot has 10 rooms set in a two-storey, *L*-shaped building. Rooms are bright and breezy, with wooden floors. There is a small beach just in front.

Sandy Bay

Oceanside Inn
$58-$70
⊗, ℜ, *bar*
next to Anthony's Key Resort
☎445-1552
⊷445-1532
oceanside@global.hn
This very friendly hotel is one of the most pleasant on the island and one of the best values. The eight rooms have a rustic character, with most furnishings made of wood with nice touches of colour. Most have sea views, and there is a big upstairs terrace. Snorkelling nearby is excellent, and diving is available.

Ships Inn
$60
⊗, ℜ, *bar*
☎445-1661
The five rooms here are bright and pleasant, housed in wooden buildings. The hotel is set on attractive, sand-covered, palm-shaded grounds reached by a rough road from the highway. The beach in front of the hotel is suitable for swimming and snorkelling. The hotel also has a dive shop.

**Islas de la Bahía Beach
Resort** *$141 room only
$235 including meals for
two people
$294 including meals and
diving*
≡, ⊗, ℜ, *bar*
☎445-1425
⇄*445-1855*
U.S. reservations
☎*800-476-2826*
The 12 rooms here are
big, bright and
cheerfully furnished.
The hotel faces a fine,
palm-shaded beach for
swimming, with a reef
suitable for snorkelling
a short swim away. The
restaurant has an out-
door terrace plus a lofty
indoor dining room.
Weekly packages are
available at reduced
rates. A dive shop and
gift shop round out the
facilities.

The Inn of Last Resort
*$230 for two including all
meals
$270 with meals and dive
package, multi-day pro-
grams offered at lower rates*
ℜ, ≡, ☎;
between West End and Sandy
Bay
☎*445-1838*
⇄*445-1848*
U.S. reservations
☎*888-238-8266*
lastresort@globalnet.hn
The Inn of Last Resort
is perched next to an
inlet called Gibson
Bight which, among
other things, is shel-
tered from hurricanes,
and also stretches over
to a lagoon with good
swimming and snorkel-
ling areas. This is a
lavish, American-run
spot with amenities that
include two dive boats,
one fishing boat, a li-
brary, a gift shop and a

big wooden deck over
the lagoon that in-
cludes a barbecue pit.
The 30 spacious, com-
fortable guest rooms,
with rustic decor, are
set in three buildings
on expansive grounds.
The hotel is reached by
a 1.5km dirt road.

Anthony's Key Resort
*$313-$360 including three
meals a day and dive package for two people*
⊗, ℜ, *bar*
☎*445-1003*
⇄*445-1140*
U.S. reservations
☎*800-227-3483*
www.aventuras.com/anthonys-key
In several important
respects, this is both
the most lavish and, at
the same time, most
nature-oriented resort
hotel in Honduras. Of
the 56 rooms, 15 are
situated on the land
side and 41 on an adja-
cent cay connected by
a 24hr boat service.
The cay is left largely in
its natural state, cov-
ered in tropical forest
with big, rustic cabins
spread over a wide
area and linked by
wooden walkways.
Each cabin has cool sea
breezes, indoor and
outdoor terraces, taste-
ful and understated
decor with wooden
furnishings, and big,
lavish bathrooms.
Rooms on the sumptu-
ously vegetated land
side are slightly
cheaper. All meals are
served buffet style, and
among the amenities
offered to guests are a
nature trail on Bailey's
Cay, visits to the mu-
seum and dolphin
shows, horseback rid-

ing, and the use of
water craft including
kayaks, canoes, pedal
boats and windsails.
There is a dive shop
and good diving and
snorkelling nearby, as
well as weekly dive
packages.

West End

An ever-shifting selec-
tion of budget accom-
modations is available
in West End, mostly set
near the main road
running parallel to the
beach and generally
priced somewhere be-
tween $5 and $15. We
hesitate to offer specific
names and locations
because they seem to
change often, although
some have been
around for a few years.
Often they consist of
groups of small, scruffy
cabins identified by
nothing more than
crude, hand-painted
signs anouncing
"Rooms for Rent" or
something similar. It is
not difficult to spot
some of these signs as
you walk along the
road; it may be more
difficult is to find someone to look after you
once you have arrived.

Following are some
other accommodations:

Chillies
$15
sb, ⊗
Half Moon Bay
☎*445-1214*
online@globalnet.hn
This hotel has seven
simple rooms set in a
handsome, two-storey
wooden building with
wide verandas. Good

value. Dormitory space is available for $7.50 per person.

Sunset Inn
$20-$50
sb/pb, ⊗/≡
north of Foster's pier
☎445-1925
The Sunset Inn is a friendly spot offering a variety of accommodations with prices varying broadly according to the level of amenities. The building is horseshoe-shaped, with a tropical atmosphere, but the area in front is rather scruffy. Some rooms are brightened by colourful Guatemalan textiles.

Hotel West Inn
$25-$35
⊗
near the southern end of the road
☎445-1615
This inn opened in 1999, has 18 rooms set in a modern, two-storey, *L*-shaped building, painted pink with wood trim. Decor is nondescript. Service is friendly.

Pinocchio Cabins
$30-$35
℟, *bar*, ⊗, *dive shop, no phone*
up the footpath from near Sueño del Mar
www.roatanet.com/pinocchio
pinocchio69@bigfoot.com
This is a small spot with four rustic, tree-shaded, high-ceilinged wooden cabins, enlivened by Guatemalan textiles. Discounts are offered for longer stays.

Casa Cálico
$25-$50
⊗, ≡, *some with K, no phone*
north of the crossroads
www.roatanet.com/casacalico
Casa Cálico is set in a handsome two-storey wooden building. It offers three spacious, hardwood-floored apartments with full kitchen as well as two smaller rooms. This American-run spot faces a bay in back and offers guests the use of kayaks.

Pura Vida Resort
$30-$40 with ⊗
$50-$60 with ≡
℟, *bar*
north of Foster's pier
☎445-1141
www.puravidaresort.com
This resort has 12 simple but elegant rooms in a central location.

Posada Arco Iris
$23-$69
⊗/≡, *some with K*
north of the crossroads
☎445-1264
roberto@bondutel.hn
This establishment offers 12 big, pleasant rooms and apartments set in a pair of concrete and wooden buildings in a wooded area. Rates vary according to the level of amenities.

Mermaid Beach Cabins
$41 with ⊗
$58 with ≡
at the southern end of the road
☎445-1335
Mermaid Beach Cabins offers 10 rooms set in three rustic wooden buildings in a wooded area near the beach. Decor is simple and

pleasant, and there is a dive shop on site.

Coral Gardens Resort
$52 with ⊗
$81 with ≡
℟
1km north of West End
☎445-1428,
www.coralgardensresort.com
Formerly Seagrape Plantation Resort, this resort is a friendly spot with 20 renovated, simply but pleasantly furnished rooms set in wooden cabins spread over spacious grounds. All face the sea. Amenities include a dive shop and shore dive facilities.

Lost Paradise Inn
$58 with ⊗
$79 with ≡
south of Foster's pier
☎445-1306
www.lost-paradise.com The Lost Paradise Inn consists of 18 attractive hexagonal wooden cabins with lofty, pointed roofs, most of them set along the beach, some of which directly face the sea.

Half Moon Bay Cabins
$64 with ⊗
℟, *bar*
☎445-1075
Fourteen rustic rooms with wooden decorative touches and splashes of colour are set near the sea, although not all have sea views. The restaurant is pleasant.

West Bay

Keifito's Plantation Resort
$29-$52
no phone on site, messages at 445-1252
www.keifitos.com
This resort offers nine plain but comfortable rooms in a series of buildings scattered over spacious grounds shaded by mango, almond and palm trees overlooking West Bay beach. This spot may be reached by boat or by a road in poor condition. Rates vary by season. Some rooms have kitchen facilities, and a restaurant operates on site during high season. Horses are available for rental.

Bananarama
$52-$64 bkfst incl.
20% less in low season
⊗
no regular phone on site, messages at 455-5799, ext 513
⇌*445-1271*
bananarama@globalnet.bm
Bananarama bills itself as a bed and breakfast and dive centre. Its four pleasant, rustic wooden cabins vary in size and are set 50m from the beach amidst gardens recalling the owners' German homeland.

Hotel Las Rocas
$81 with ⊗
$93 with ≡
☎*445-1841*
info@lasrocasresort.com
HotelLas Rocas offers six rooms set in rustic wooden *cabañas* clustered close together on landscaped grounds near the beach. Decor

is nondescript. Breakfast is included in room rates.

Cabañas Roatana
$70-$111, minimum two-night stay
⊗
10% more for ≡
⇌*445-1271, U.S. reservations 888-626-9531*
beatman@globalnet.bm
This a friendly spot set right on the beach that has eight rooms that vary in size and decor. All include a refrigerator and microwave oven.

Island Pearl
$116
≡
www.roatanpearl.com
Island Pearl is a French-run beachfront establishment offering four two-storey, two-bedroom wooden beach houses with Mexican decorative touches, sea views, and balconies with hammocks. Bathrooms have interesting tilework.

Henry Morgan Resort
$174 per person including meals, drinks and sporting activities except diving
≈, ℜ, *bar, tv,* ≡, ☎;
phones pending, reservations in Italy ☎39-02-290461)
Henry Morgan Resort is Honduras's biggest resort hotel and one of its most lavish. The 128 rooms here can house 300 guests and are set in 16 almost identical wooden buildings, painted in pastel shades and attractively furnished. Facing gorgeous West Bay beach, this hotel would not be

out of place in some of the Caribbean's bigger resort towns. It is managed by a Milan-based tour company, I Grandi Viaggi, which often fills all rooms with visitors travelling from Italy on package tours. Cuisine is primarily Italian.

Brick Bay

Brick Bay Resort
$52
≈, ℜ, *bar, tv,* ⊗
☎*445-1337* or *445-1127*
⇌*445-1594, U.S. reservations 800-535-3483*
Formerly Romeo's Resort, the Brick Bay Resort has 25 high-ceilinged rooms with balconies facing a quiet inlet of the sea set well back from the road. Many rooms have been renovated and sport new tile flooring and rattan furniture. There is no beach close by, but dive packages are available.

French Harbour

Hotel Joee
$8 sb, $13 with pb
facing the harbour
The 10 rooms here are rather rudimentary. Some have harbour views.

Hotel Harbour View
$18 with ⊗, *$19 with* ≡
facing the harbour
☎*455-5390*
⇌*455-5379*
The nine rooms here are pleasant, simple and comfortable. Many of the guests are business travellers. There is a television lounge facing the sea.

Hotel Casa Romeo
$45
≡, *tv*, ☎, ℜ, *bar*
facing the harbour
☎*455-5518*
⇌*455-5645*
The seven rooms here
are pleasant, simple
and breezy, and all
have harbour views.
The downstairs restau-
rant is attractive.

Gio's
$56
ℜ, *bar*, ≡, *tv*
facing the harbour
☎*455-5215*
⇌*455-5536*
This place offers nine
big, bright wood-
trimmed rooms, some
with sea views, upstairs
from one of Roatán's
better restaurants.

**Fantasy Island Beach
Resort**
$120
≡, *tv*, ☎, ℜ, *bars*, ≈
on an island outside French
Harbour
☎*455-5222*
⇌455-5268
U.S. reservations
☎*800-676-2826*
This is one of the most
lavish hotels in Islas de
la Bahía, with 76 rooms
spread through three
buildings. It occupies a
whole island, linked to
the mainland by a short
wooden bridge. Rooms
are carpeted and ele-
gantly decorated in
shades of blue and
pink, most facing the
pool and the beach.
The water is very calm.
The main building has
eaves and turrets that
give it the appearance
of a castle. A variety of
dive packages are avail-
able. The hotel also
boasts tennis courts, a

dive shop, a gift shop,
a conference room and
water-sports opportuni-
ties of all kinds.

Oak Ridge

Oak Bay Resort
*$200/person for four nights,
including open-water diving
course, six training dives
and use of equipment
$335 per person for seven
nights, including eight boat
dives and unlimited shore
dives*
⊗
outside Oak Ridge
☎*435-2337*
www.2extreme.net/scuba
Accessible by water taxi
or by road, this spot
provides remarkable
value for diving enthu-
siasts who can manage
without the amenities
of a fancy resort hotel.
Its four apartment-style
units are adequately
furnished and spacious,
some with big living
and dining areas. There
are food shops and a
small restaurant nearby.
Diving instruction is
available from the on-
site dive shop.

Reef House Resort
*$193 including three meals
a day for two people and
shore dives
$263 including meals and
boat dives*
⊗, ℜ, *bar*
across the lagoon from Oak
Ridge
☎*435-2294*
⇌*452142, U.S. reservations
800-328-8897*
This rustic, romantic
spot, is accessible only
by boat across a peace-
ful lagoon. It caters
mostly to divers and to
visitors with an interest
in fishing, with boats

and guides available
separately or as part of
a package. Multi-day
dive packages are also
offered through the
dive shop on site.
Good diving and
snorkelling are an easy
swim away, just 200m
from shore, with a wall
marked by a buoy.
Several other dive sites
are just 5 to 15min
away by boat. The 12
rooms here have high
wooden ceilings and
mixed rustic and mod-
ern decor. All face the
sea and are cooled by
sea breezes and fans.

Punta Gorda

Hotel Henry's Cove
$90
≈, ℜ, *bar*, ≡, ⊗, ☎
1km from village of Punta
Gorda
☎*435-2187*
⇌*435-2709*
This hotel is set in a
big, bright, airy
wooden building on a
hillside above the sea.
Amenities include a
handsome dining room
and a broad wood-
planked terrace facing
the sea. The 14 com-
fortable rooms located
upstairs in the main
building offer simple
wooden decor, some
with balconies looking
out to sea. Twenty ad-
ditional rooms, slightly
bigger than those in the
main building, are lo-
cated in a group of 10
cabañas set in a
wooded area. Below
are a beach and a div-
ing dock that was re-
built following Hurri-
cane Mitch.

Guanaja

Some hotels in Guanaja suffered very extensive damagae during Hurricane Mitch. Most have been rebuilt and reopened, but a couple of hotels may be gone for good. Hotels in town and by the airstrip tend to be simple, while the resorts scattered around the island tend to be more lavish even though some maintain a rustic motif. Most rely on fans and sea breezes for ventilation rather than air conditioning.

Hotel Rosario
$24
≡, tv
in the centre of Bonacca
☎*453-4240*
Hotel Rosario offers five freash, clean rooms. The family that runs this hotel observes the Adventist sabbath and does not receive guests Friday evening or during the day on Saturday.

Hotel Alexander
$33 with ⊗
$41 with ≡
near the centre of Bonacca
☎*453-4326*
Hotel Alexander's 13 rooms are big and adequately furnished but not well maintained. Seaside rooms face a scruffy terrace. Only the rooms facing inland have air conditioning. The hotel is situated in a quiet area at the end of the main street. Overpriced.

Hurricane Hillton
$50
ℜ, ⊗, tv, ℝ, *no phone*
next to the airstrip
Formerly the Hotel Airport Hillton, this hotel has no connection with the international chain spelled with a single *L*. This is the lair of the redoutable Captain Al Veverica, an American who has lived here many years and become known fondly as a local character. The hotel was totally destroyed by Hurricane Mitch and is being rebuilt a couple of rooms at a time. Located just at the edge of the airstrip, it appears to be perched in the middle of a scrapyard, but the warm hospitality of Captain Al and his family provide ample compensation for anyone who may be put off by this. Meals (available also as part of a package) are home-cooked and generous. Simple, comfortable rooms are set on stilts above the water.

Nautilus Dive Resort
$212 including three meals a day and two dives for two people
⊗, ℜ, *bar*
on the west side of Guanaja
☎*454-4389, U.S Reservations 800-535-7063*
The seven rooms here, decorated in Mexican and Central American motifs, are situated in a building set well back from the beach on grassy, poorly kept grounds. Weekly rates are available and there is a dive shop.

Under the same management is **Dunbar Rock**, with six rooms, as well as a restaurant and bar, perched atop a rock about 400m from shore. Rates are just slightly higher

Bayman Bay Club
$186 including three meals a day for two people, $232 including two dives a day
⊗, ℜ, *bar, no phone*
on the north side of Guanaja, reached by an inner passage across the west side of the island
☎/≈ *454-4179*
U.S. reservations
800-524-1823
Fourteen handsomely decorated rooms with splendid views and good cross-ventilation are set in rustic wooden cabins. These are scattered throughout a tropical forest perched high on a hillside above a small but attractive beach. Kayaks are available for the use of guests, and the hotel boasts a dive centre and gift shop. Hiking trails are nearby.

Posada del Sol
$321-$353 including three meals a day for two people, $364-$385 including meals and three dives a day
⊗, ≈
on the south side of Guanaja
U.S. reservations
800-642-3483 or
(561) 624-3483
Most of the 23 bright, comfortably furnished rooms in this gorgeous spot are set in a Spanish colonial-style building, with pleasant use of wood and painted tile. A beautiful pool area is surrounded by palms and bougainvil-

laea, with a wooden deck. There is a small beach just below. Although the hotel has a formal dining room, most meals are served outdoors. Oceanfront or hillside rooms cost slightly more than poolside rooms. Weekly rates and honeymoon packages are available. The hotel also boasts tennis courts, fishing, a dive centre and a gift shop.

Utila

Lodgings in Utila are mostly inexpensive and situated in town, but at least one resort-style hotel is up and running.

Seaside Inn
$5 with sb
$7 with pb
facing Economarine
☎425-3150
This inn has 11 small, very basic rooms in a two-storey building.

Celena Hotel
$5
⊗
near the airstrip
☎453228
The seven rooms here are bright, simple and clean. Very good value.

Margaritaville Beach Hotel
$10
⊗
at the western end of the road
☎425-3366
This hotel has 16 bright, airy, simple rooms in a big two-storey wooden building with sea views. A

beach is nearby. Excellent value.

Freddy's Place
$17
⊗
near the bridge toward the airstrip
Freddy's Place offers simple, breezy rooms and a broad wooden terrace facing the water. If nobody is there, ask for Lucille at the red-roofed house across the road.

Mango Inn
$10 with sb and ⊗
$15 with pb and ⊗
$35 *for cabañas with* ☰
ℜ, *bar*
about 300m north of the crossroads
☎425-3335
Mango Inn offers 19 simple, comfortable rooms in a two-storey, L-shaped wooden building. The *cabañas* are pleasant and wood-panelled.

Utila Lodge
$54
ℜ, ☰
just off the main street
☎425-3143, U.S. reservations 800-282-8932
www.roatan.com/utilalodge.htm
This intimate spot was the first resort-style hotel in Utila and offers dive packages that include buffet meals coordinated to diving schedules. Its two-storey wooden building house eight guest rooms with rustic furnishings and screened-in porches facing the sea. The dining area is especially attractive and also faces the sea.

Restaurants

Roatán

Coxen Hole

The restaurants at the **Hotel El Paso** and the **Hotel Cay View**, almost directly adjacent to one another in the centre of town, are both open from 7am to 10pm and have pleasant seafront terraces ideal for simple, relaxing meals. The menus are centred on fish and seafood, and prices are moderate. Both offer full breakfasts.

Sandy Bay

Rick's American Café
$$
every day 5pm to 10pm except Wed
Located along the highway, specializes in steaks, burgers and fajitas. A parabollic antenna beams in sports broadcasts from the United States. Full bar service is available

West End

The dining scene here is lively and casual. Most restaurants are open-air, usually sheltered by a thatched roof. Visitors strolling along the main road next to the beach will find a good variety of spots.

Papagayo's Safari Sea Club and Safari Sea Japanese Garden

$-$$
every day except Tue 7am to 3pm and 6pm to 11pm
in front of Sunset Inn

Two different restaurants sharing the same quarters but operating at different hours. Papagayo's offers interesting breakfasts and lunches, including such items as breakfast burritos and smoked-chicken quesadillas, while the Japanese Garden offers evening meals of sushi and tempura dishes, as well as some Thai items, including curries.

Foster's Restaurant

$$
every day 8am to midnight
☎445-1124 or 445-1008
This place is a local landmark set on a large pier jutting into the sea. It offers a broad menu and a lively atmosphere in the evening, with live island music on Friday evenings.

Eagle Ray's Bar & Grill

$-$$
every day 7:30am to midnight
upstairs from Sueño del Mar dive shop
☎445-1717
With a breezy open-air terrace upstairs on a big pod at the end of a pier, this bar and grill offers a big breakfast menu plus selections of sandwiches and snacks including Buffalo wings and enchiladas, as well as full meals of fish, shrimp, meat and vege-tarian items. The drink list is impressive.

Lighthouse Restaurant

$$
every day 7:30am to 10pm
along the beach, may be reached by the road behind the Baptist Church
The Lighthouse Restaurant is a humble open-air spot with a varied menu featuring local dishes and daily specials. Menu items include fish cooked with coconut, garlic squid, conch soup and vegetable stir fry.

Cindy's

$$
Mon to Sat 11am to 10pm
near Sueño del Mar dive shop
Cindy's is a very casual fish and seafood restaurant run by a fisher and his wife. Items include red snapper, mahi-mahi, tuna, wahoo and barracuda. "We bring it in fresh and grill it," the owners say. It can also be broiled or fried.

Pinocchio Restaurant

$$
every day except Wed 6pm to 9pm
up the footpath by Sueño del Mar dive shop
This restaurant is Italian-run and has a fascinating menu that ranges from crepes to stir-fried seafood, grouper with coconut, chicken with gorgonzola or ginger, or calamari. The open-air, wood-planked dining area is surrounded by forest.

Tony's Bamboo Hut

$$-$$
every day 5:30pm to 11pm
south of Foster's pier
This place offers an interesting variety of pasta and pizza, such as spaghetti with lobster, as well as grilled kingfish, snapper and shrimp. It is set beneath a big thatched shelter facing the sea.

Pura Vida Restaurant

$$-$$$
every day except Tue 7:30am to 9:30pm
north of Foster's pier
☎445-1141
Pura Vida offers pizza, pasta, fish and meat in an attractive open-air dining area facing toward the sea.

West Bay

Bite on the Beach

$$
Wed to Sat noon to 8pm, Sun 11am to 5pm
This is an open-air beachfront restaurant offering varied fish and meat dishes.

Restaurant Neptuno

$$-$$$
every day 7:30am to midnight
Neptuno offers a broad menu, including burgers, *ceviche* and lobster, as well as breakfasts served at tables and a bar on the beachfront.

Islas de la Bahía

French Harbour

Romeo's
lunch $$
dinner $$$-$$$$
Tue to Sun 7am to 10pm
in Hotel Casa Romeo
☎455-5215
Romeo's is an elegant, breezy dockside restaurant with purple tablecloths. The lunch menu consists mostly of sandwiches, pasta and simple seafood dishes, while the more elaborate evening menu includes seafood, steaks, several varieties of pasta with seafood, and a big seafood platter.

Gio's
$$$-$$$$
Mon to Sat 10am to 2pm and 5pm to 10pm
facing the harbour
☎455-5215
Gio's offers an attractive seafront dining room and outdoor terrace with a seafood-centred menu that includes interesting sauces such as jalapeño and coriander. Specialties include king crab and lobster.

Guanaja

Pirate's Den
$-$$
every day 7:30am to 2pm, 6pm to 10pm
Bonacca
☎453-4308
Also known as the Silver Dollar, this establishment offers varied meat and fish dishes, including hamburgers, tacos and some local dishes. The dining room is bright and simple, with plenty of fans.

Ashley's Restaurant
$$-$$$
Sun to Fri 7:30am to midnight, Sat 5pm to midnight
Bonacca
☎453-4139
This restaurant presents a variety of meat, fish and seafood dishes, including shrimp and lobster, in a simple, airy dining room along a canal.

Utila

Restaurant Exiendhouse
$
7am to 10pm Sun to Fri
centre of town
☎425-3301
Exiendhouse offers fish and burger plates, as well as conch soup and varied breakfasts, in a small, rather curious, open-air streetfront spot.

Bundu Café
$
7:30am to 3pm, days of operation vary
centre of town
Bundu Café offers sandwiches, fruit salad, pancakes, granola and juices, as well as a book exchange and video rentals.

Mermaid's Corner
$
Sun to Thu 11:30am to 10pm, Fri 11:30am to 3pm, Sat 6:30pm to 10pm
main street
☎425-3299
Here they serve pizza, pasta, burgers and salads in a pleasant open-air dining room. A variety of dishes are also served from a hot buffet.

Las Delicias Café
$-$$
Mon to Sat 7am to 11pm
north of the crossroads
This is an open-air spot with good breakfasts and a menu that stretches from burgers and spaghetti to shark and barracuda.

Frosty Sea Frog
$-$$
every day 10am to 10pm
centre of town
A simple streetfront spot with an extensive menu that includes soup, sandwiches, fajitas, fish, meat, pasta, pizza, rice dishes and shrimp.

Mango Inn
$$
every day 6:30am to 10pm
about 300m north of the crossroads
☎425-3335
The Mango Inn has an open-air restaurant set in a grassy area. It provides varied breakfasts, including a Sunday breakfast buffet. Lunch and supper offerings include fresh fish, spaghetti and sandwiches. Tuesday is paella night, and Thursday is kebab night. Barbecued fish is available most nights.

Jade Seahorse Restaurant & Gardens
$$
Fri to Wed noon to 11pm
about 200m north of the crossroads
☎425-3270
An extraordinary spot with an indoor dining in a room lined with original art and imaginative figurines, as well as al fresco dining

amidst fanciful gardens, with a bar (reached by wooden steps) set in the branches of a large tree. Menu items include grilled or baked fish (often snapper or kingfish), grilled conch, fish or conch soups, spaghetti with pesto, and vegetarian plates, as well as fruit shakes and freshly baked breads, including banana nut loaf. The selection of music is also good.

Entertainment

Evening activity on Islas de la Bahía centres around restaurants and bars. Cultural events are few and far between, although certain restaurants may occasionally offer video showings. If anything special is happening (particularly in West End or Utila), it will usually be signposted several days in advance. One or two discos have operated sporadically on Roatán.

Shopping

Prices are higher on Islas de la Bahía than elsewhere in Honduras. Most food, apart from fish and seafood, has to be shipped from the mainland, adding to the cost, and the same applies to a variety of other items. The **B. Warren** supermarket on the main street of Coxen Hole in Roatán offers the best selection of food and general merchandise.

Visitors headed to West End or other parts of the island should consider stocking up on necessities in Coxen Hole before heading out.

Islas de la Bahía offer little by way of original handicrafts. Visitors looking for items from elsewhere in Honduras and Central America generally will find several small gift shops along the main street of Coxen Hole and two or three along the main road in West End.

There are gift shops also in several of the resort hotels on Roatán and Guanaja.

Librería Casi Todo in West End provides the sale and exchange of books in English and Spanish.

A shop with no sign, almost directly facing the Sueño del Mar dive shop, offers a superb variety of Guatemalan handicrafts. This shop, run by Mayas from Guatemala, includes a broad selection of hand-dyed textiles and clothing among the items it sells.

In Utila, **Gunther's Gallerie** offers original works of art.

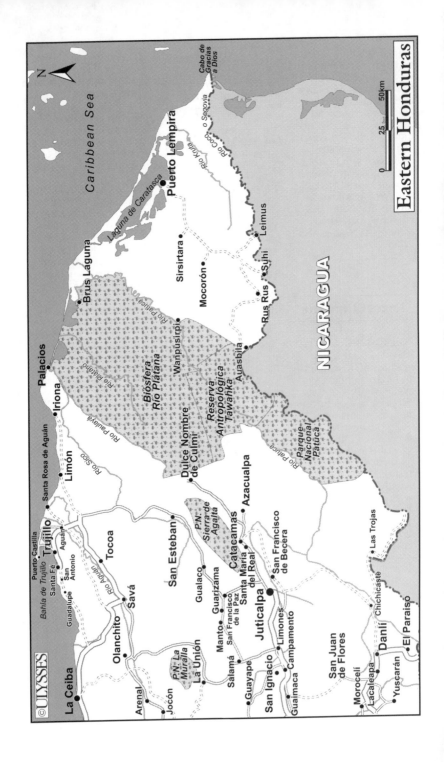

Central and Eastern Honduras ★

The central and eastern portions of Honduras are something of a grabbag. Here we include the area between Tegucigalpa and San Pedro Sula, most notably the city of Comayagua, a former capital with many colonial-era buildings, and Lago de Yojoa, which offers the usual lakeside pleasures. Nearby are the Pulhapanzak waterfalls.

To the east of Tegucigalpa, near the border with Nicaragua, lies the town of Danlí, an important centre of cigar production where visitors can watch a variety of fragrant smokes being hand-rolled in time-honoured fashion.

Within the sweep of this chapter we also cover Juticalpa and Catacamas (near an archeological site that features glowing skulls; see box on page 182) in the eastern depart-

ment of Olancho, as well as La Muralla and Sierra de Agalta National Parks, enticing spots for lovers of wilderness and mountain air. Finally, we also mention La Mosquitia, the vast, sparsely populated area sprawling over northeastern Honduras that is mostly covered with jungle.

Much of what is mentioned in this chapter consists of

spots that visitors are likely to see on their way to or from somewhere else. This hardly means to suggest that little here merits a detour, but it does hint that many readers planning their Honduran itineraries will choose to devote more of their time to other regions. Except for Danlí and spots along the Tegucigalpa-San Pedro Sula highway covered in the early part of the Exploring section, this chapter will be of greater interest to those who choose to venture off the beaten track, away from the beaches, reefs and Mayan ruins that draw the greatest number of visitors. This is indeed the back country of Honduras. But with its ruggedness and unpretentious earthiness, it does offer enchantments of its own.

Finding Your Way Around

By Car

The main highway running the 241km between Tegucigalpa and San Pedro Sula crosses some mountainous terrain but is well paved and well marked. It comprises two lanes most of the way, with a short four-lane stretch south of San Pedro Sula. This highway also connects **Comayagua**, **Siguatepeque** and a portion of **Lago de Yojoa**. A secondary road branching from the main highway links other parts of the lake.

Danlí lies 92km east of Tegucigalpa, along a highway running to the Nicaraguan border at Las Manos, 30km to the south. On the other side of the border, the highway continues to Estelí and Managua.

Travellers bound for **Juticalpa**, **Catacamas**, **Parque Nacional La Muralla or Sierra de Agalta** will more than likely find themselves on the paved highway running northeast from Tegucigalpa (although it runs from the southwestern part of the city to avoid the mountains directly to the north). The cutoff north to La Muralla runs from the village of Limones near Km 126 of the highway. This road is rutted and unpaved (and slippery in wet weather), but still suitable for regular cars. La Muralla can be reached by a side road from the town of La Unión. The main road continues north to Olancho, where paved roads provide links to La Ceiba and Trujillo.

La Mosquitia is distinguished, among other things, by a total absence of highways. There are a few rough tracks (barely suitable even for all-terrain vehicles), and some crude roads running southwest from Puerto Lempira (again, fit only for all-terrain vehicles), but nothing suitable for long-distance land travel. Most travel in this region is done by air or by water.

By Bus

Comayagua, Siguatepeque and the portion of **Lago de Yojoa** abutting the main highway are served by most of the buses running between Tegucigalpa and San Pedro Sula, with service several times an hour throughout the day. For information on schedules, fares and terminals, please see pages 66 and 94. (Deluxe services do not make intermediate stops.) Passengers are dropped along the highway and taxis are available for short hops into Comayagua or Siguatepeque. To return to Tegucigalpa or San Pedro Sula, buses can be flagged at fixed stops along the highway. Sometimes the buses arrive full or have space for only a few passengers, but usually it is not a very long wait until everyone is looked after (except, of course, during peak holiday periods). Local services run to Tegucigalpa once or twice an hour from the centres of Comayagua and Siguatepeque, but these buses make many stops and tend to be slow and uncomfortable. There are also local services from Comayagua and Siguatepeque to San Pedro Sula.

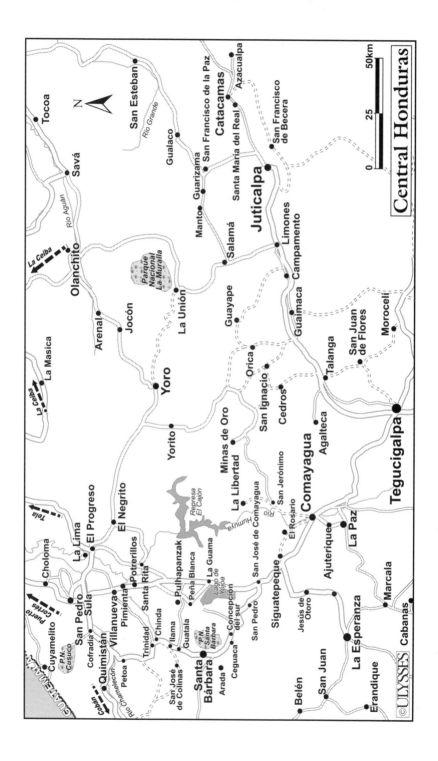

Central Honduras

For portions of **Lago de Yojoa** northwest of the main highway, local buses run at 30min intervals until 6pm from the highway junction at La Guama to the town of **Peña Blanca**. Peña Blanca is also served twice an hour by direct buses from San Pedro Sula that continue to El Mochito. These same buses serve **Pulhapanzak**. Passengers should disembark in the village of Buenaventura, near the entrance to the falls. The trip takes about 1.5hrs. The terminal in San Pedro Sula is on 2a. Avenida between 5a. and 6a. Calles S.E. The last bus from Buena-ventura is at 5:30pm, but this is subject to change so check first.

Between Tegucigalpa and **Danlí**, buses leave every 30min in each direction from 5:30am to 6pm. The Tegucigalpa terminal is situated in Colonia Kennedy, nowhere near most of the other terminals. Three companies, Discua, Litena and Extraoriente, have merged to form an abusive near-monopoly on this route, providing tattered vehicles and surly staff. Additional service is provided by El Dandy, operating from a terminal along 6a. Avenida in Comayagüela. Travel time is about 2hrs. Some buses continue onward to El Paraíso, just a short hop from the Nicaraguan border

at Las Manos. The terminal in Danlí is situated at the edge of town, with several small eating spots nearby.

Two companies, Discovery and Aurora, link Tegucigalpa and **Juticalpa**, both with reasonably comfortable vehicles. Each has its terminal in Comayagüela (*Aurora on 8a. Calle between 6a. and 7a. Avenidas; Discovery on 7a. Avenida between 12a. and 13a. Calles*), with departures about an hour apart through most of the day. Discovery also has services continuing onward to Catacamas. In addition, there are local services between Juticalpa and Catacamas. To **La Muralla**, Cotraipbal runs at least twice a day between Tegucigalpa (*7a. Avenida between 11a. and 12a. Calles in Comayagüela,* ☎ *237666*) and Trujillo via Olanchito. Passengers heading to the national park should disembark at La Unión and seek local transport for the final short hop.

There are no bus services in the **Mosquitia** region.

By Taxi

Taxis are available to meet arriving passengers at Comayagua, Siguatepeque and Danlí. They also provide service to outlying

towns. There are no taxis based at Lago de Yojoa.

By Plane

Air travel is the main way of getting to or from points in La Mosquitia. Fares generally are quite cheap (for example, $40 one-way from La Ceiba to Palacios). Flights radiate from La Ceiba where connections are available to or from San Pedro Sula, Tegucigalpa and the Islas de la Bahía.

Isleña, Sosa and Rollins all fly to La Mosquitia on a shifting basis, adding or dropping routes on short notice. Direct service is provided from La Ceiba to Palacios and Puerto Lempira daily, except for Sunday, with less frequent service to Brus Laguna. Some of the Palacios flights make stops at Trujillo. See p. 127 for airline information in La Ceiba.

By Boat

Small dories ferry passengers between the main towns in La Mosquitia and some of the outlying villages. Freight vessels, some of them with space for passengers, operate on a very irregular basis between La Ceiba or Puerto Castilla and Palacios, Brus Laguna or Puerto Lempira.

Exploring

Comayagua

Situated 84km northwest of Tegucigalpa, Comayagua was the capital of Honduras from 1543, a few years after the country's founding, until 1880, when the seat of government was moved to its current location. Rumour has it that the president of the day decided to move the capital away from Comayagüela to punish the townspeople for snubbing his Amerindian mistress. Although many of the oldest buildings were destroyed in an earthquake in the late 18th century or in fires set by invading Guatemalan troops several decades later, many colonial-era buildings can still be found. Despite its architectural wealth and historical importance, however, Comayagua will strike many visitors as being much less than the sum of its parts, with a decidedly nondescript air. It does, though, have churches and museums that are worth a brief visit.

Both the *parque central* and the Museo de Arqueología have recently been renovated.

The **Catedral de Comayagua** ★, built in the early 18th century and facing the central plaza, has an ornately carved, multi-tiered facade with niches containing sculpted images of Christ and several saints. Jutting forward on one side is a bell tower topped by a colourful cupola and housing a 12th-century Moorish clock that once graced the Alhambra in Granada and was donated to Honduras by King Phillip II of Spain. This is one of the oldest working clocks in the world. The interior of the cathedral has simple lines, decorated with religious paintings, a richly carved altar and pulpit and many altarpieces.

Iglesia La Merced, three blocks away, is the oldest church in Comayagua, built in stages starting in 1550.

It is a simple structure of stone and adobe with a carved altar and a single surviving bell tower (the other one was destroyed in an earthquake). Other churches in Comayagua include **San Sebastian** and **San Francisco**, both partly reconstructed after suffering damage throughout the centuries; and the humbler **Caridad Illescas**.

The **Museo de Arqueología** ★ (*$2; Wed to Sun 9am to 4pm; one block from the central plaza*) has a small but interesting pre-Hispanic collection of carvings, pottery, jewellery and utensils.

The **Museo Colonial** (*$1; every day 9:30am to 4:30pm; half a block from the cathedral*) is housed in the 16th-century Casa Cural and presents a collection consisting mostly of religious objects.

Central and Eastern Honduras

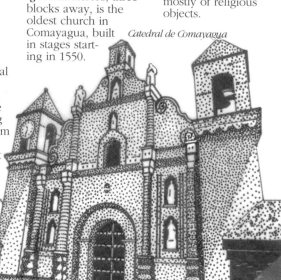

Catedral de Comayagua

Ajuterique

Situated 11km south of Comayagua along the poorly surfaced gravel road that continues to La Paz, Ajuterique has a timeless feel to it, with its many colonial-style wood and stucco buildings roofed in red tile. The **Iglesia Jesús Nazarena** has a distinctive white and black facade, a hardwood ceiling, and a small but elaborate altar. Tourists are a rarity in this friendly, dignified town. Buses run twice an hour from Comayagua.

Siguatepeque

Siguatepeque lies 2km off the main highway near the halfway point between Tegucigalpa and San Pedro Sula. This is a friendly but nondescript town lying at an altitude of 1,140m, giving it a pleasant climate. It has a lovely, tree-shaded central plaza facing a big modern church, and several places to stay.

Danlí

This otherwise unprepossessing spot in southeastern Honduras near the border with Nicaragua, is rendered interesting by the many **cigar factories ★★** that can be found in this town. Cigar factories, big and small, employ many thousands of people, most of whom seem to get to and from work by bicycle, making this one of the most bicycle-intensive towns in Central America.

Soil and climate conditions on both sides of the Honduras-Nicaragua border render this area well suited to the production of fine tobaccos. These are stripped, rolled and packaged by hand in the same way they have for centuries. Most factories are pleased to show visitors around (and entice them with boxes of cigars) during normal working hours, usually from about 7:30am to 4pm Monday to Friday, with a 1hr lunch break. Many also open Saturday mornings. Row upon row of workers sit at long tables rolling cigars, in what seems like a scene from another era.The Spanish-owned San Cristóbal cigar factory, near the entrance to town, is probably the largest of these factories. Tabácos de Oriente (*3km out of town on the road to San Marcos*) is another big operation; it is part of Tabácos Placencia, owned by a Cuban family. A number of smaller factories dot the town, although some of them have no outdoor signposts. Local taxi drivers, charging hourly rates, can show visitors the different factories.

Danlí's quiet ***parque central*** is tree-shaded and attractive, bordered by the massive Iglesia Inmaculada Concepción.

The **Museo Municipal ★** (*free admission; Mon to Fri 8am to 4pm; facing the central plaza*) is housed in a wooden building from the mid-19th century and contains a variety of bric-a-brac as well as a few pre-Hispanic and colonial objects. Most interesting is the *sala de maiz*, which displays a collection of objects used to prepare corn.

Balneario Los Arcos, in the mountains outside town, has a series of natural pools for swimming as well as a small zoo.

La Unión

This friendly but sleepy town is notable mainly for its proximity to Parque Nacional La Muralla (see below), 14km uphill. La Unión is situated 70km north of the main highway connecting Tegucigalpa with Juticalpa and is reached by a rutted gravel road. Buses between Tegucigalpa and Trujillo pass here (see page 178), with the last departure to Tegucigalpa at about 1pm from La Unión. The town has a small

Cigars: The Vagaries of Supply and Demand

Special combinations of soil and climate found in only a few places in the world produce the tobacco leaf required to create fine cigars. The region around Pinar del Río, in western Cuba, is one such area. The countryside around Danlí, in southeastern Honduras, is another. Cigars had undergone a long, slow decline in popularity in the United States and other western countries but suddenly became fashionable again in the 1990s. Because of a U.S. ban on trade with Cuba, cigar distributors in the United States had to look to other sources, and Honduras was a natural.

In the mid-1990s, Danlí was a boom town. Existing cigar factories expanded rapidly to meet mushrooming demand, and many new ones opened in this very labourintensive industry, creating a hiring bonanza. This could not last indefinitely. Several major U.S. distributors overestimated the growth in demand and found themselves with large unsold supplies of cigars. They responded with sharp reductions in orders to eliminate excess inventories. One result was massive layoffs in Danlí. A factory that a couple of years earlier employed more than 2,000 people cut its workforce to only 600 in 1999. Some factories shut their doors completely. Once inventories fell to acceptable levels, however, fresh orders came flooding in and Danlí resumed its modest prosperity.

hotel situated on the main street. One block behind the main street is the office of COHDEFOR, the government forestry department, where visitors should stop to make arrangements before heading to the national park.

Yocón is a simple, idyllic-looking village just off the road a few kilometres south of La Unión. You'll feel as if you've stepped into another era.

Juticalpa

This is the main administrative centre of the Olancho department, but has no special charm. Juticalpa is situated in frontier country, where cattle ranching, forestry and gold mining are the main activities. Visitors will find some modest hotels and one or two decent places to eat, but not much else.

Catacamas

This pleasant, picturesque town is characterized by cobbled streets and red-tile-roofed houses in traditional Honduran style. Apart from its neoclassical church, there are few buildings of special distinction, but the general atmosphere makes this an enchanting spot, at least during daylight hours. (See inset p182) Although the town

Central and Eastern Honduras

The Glowing Skulls of Talgua

In 1994, a group of amateur cave explorers came upon an amazing sight. They were about 600ms inside a cave near the village of Talgua, 4km north of Catacamas, when two members of the group noticed an opening in a limestone wall high above the floor of the cave. They were able to scale the wall and found something that went beyond science fiction. Reflected in the glow of their headmounted lamps were hundreds of skulls and bones that seemed crystalline and almost appeared to be glowing themselves. After they reported their discovery, a team of archeologists visited the cave and determined that this chamber contained about 200 human remains, carefully stripped of their flesh and painted in an ochre hue, as well as ritual offerings of ceramic and jade, dating back about 2,500 years. Calcite drippings over many centuries coated these bones and ceremonial objects with a layer of luminous stone that kept them in an almost perfect state of preservation. It was later determined that they belonged to a previously unknown Mesoamerican civilization, and it was speculated that the bodies were placed in a cave to speed their way to the next world. Two other caves were later discovered nearby. One held more bones, as well as pictographs on the walls.

Work on the Cuevas de Talgua archeological park, set to open in December 1999, included a new road to the site, a visitor's centre, walking paths and a footbridge, as well as ladders and platforms to help visitors make their way through the caves.

boasts a couple of small hotels and restaurants, it receives few visitors. This seemed likely to change following the opening of the **Cuevas de Talgua** archeological park, 4km north of Catacamas.

La Mosquitia

La Mosquitia (sometimes spelled Moskitia) is the name given to the vast swath of sparsely populated forest, savana, swamp, lagoons and river basins stretching across northeastern Honduras and into Nicaragua. There are mountains in the southwestern part of La Mosquitia and low hills in several areas. The climate is wet all year, with the heaviest rainfall in October and November.

The region takes its name from the Misquito Indians who form a large part of the population. The rest include Pech, Tawahkas, Garífunas and, of course, *mestizos*. It is easy to assume, although it is a fallacy, that the name is derived from the pesky insect with the similar-sounding name, especially since mosquitoes do abound in the area year-round, particularly

The Legend of the White City

Somewhere beneath the jungle of La Mosquitia lies buried an ancient city of gleaming white stone, according to interpretations of writings from the Toltec and Maya cultures. The legend of the "Ciudad Blanca," or White City, has been kept alive by several explorers and writers who have developed several theories as to where this city may lie. Areas near the confluence of certain rivers are considered the likeliest possibilities, if indeed this is more than legend. A lack of financial support for necessary excavation has been blamed for the absence of any recent evidence. The capital of the long vanished kingdom of Tlapalan has been linked with a human deity much revered by pre-Columbian cultures in Mesoamerica.

Articles written by Ricardo Madrid, a U.S.born Honduran who leads tours in the Mosquitia, help provide some of the historical background. In a report to the king of Spain in 1544, Cristóbal Pedraza, bishop of Honduras, alluded to a land called Veragua, glimpsed from a mountaintop, whose main city was said to have been filled with treasure. In 1939, a fivemonth expedition led by American explorer Theodore Morde found remains of a temple dedicated to a monkey god, part of a series of ruins enclosed within a wall and covering a large area. In an account published several years later, Morde spoke of a pyramidshaped building with large stone columns bearing effigies of monkeys and other animals. Nearby were a waterfall and rapids, with pure white sand along the course of the river. White stone from the area may have been used in construction. Morde kept the exact location a secret to keep looters away. While in London to seek support for a new expedition, he was hit and killed by a car. A subsequent Britishled expedition failed to locate the site.

Some archeologists are sceptical about the existence of the White City, but several scholars say it should not be dismissed out of hand. After all, the "mythical" Greek city of Troy was only found in 1870, and the lost Inca city of Machu Picchu was uncovered in 1911. Perhaps the Mosquitia jungle really does conceal significant archeological treasures.

Central and Eastern Honduras

after heavy rains. Any-body planning to spend much time outdoors, particularly at night, should stock up on insect repellent and should probably take anti-malaria medication. Given the sporadic electricity supply even in the towns, flashlights are also highly useful. In many areas, travellers will need water purification tablets and a good supply of food. Local fish can be delicious but often is the only thing available.

The **Biósfera del Río Plátano**, with its rivers and varied ecosystems, is the Mosquitia's most important draw and is described on page 186. Rafting on the Río Sico also attracts visitors. Several tour companies offer programs covering portions of the Mosquitia. (see p 60.)

Do-it-yourselfers will find the Mosquitia daunting. It`s one thing to hop on a plane in La Ceiba and get off in one of the region's small towns. It is quite another matter, however, to head upriver or hike into the jungle without the assistance of a qualified boatman or guide whose prices may leap skyward – or who may not exist at all. A self-guided tour of the Mosquitia is recommended only to the most hardy and hardened of travellers.

Palacios

This fishing village near the northwestern corner of the Mosquitia is perched at the edge of a coastal lagoon and is served by flights six days a week. Palacios is often used as a starting point for visits to the Biósfera del Río Plátano. This used to be the Black River colony established by British loggers in the 19th century. The last remnants of crumbling British-built wooden mansions were bulldozed in 1939 to make way for the airstrip, which to this day remains covered in grass. The remains of an earthen fort may still be seen, along with some cannons. Food and lodging are available.

Puerto Lempira

This rustic town, laid out in neat rectangular blocks, sits at the southeastern edge of the Laguna de Caratasca in the eastern Mosquitia. It is the biggest town in the region and offers no special attractions apart from sport fishing in the lagoon. Small launches radiate to several villages, including **Cauquila** across the lagoon not far from the Caribbean coast. Winds can come up suddenly, though, especially in the afternoon, making the lagoon treacherous at times. There are several places to eat or

sleep. A bar called Yampus, set in a big wooden building on stilts over the lake with booming country music and a pleasant lakeside terrace, is a social centre of sorts. The local banks do not change dollars but the Agencia Matra, a shipping company, will help out, though at less than the official exchange rate.

Parks

Parque Nacional La Muralla

This vast and mountainous national park in the geographic heart of Honduras contains an impressive variety of flora and fauna along with an incipient network of hiking trails and two rudimentary campsites. This is frontier territory, large parts of which are completely undisturbed by human encroachment. The park sprawls over 21,935ha, 13,850 of which are fully protected, while the rest forms a buffer zone, part of which is given over to subsistence agriculture. Only the southwestern corner of the park has been developed for visitors. In the near future, the network of trails and other facilities may be extended to cover more of the park's broad reaches, including several mountain peaks, but for the moment the scale of development has been decidedly modest.

The park includes the headwaters of the Río Aguán, which flows into the Caribbean near Trujillo. The park entrance, 14km from the town of La Unión, is situated at an altitude of 1,430m. Of the mountains found within the park's boundaries, only La Muralla itself has a trail reaching the summit at an altitude of 1,650m. The highest peak is Montaña de las Parras (2,064m high) but is almost impossible to reach. Montaña Los Higuerales, reaching about 1,800m, is also inaccessible.

Within the park's boundaries, biologists have counted 853 species of plants, 179 species of birds, 58 species of mammals, 51 species of reptiles and amphibians, and 294 species of insects. Birdlife includes the mystical quetzal, with its long tail and splendid plumage, along with wild turkeys, several types of toucan, and an almost invisible songbird called the jilguero. Trees include tropical hardwoods such as caboa, as

well as a variety of oaks.

The visitor's centre at the park entrance is housed in an elaborate wooden structure and is staffed around the clock. In the main hall, there are a small nature exhibit, a slide show and a mock-up showing the park's topography, but no maps are available. Visitors to La Muralla are asked to report first to the office of COHDEFOR, the government forestry department in La Unión, open during regular office hours. The COHDEFOR office stays in radio contact with the visitor's centre and will arrange to have a local guide meet tourists. Although the use of a guide is not obligatory, the park administration prefers it. It only costs about $8 a day for a group of up to 10 people. At the moment, there are four hiking trails ranging in length from 1km to 10km, none extending beyond the park's southwestern corner. The two campsites have running water, outhouses and cooking grills.

Reaching the park

entrance can be a bit of an adventure in itself. A narrow dirt road runs 14km from La Unión, mostly uphill, with three crossings where rivers have to be forded. The road runs through pine-clad mountain scenery, with small coffee plantations, cattle ranches and subsistence farming. It is possible to drive up in a regular car, but a high truck or four-wheel drive vehicle is preferable, especially in wet weather. For those without transportation, COHDEFOR vehicles make the trip several times a day and employees will usually agree to carry passengers, although there are no guarantees. Hotels in La Unión can sometimes arrange transportation for their guests.

One of the most impressive sights in the park, completely separate from the main area, is a high, rocky and misty waterfall called Cascada de Mucupina. This can be reached by walking 3 to 4hrs from the tiny village of Los Planes de Mucupina, situated 25km north of La Unión, along the road to Olanchito. A local man named Don Jerónimo Menocal provides guide services.

Parque Nacional Sierra de Agalta

This is one of the harder-to-reach national parks in Honduras, with few amenities, but for many hikers and nature lovers it will prove to be worth the effort. Its main attractions are the peak of La Pichuca, 2,354m above sea level with splendid panoramas on clear days, several streams and waterfalls, and a variety of ecosystems including an area of cloud forest with several truly unique plant species. The constant high humidity makes this the headwaters of many creeks, and creates the perfect environment for typical cloud forest vegetation, which consists of abundant epiphytes as well as orchids, bromeliads, moss, lichens and tree-like ferns. Fauna include quetzals, green toucans, jaguars, cougars, tapirs and ringtails.

The nearest village is **Gualaco**, a little to the north along the Juticalpa-San Esteban road. From there, access is by foot or by mule. The park can also be reached from **Catacamas** to the south. Independent visitors must be completely self-reliant. Camping is permitted and, indeed,

necessary. A visit will take several days. Count on two days to ascend to the summit which you will reach by a good but occasionally steep trail. COHDEFOR, the government forestry service, can sometimes provide information at its offices in Juticalpa, Gualaco, San Esteban or Catacamas. La Moskitia Eco-aventuras (see page 60) offers organized tours.

Biósfera del Río Plátano

The Biósfera del Río Platano (Río Plátano biosphere reserve) sprawls across the northwestern portion of La Mosquitia. In theory, it is a protected area, although illegal encroachments by farmers and hunters seem to go unpunished. The reserve includes large areas of tropical rain forest, pine savannah and mangrove swamp. Its rich diversity of wildlife includes howler monkeys, river otters, tapirs, jaguars, crocodiles, parrots, macaws, kingfishers, herons and giant blue butterflies.

Tour programs to the Biósfera del Río Plátano, and to the zone further south designated as the **Reserva Antropológica**

Tawahka usually run for a week or longer and include jungle hikes, rafting and visits to traditional indigenous villages. Scattered through the area are several tiny archaeological sites featuring groups of petroglyphs, with designs carved into rocks in ancient times.

Some tour groups set out from the town of **Palacios** next to a coastal lagoon, arriving by air and heading upriver by motorboat, while others cross over from Tegucigalpa and enter the reserve further south near the headwaters of the Río Plátano, paddling downriver by raft or canoe a good part of the way from there.

Outdoor Activities

Lago de Yojoa

Lago de Yojoa (pronounced yo-KHO-a), 81km south of San Pedro Sula, is a big freshwater lake surrounded by mountains. The water is clear and deep, suitable for swimming, bass fishing and a variety of other water sports. Arrangements can be made at the bigger hotels along the shore. The lake is extensive, about 22km long, 10km wide and 40m deep. There are literally hundreds of varieties of birds.

The southeastern portion of the lake lies along the main highway between San Pedro Sula and Tegucigalpa, while another road runs parallel to the northeastern shore of the lake, continuing to the nearby town of **Peña Blanca**. This road is served by twice-hourly buses from La Guama at the junction with the main highway. Peña Blanca is a fair-sized town, with banks, a pharmacy, a gas station and other services. Those staying by Lago de Yojoa are not far from the Parque Nacional Santa Bárbara (see p 110) and other parks in the area.

Pulhapanzak

This series of waterfalls plunges 43m in a spectacular setting bordered by tropical vegetation. This is a popular spot for day excursions from San Pedro Sula and can get crowded on weekends and holidays. The entrance, near the village of Buenaventura 11km north of Peña Blanca by unpaved road, is open from 6am to 6pm. Admission is $1 for adults, $0.70 for children. Young boys will offer to act as guides for a few lempiras.

Balneario Las Gradas, a short distance upriver, has a natural pool for swimming as well as picnic grounds and other facilities.

Río Sico and Río Plátano

Several tour companies offer river rafting and other expeditions along the Río Sico, near the western edge of the Mosquitia, and along the Río Plátano within the biosphere reserve of the same name. Please see p 186 for more information.

Accommodations

Comayagua

Hotel Libertad
$5
sb
facing the parque central
☎ *772-0091*
Hotel Libertad offers 18 dark, rudimentary rooms in a mid-19th-century building set around a garden courtyard.

Hotel Imperial
$12
⊗
one block from the main boulevard
☎ *772-0215*
There are 25 bright, simple rooms here, many of them set around a dark interior

courtyard. There is no hot water.

Hotel Emperador
$18
≡, *tv*
just off the main boulevard
☎ *772-0332*
This establishment has 38 bright, homey rooms with private balconies.

Hotel Quan
$12 with ⊗
$22 with ≡ *and tv*
1½ blocks from the main boulevard
☎*772-0070*
This modern building on a quiet side street has 20 ordinary but reasonably comfortable rooms. The air-conditioned rooms are bigger.

Siguatepeque

Lago de Yojoa

Hotel Los Remos
$18
⊗, ≈, ℜ, bar
at the southern end of the lake, along the main highway
no phone on site reservations
☎*898-8775*
Hotel Los Remos has 12 very plain rooms, some of them suitable for family groups. The grounds are not very well kept, and service is slow.

Hotel Agua Azul
$23
⊗, ℜ, *bar*, ≈
Km 8 on the Peña Blanca road
☎*991-7244*
The 18 rooms here are set in cabins scattered over well-landscaped

and forested grounds. Rooms are bright and airy. Those closer to the lake are more pleasant and nicely decorated with wood and tiles. The dining area faces the lake and is very appealing. Service is not as good as it once was, however. Guests have the opportunity to fish and go horseback riding, and can use the motorboats and billiard tables.

Hotel Brisas del Lago
$38-$46
≡, *tv*, ℜ, *bar*
☎*992-2937*
This hotel has 72 rooms set in a series of big, boxy buildings some distance from the lake on minimally landscaped grounds. Rooms are bright and pleasant, with ceramic floor tiles and individual balconies. The hotel boasts tennis courts and a games room. Guests can fish on the lake and enjoy the use of motorboats and pedalboats.

Danlí

Accommodations are generally better in Danlí than in nearby Nicaraguan towns such as Estelí.

Hotel Apolo
$7
centre of town
☎*883-2177*
This spot has 18 very simple rooms.

Hotel La Esperanza
$6 per person with sb
$20 per person with pb
≡, *tv*
centre of town
☎*883-2106*
The 26 rooms here are rather plain.

Gran Hotel Granada
$42 with ⊗
$78 with ≡
tv, ≈, ℜ, *bar*
at the edge of town on the highway to Tegucigalpa
☎*883-2499* or *883-2784*
⇄*883-3224*
Gran Hotel Granada has 69 rooms set in two wings. Rooms in the new wing are bigger and more comfortable but face the parking area, whereas most rooms in the old wing face a garden terrace. This modern single-storey building houses 36 pleasant rooms with high wooden ceilings. Most rooms face a luxuriant garden-terrace with lounge chairs in front.

La Unión

Hotel La Muralla
$4
⊗, *sb*
on the main street
The 12 rooms in this friendly, family-run spot are clean but very basic. All face an outdoor passageway, with washrooms at one end.

Juticalpa

Boarding House Alemán
$5
⊗
near the central plaza
☎*885-2783*
This spot is friendly, with a small garden courtyard and six small, simple rooms.

Hotel Antúnez
$7-$11
⊗, *some rooms with tv*, ☎
one block from the central plaza
☎*885-2250*
The 43 rooms here are simple and rather dark; a few have lounge chairs facing a patio. Service is slow.

Apart-Hotel La Muralla
$9-$13
⊗, *tv*, ☎
one block from the central plaza
☎*885-1270*
This friendly spot has good service and 17 modern but plain and dark rooms, some of them more spacious than others.

Catacamas

Visitors can choose from among several small, fairly basic hotels, all charging under $10. They include the **Hotel Colina**, **Hotel Central** and the simpler **Hotel Rapalo**.

Palacios

Río Tinto Lodge
$9
no phone
Río Tinto Lodge offers 10 rooms with running

water and electricity in the early evening. The upstairs rooms are preferable, with good cross-ventilation and a broad porch with views of the lagoon. The owner, Félix Mármol, is an important local personality.

The superior **La Moskitia Ecolodge** closed its doors in 1999 because of the post Mitch drop in business. It is uncertain if it will reopen.

Puerto Lempira

Hospedaje Flores
$4-$6
near the centre of town
Some rooms have fans. All are very rudimentary.

Hotelito Central
$5-$7
centre of town
☎898-7454
The 19 rooms here are clean but tiny and very spartan, with shared bath. Most have no fan.

Gran Hotel Flores
$17 with sb
$22 with pb and ⊗
$27 with ≡ and tv
near the centre of town
☎898-7421
The 23 rooms here are simply but adequately furnished. Electricity is only available part of the day.

Restaurants

Comayagua

Several simple restaurants are scattered around the centre of town, including spots specializing in grilled chicken or Chinese food.

Along the main thoroughfare referred to simply as "El Boulevard" are three more elaborate restaurants: **Pájaro Rojo**, **Hanemann's** (upstairs in the mall across the street, open for supper only and for Sunday lunch), and the more expensive **La Torre Latina**.

Siguatepeque

China Palace
most dishes $3-$6
near the bus terminal
China Palace has a pleasant, air-conditioned dining room and the usual assortment of Central-American-style Chinese dishes. Other spots in the centre of town include **La Villa** for Mexican dishes, **Alby's** for fried chicken and pupusas, and **Pizzería Venezia** for guess what.

Pizzería Venezia also has a branch along the highway.

Lago de Yojoa

A big cluster of simple restaurants along the main highway near the southeastern corner of the lake offer fresh lake fish with tortillas and condiments for just a couple of dollars. There is a smaller but similar group of restaurants a little farther north along the highway. Apart from these, the best options are hotel restaurants along the shore.

Hotel Agua Azul offers a dining room facing the lake, with terrace, with most items priced from $3 to $6 and lake bass priced according to size.

Danlí

Restaurant Rincón Colonial, in the centre of town one block from the *parque central*, and **Restaurant El Torito**, in a new location just beyond the edge of town along the highway to Tegucigalpa, both specialize in meat dishes, with most items priced under $7.

Juticalpa

Several restaurants, among them **Los Arcos**, **La Fonda** and Pampas Olanchanas, are clustered along the highway about 1km west of town, with a heavy emphasis on beef and most dishes in the $3-

$6 range. **La Gran Vía**, 2km west of town, is a pleasant open-air spot with meats and pinchos, including excellent smoked sausage pinchos, as well as fish and shrimp, in the same price range.

Catacamas

This is beef country. The better restaurants, including **As de Oro** and **The Rodeo**, are situated away from the centre of town.

Palacios

The Garífuna-run **Restaurant Victoria** offers fish and seafood, as well as simple meat dishes. At the **Río Tinto Lodge**, meals can be taken with advance notice.

Puerto Lempira

There are three or four restaurants scattered around town. The most agreeable by far is **Merendero Gladys**, a friendly spot next to the pier facing the lake in a simple, tin-roofed, open-sided shack set on stilts over the water. Fried fish, grilled pork or roast chicken each cost about $2.

Southern Honduras

The southern part

of Honduras is more often traversed than truly visited. Many travellers pass through en route between El Salvador and Nicaragua or on their way from these countries to Tegucigalpa and points beyond, but few take the trouble to explore the area.

Points of interest are admittedly few, though some hidden treasures lie here, notably the well preserved colonial town of Pespire, the attractive but often overlooked colonial district of Choluteca, and the casual, little visited beach resort of Amapala on Isla del Tigre.

The area covered in this chapter comprises the narrow neck of land squeezed between the borders with El Salvador and Nicaragua, stretching down to the Gulf of Fonseca, a shallow inlet of the Pacific Ocean shared by all three countries.

Honduras's southern coastline extends only 124km, and very little of this is fringed by beach.

This area, situated well away from the normal hurricane zone and with a generally hot, dry climate, had scarcely ever experienced the high winds and torrential rains associated with Caribbean storms. It was hit especially hard by Hurricane Mitch in 1998. The Choluteca and Nacaome rivers crested many metres above

their normal levels, and several villages were completely wiped out. In the city ofCholuteca, some lower-lying parts of the colonial-era historical centre were destroyed forever.

Two main thoroughfares pass here: the Carretera Panamericana, which links the capitals of most Central American countries (though it bypasses Tegucigalpa), plus the road that winds its way north through the mountains, connecting the

Carretera Panamericana with Tegucigalpa. The two roads meet at the tiny crossroads town of Jícaro Galán.

Visitors arriving from El Salvador, and more particularly from Nicaragua, will find accommodations on the Honduran side generally of higher standard. Comfortable lodgings are available in both Choluteca and Jícaro Galán as well as in the port city of San Lorenzo, in between. With one or two exceptions, hotels in western Nicaragua are mostly quite bleak, and the same applies to El Salvador east of the city of San Miguel.

Because the easiest international road access to Honduras lies through the southern part of the country, many visitors will find themselves passing through here, and it is worth considering stopping briefly along the way.

Beachgoers are largely (though not entirely) justified in skipping this region. They are likely to have a better time on the Caribbean coast in the

north. The beach town of Cedeño, on the Pacific coast, is popular among Hondurans of limited means, but it is a seedy and depressing spot. Punta Ratón, farther west, has better beaches, but it is hard to reach and almost bereft of services.

Certainly the most attractive beach resort on the Pacific side of Honduras is Amapala, on Isla del Tigre, though it is not for everyone. This former seaport, small but handsome, has a semi-abandoned, off-the-beaten-track feel to it. Its halcyon days are past, but there are at least three hotels on the island, and several secluded beaches where swimming is pleasant and camping is possible.

Finding Your Way Around

By Car

Southern Honduras is crossed by the **Carretera Panamericana** on its short hop between the Salvadoran border at **El Amatillo** and the Nicara-

guan border at **El Espino**, where the road continues to Managua via Estelí. **Choluteca**, the biggest town in the region, lies closer to the Nicaraguan side, and there the highway branches with an alternate route going to the more southerly border town of **Guasaule**, reaching Managua via Chinandega and León.

The other main road in this part of the country is the highway from Tegucigalpa, which meets the Carretera Panamericana at the small crossroads town of **Jícaro Galán**.

Another road, running southwest from a point 4km west of the port city of **San Lorenzo**, goes as far as **Coyolito**, where boat connections (passengers only) depart for **Amapala** on Isla del Tigre. Another paved but potholed 32km road, running southwest from the Carretera Panamericana at a junction between San Lorenzo and Choluteca, goes to **Cedeño**.

All the roads mentioned here are paved and maintained in reasonably good shape.

There is a rudimentary road network on Isla del Tigre, but few vehicles.

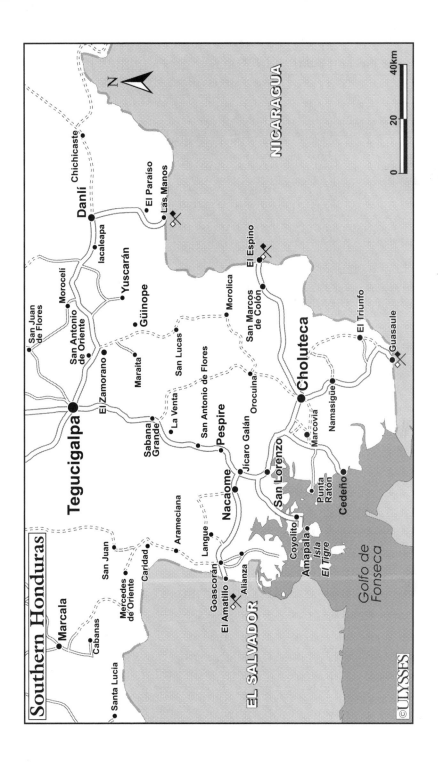

Southern Honduras

N

0   20   40km

NICARAGUA

EL SALVADOR

Golfo de
Fonseca

Marcala
Cabanas
Santa Lucia
San Juan
Mercedes
de Oriente
Caridad
Arameciana
Langue
Goascorán
El Amatillo
Alianza
Coyolito
Amapala
Isla
El Tigre

Tegucigalpa
San Juan
de Flores
San Antonio
de Oriente
El Zamorano
Maraita
La Venta
Sabana
Grande
San Antonio de Flores
Pespire
Nacaome
Jícaro Galán
San Lorenzo
Cedeño
Punta
Ratón
Marcovia
Namasigüe

Moroceli
Iacaleapa
Yuscarán
Güinope
San Lucas
Orocuina
Morolica
San Marcos
de Colón
Choluteca
El Triunfo
Guasaule
El Espino

Danlí
Chichicaste
El Paraíso
Las Manos

© ULYSSES

By Bus and Boat

International buses between El Salvador and Nicaragua cross southern Honduras, as do the direct services on the Tegucigalpa-San Salvador and Tegucigalpa–Managua routes (see pp 66 - 67)

The route between Tegucigalpa and **Choluteca** is well served, with comfortable buses at intervals of 45 to 60min most of the day, stopping upon demand at **Pespire**, **Jícaro Galán** and **San Lorenzo**. These are supplemented by premium-fare air-conditioned express buses (categorized as *servicio ejecutivo*) operating at 2hr intervals between Tegucigalpa and Choluteca with no intermediate stops. Travel time is about 2hrs on express buses, slightly longer on regular buses. From Tegucigalpa these buses operate from separate sections of the Mi Esperanza terminal, at the far end of 6a Avenida near 23 Avenida on the Comayagüela side (☎225-1502). In Choluteca they leave from small, separate terminals a couple of blocks apart near the main market toward the edge of town (☎882-2712). Some buses provide through service between Tegucigalpa and **San Marcos**, closer to the Nicaraguan border, from where

frequent local buses operate to the crossing point at **El Espino**. Additional service between Tegucigalpa and Choluteca is provided by slow, multiple-stop buses (often with many standing passengers) operated two to three times an hour by El Dandy and other companies. These buses should be avoided unless it is impossible to get space on the faster services.

To **Nacaome** and El Amatillo on the Salvadoran border, direct (though less comfortable) buses operate from Mercado Belén in Comayagüela.

From Choluteca, buses and minibuses radiate in several directions, including local services along the Carretera Panamericana to **El Amatillo**, to the Nicaraguan border crossings at **El Espino** and **El Guasaule**, and to **Cedeño**. The municipal terminal in Choluteca lies near the edge of town and is served by cheap local taxis. The Mi Esperanza terminal is located 1.5 blocks away.

Routes from San Lorenzo include hourly service until 5pm to **Coyolito**, taking 1hr 15min for the trip, compared to about 30min by car. Buses northbound from Coyolito leave hourly from 5am to 4pm. There is also a direct bus to Tegucigalpa leaving at 3:30am. Boats between Coyolito

and **Amapala**, on Isla del Tigre, leave whenever a minimum of 10 passengers has assembled; the fare is $0.70 per passenger, or $5 for a private trip. The crossing takes 20min at low speed. Boats are also the most useful way to reach certain points on the island.

By Taxi

Taxis are available at most of the larger towns in southern Honduras and at the main border crossings. Fares are generally cheap. Collective taxis operate on certain intercity routes, notably **Nacaome-Jícaro Galán**. There are no taxis based at Coyolito or Cedeño, making it essential to check the departure times of the last buses. After that, the occasional taxi may come bearing arriving passengers, but this cannot be counted upon. There are no taxis, at Pespire, either but buses operate until mid-evening, both northbound and southbound, and may be flagged along the highway.

Exploring

South from Tegucigalpa

Heading south from the capital, the town of **Ojojona**, a craft centre noted for its quiet colonial air, is located along a side road 7km off the main highway (see p 66) in the Teguicigalpa chapter. Further south, along the main highway, **Sabanagrande** has a newly restored church, built in the 19th century, with an altar of a transitional style between the baroque and neoclassical and a facade modelled after that of the Tegucigalpa cathedral, though on a smaller scale. Two stone wheels displayed in the town plaza recall earlier mills. A few kilometres south, near the village of **La Venta**, El Salvador's spectacular San Miguel volcano is visible on a clear day.

Pespire

This little gem of a colonial town, with its steep, stone-paved streets and its wealth of traditional architecture, is perched in a picturesque valley down a short hill from the highway, 80km south of Tegucigalpa. Pespire is wedged between the highway and the Río Nacaome to the west. The triple-domed **Iglesia San Francisco** is plainly visible from the highway above. Inside it has an intricately carved wooden altar and an arched wooden ceiling. Across from the church is the handsome **Alcaldía**, or town hall, with its arched wooden colonnade.

A bridge crosses the river near a series of rapids and leads to the village of **La Laguna**. It is 8km along a poor road which makes for an easy and pleasant walk. There is a lake near the village, though the water is not suitable for swimming.

Pespire is utterly unspoilt and makes no concessions to tourism, making it all the more attractive to those who wish to stroll for an hour or two amid surroundings that have changed little over the years. The nearest spot for decent food and lodgings is Jícaro Galán 12km to the south.

Jicaro Galán

This is a dusty, bedraggled little town centred around a triangular highway junction. The main attraction is the Turicentro Oasis Colonial, a comfortable hotel with a pool and restaurant.

San Lorenzo

This is the only important commercial seaport on the Pacific coast of Honduras. It is also an important shrimp-farming centre. Although the town itself offers little of special interest, there are several seafront restaurants. San Lorenzo faces the Gulf of Fonseca in an area crisscrossed by an intricate network of mangrove-lined canals and estuaries, with a wealth of vegetation and marine life, forming the Lagunas de Invierno y Manglares de Fonseca nature reserve. Besides several varieties of mangroves, thickets and trees, this protected area is home to many bird species and also to turtles. Its attractions also include a dark volcanic sand beach, Playa del Amor, situated on an island. There are also interesting views of a portion of Central America's volcano chain. The sunsets are said to be spectacular. This area falls under the protection of the Comité para la Defensa y Conservación del Golfo de Fonseca, which has adopted the unwieldy acronym Cooddeffagolf. This foundation has an office in San Lorenzo and is supposed to provide information, but the staff is not always friendly. A better bet is San Lorenzo Tours (*facing*

Southern Honduras

the waterfront near the Hotel Miramar, ☎881-2650), which offers boat tours on demand. Rates are $21 an hour (subject to change) for a maximum of eight passengers.

Choluteca

Choluteca is the biggest city in southern Honduras and has often been dismissed as a hot, sweltering and rather uninteresting commercial town. These adjectives all apply to the modern city centre, but only a few hundred metres away lies one of the finest clusters of colonial architecture in Central America, stretching several blocks in each direction. This area of town is quiet, elegant, and not at all pretentious. Buildings look well cared for but not heavily tarted up, and residents go about their normal day-to-day activities.

The focal point of Choluteca's *barrio colonial* is **Parque Valle**. On one side is the restored house of José Cecilio del Valle, a co-author of the Central American declaration of independence. Occasional art exhibits are held there. Across the park is the big, whitewashed and rather austere **Cathedral**, which locals say has no particular name. Next to the Cathedral, and sepa-

rated by a pleasant terrace with a large fountain, is the **Alcaldía**, or town hall, a gorgeous colonial building with a big garden courtyard. Two blocks behind the Cathedral is the 17th-century **Iglesia La Merced**, generally open only in the early evening hours, with an unprepossessing exterior and simple objects of religious art inside. In between are several houses of similar antiquity. Some lower-lying parts of the historical area suffered disastrous flooding as a result of Hurricane Mitch in 1998 and are now irrecuperably lost.

Choluteca is an important market town serving an area with a heavy dependence on the cattle, sugar cane, fruit, and shrimp farming industries. It also serves the heavy passing traffic and offers a good range of hotels, along with several decent restaurants. Those arriving from the west enter by way of an impressive suspension bridge over the Río Choluteca. When crossing this bridge, you can get some idea of the amplitude of the Mitch-induced flooding: the river actually rose above the level of the bridge's roadway, high over the normal riverbed.

Cedeño

This fishing town and beach resort will disap-

point anyone expecting fine beaches or a pleasant atmosphere. To put it bluntly, Cedeño is a place best left to those who really cannot afford anything better. The beaches in town virtually disappear at high tide, though there are broader beaches nearby. There are many small but not very appealing restaurants set on stilts over the water. Pigs rummage around the streets, and the local hotels, almost without exception, are sordid and dirty.

Punta Ratón

Just south of this village is a wildlife reserve including a strip of beach where sea turtles lay their eggs from August to November. Dense forest nearby is home to many varieties of birds.

Amapala

Amapala is a former seaport and the only town on **Isla del Tigre** in the Gulf of Fonseca. Port activity moved to San Lorenzo long ago, leaving Amapala just a shell of its former self, looking and feeling a little like a ghost town. It is a bit surprising to travel through very rustic surroundings on the road to Coyolito and then take the boat to an island that may as well be in the middle of nowhere, only to land at a fine pier and discover what looks like a typical mainland Honduran town with red-tile-roofed buildings clustered around narrow streets. Some of these buildings lie abandoned, contributing to Amapala's ghost-town atmosphere.

There are several hotels in or near Amapala, and camping is permitted on the beaches, which for many visitors are the island's main attraction (see below). At the centre of the island lies an extinct volcano, part of the great Central American chain of volcanoes.

Nacaome

This town, 6km west of the highway junction at Jícaro Galán, was the scene of several important battles in the course of its long history. Nevertheless, apart from a rather ordinary colonial church, it will not be of interest to most visitors.

Beaches

San Lorenzo

Playa del Amor, situated on an island about 10min by boat from San Lorenzo amid mangrove-lined estuaries, offers dark volcanic sand and interesting

views of a portion of Central America's volcano chain.

Isla del Tigre

Several small, secluded beaches are scattered around the island. The two biggest are Playa Grande, 1.5km from Amapala, and Playa Negra, 3km from Amapala. Both have dark volcanic sand. Towards the other side of the island are several small, white-sand beaches, reachable on foot or by boat. Topless sunbathing and swimming are accepted in some secluded spots. Waves are gentle and, since the Gulf of Fonseca is shallow, water temperatures are quite high. For information on getting to Isla del Tigre, please see the section on Amapala on p 195.

Punta Ratón

Punta Ratón may be reached by a long and very bumpy branch off the road to Cedeño, 44km from the Carretera Panamericana. The beach is better here than at Cedeño, but the road is poor, there is no regular bus service, and the availability of food and drink is limited.

Outdoor Activities

Hiking

An extinct volcano lies in the centre of Isla del Tigre. There is a trail to the top that can be climbed in 1.5 to 2hrs.

Accommodations

Jícaro Galán

Hotelito Sirleny
$8/person.
⊗, *tv*, ℜ
☎*895-4019*
The seven rooms at this comfortable hotel are small and simple, but pleasantly decorated.

Turicentro Oasis Colonial
$47
≡, ℜ, ≈, ☎, *tv, bar, billiards*
☎*895-4006 or 895-4008*
⇜*895-4007*
The 51 rooms here are bright and pleasantly furnished, most with high wooden ceilings and many set around a quiet garden courtyard. Passageways are tiled and colonnaded. There is a big pool in a resort-like setting.

San Lorenzo

Hotel Mandarín
$12
along the highway near the bus stop
☎*881-2316*
The 38 rooms in this motel-style spot are very basic, some facing an inner corridor.

Hotel Morazán
$18, bigger rooms $24
≡
on a quiet side street north of the highway
☎*881-2400*
This hotel has 18 quiet simply furnished rooms. Staff is friendly.

Gran Hotel Miramar
$28
≡, *tv*, ℜ, *bar*
on the waterfront
☎*881-2138*
The 25 rooms here are small and bright but gaudily furnished. Upkeep and service are not up to scratch. Rooms facing the sea have balconies and are far preferable. A small but not very attractive beach lies nearby. The restaurant has a terrace facing the sea.

Choluteca

Hotel Santa Rosa
$7
near San Antonio market in the centre of town
☎*882-0884*
The 31 large rooms at this friendly spot are somewhat scruffy but not unpleasant. Most face an attractive terrace with many plants.

Hotel Pacífico
$8 with ⊗
annex $14 with ≡, *tv*
on a side street near the Hotel Centroamérica
☎*882-3249*
These twin hotels, the original and the annex, face each other across the street. They are clean, simple and comfortable. The annex is built motel-style, with a concrete courtyard.

Hotel Flamingo
$11 with ⊗
$17 with ≡, *tv*
Avenida Valle in the centre of town
☎*882-3876*
The 14 rooms at this hotel are small, simple and fresh, facing a small courtyard. The entrance lies through a driveway.

Hotel Centroamérica
$27
≡, ℜ, ≈, *tv*, *bar*
near the edge of town on the Carretera a San Marcos
☎*882-3940*
⇌*882-2667*
The 28 rooms are big and bright but rather simple and are set around a three-storey courtyard. Formerly called Hotel Imperio Maya.

Hotel La Fuente
$45
≡, *tv*, ☎, ℜ, ≈, *bar*
near the edge of town on the Carretera a San Marcos
☎*882-0253*
⇌*882-2273*
This spot has 43 big, pleasant rooms. They are set around a large pool with many palm trees and comfortable lounge chairs. The

restaurant is rather dark, however.

Hacienda Gualiqueme Hotel y Club
$59
≡, ☎, ℜ, ≈, ⊘, △, ⊛, *tv*, *bar*
west of town just past the suspension bridge
☎*882-2750*
⇌*882-3620*
A series of attractive, single-storey, red-tile-roofed buildings are set around landscaped grounds and a pool. The 31 rooms, renovated following flood damage, are pleasant, with tile floors. The restaurant, however, is small and ordinary. Guests are offered tennis, racquetball and horseback riding.

Amapala

Pension International
$4
near the pier
☎*998-8585*
This spot can best be described as colourful and very dilapidated. Upstairs rooms have terraces, sea views and cross-ventilation. Downstairs rooms are dark and stuffy.

Hotel Villas Playa Negra
$32 with ⊗
$46 with ≡ *for up to four people*
5km from Amapala Tegucigalpa
☎*232-0632*
The 14 rooms here, half with air conditioning, are set in a series of multi-room villas with modern furnishings. The hotel offers a

private beach, pool, fishing, horseback riding, a discotheque on weekends, and launch service to and from Coyolito. The restaurant concentrates on fish and seafood, with most dishes priced at $5-$8.

Restaurants

Jícaro Galán

Turicentro Oasis Colonial
$$
every day 6am to 10pm
☎*895-4006*
Turicentro Oasis Colonial offers a selection of meat and seafood dishes both in an air-conditioned dining room and on an outdoor terrace facing a swimming pool.

San Lorenzo

Carpa Restaurant
$$
every day 10am to 11pm or later
☎*881-2650*
Several restaurants face the estuary near the Hotel Miramar, most with outdoor terraces and all specializing in fish and seafood, as well as seafood soups. This pleasant restaurant is among the better choices.

Choluteca

El Rancho de José
$
just outside town on the Carretera a Guasaule
El Rancho de José is a pleasant, open-air restaurant bordered by high shrubs and furnished with wooden tables and chairs. The menu includes a variety of seafood soups, seafood dishes and meats.

El Emporio
$-$$
just outside town on the Carretera a Guasaule
El Emporio has separate open-air and air conditioned dining areas and a menu that includes Mexican specialties as well as the regular meat and seafood dishes.

El Conquistador
$-$$
at the edge of town near Hotel La Fuente
El Conquistador has a pleasant outdoor dining area decorated with paintings. The emphasis is on meat, but there are also some seafood offerings.

Amapala

There are a couple of small, open-air restaurants near the pier, emphasizing fish and seafood. The Hotel villas Playa Negra offers full dining service.

Shopping

Shopping opportunities in southern Honduras are rather limited. Some roadside stalls offer a selection of ceramics and basketry.

GLOSSARY

GREETINGS

Goodbye	*adiós, hasta luego*
Good afternoon and good evening	*buenas tardes*
Hi (casual)	*hola*
Good morning	*buenos días*
Good night	*buenas noches*
Thank-you	*gracias*
Please	*por favor*
You are welcome	*de nada*
Excuse me	*perdone/a*
My name is...	*mi nombre es...*
What is your name?	*¿cómo se llama usted?*
no/yes	*no/sí*
Do you speak English?	*¿habla usted inglés?*
Slower, please	*más despacio, por favor*
I am sorry, I don't speak Spanish	*Lo siento, no hablo español*
How are you?	*¿qué tal?*
I am fine	*estoy bien*
I am a tourist	*Soy turista*
single (m/f)	*soltero/a*
divorced (m/f)	*divorciado/a*
married (m/f)	*casado/a*
friend (m/f)	*amigo/a*
child (m/f)	*niño/a*
I am hungry	*tengo hambre*
I am ill	*estoy enfermo/a*
I am thirsty	*tengo sed*

DIRECTIONS

beside	*al lado de*
to the right	*a la derecha*
to the left	*a la izquierda*
here, there	*aquí, allí*
into, inside	*dentro*
outside	*fuera*
behind	*detrás*
in front of	*delante*
between	*entre*
far from	*lejos de*
Where is ... ?	*¿dónde está ... ?*
To get to ...?	*¿para ir a...?*
near	*cerca de*
straight ahead	*todo recto*

MONEY

money	*dinero / plata*
credit card	*tarjeta de crédito*
exchange	*cambio*
traveller's cheque	*cheque de viaje*
I don't have any money	*no tengo dinero*
The bill, please	*la cuenta, por favor*
receipt	*recibo*

SHOPPING

store	*tienda*

market	*mercado*
open, closed	*abierto/a, cerrado/a*
How much is this?	*¿cuánto es?*
to buy, to sell	*comprar,* vender
the customer	*el / la cliente*
salesman	*vendedor*
saleswoman	*vendedora*
I need...	*necesito...*
I would like...	*yo quisiera...*
batteries	*pilas*
blouse	*blusa*
cameras	*cámaras*
cosmetics and perfumes	*cosméticos y perfumes*
cotton	*algodón*
dress jacket	*saco*
eyeglasses	*lentes, gafas*
fabric	*tela*
film	*película*
gifts	*regalos*
gold	*oro*
handbag	*bolsa*
hat	*sombrero*
jewellery	*joyería*
leather	*cuero, piel*
local crafts	*artesanía*
magazines	*revistas*
newpapers	*periódicos*
pants	*pantalones*
records, cassettes	*discos, casetas*
sandals	*sandalias*
shirt	*camisa*
shoes	*zapatos*
silver	*plata*
skirt	*falda*
sun screen products	*productos solares*
T-shirt	*camiseta*
watch	*reloj*
wool	*lana*

MISCELLANEOUS

a little	*poco*
a lot	*mucho*
good (m/f)	*bueno/a*
bad (m/f)	*malo/a*
beautiful (m/f)	*hermoso/a*
pretty (m/f)	*bonito/a*
ugly	*feo*
big	*grande*
tall (m/f)	*alto/a*
small (m/f)	*pequeño/a*
short (length) (m/f)	*corto/a*
short (person) (m/f)	*bajo/a*
cold (m/f)	*frío/a*
hot	*caliente*
dark (m/f)	*oscuro/a*
light (colour)	*claro*
do not touch	*no tocar*

expensive (m/f)	*caro/a*
cheap (m/f)	*barato/a*
something (m/f)	*algo/a*
quickly	*rápidamente*
slowly (m/f)	*despacio/a*
What is this?	*¿qué es esto?*
when?	*¿cuando?*
where?	*¿dónde?*

TIME

in the afternoon, early evening	*por la tarde*
at night	*por la noche*
in the daytime	*por el día*
in the morning	*por la mañana*
minute	*minuto*
month	*mes*
ever	*jamás*
never	*nunca*
now	*ahora*
today	*hoy*
yesterday	*ayer*
tomorrow	*mañana*
What time is it?	*¿qué hora es?*
hour	*hora*
week	*semana*
year	*año*
Sunday	*domingo*
Monday	*lunes*
Tuesday	*martes*
Wednesday	*miércoles*
Thursday	*jueves*
Friday	*viernes*
Saturday	*sábado*
January	*enero*
February	*febrero*
March	*marzo*
April	*abril*
May	*mayo*
June	*junio*
July	*julio*
August	*agosto*
September	*septiembre*
October	*octubre*
November	*noviembre*
December	*diciembre*

WEATHER

It is cold	*hace frío*
It is warm	*hace calor*
It is very hot	hace mucho calor
It is sunny	hace sol
It is cloudy	*está nublado*
It is raining	*está lloviendo*
It is windy	*hay viento*

COMMUNICATION

air mail	*correos aéreo*

collect call	*llamada por cobrar*
dial the number	*marcar el número*
area code, country code	*código*
envelope	*sobre*
long distance	*larga distancia*
post office	*correo*
rate	*tarifa*
stamps	*estampillas*
telegram	*telegrama*
telephone book	*un guia telefónica*
wait for the tone	*esperar la señal*

ACTIVITIES

beach	*playa*
museum or gallery	*museo*
scuba diving	*buceo*
to swim	*bañarse*
to walk around	*pasear*
hiking	*caminata*
trail	*pista, sendero*
cycling	*ciclismo*
fishing	*pesca*

TRANSPORTATION

arrival, departure	llegada, *salida*
on time	*a tiempo*
cancelled (m/f)	*anulado/a*
one way ticket	*ida*
return	*regreso*
round trip	*ida y vuelta*
schedule	*horario*
baggage	*equipajes*
north, south	*norte, sur*
east, west	*este, oeste*
avenue	*avenida*
street	*calle*
highway	*carretera*
expressway	*autopista*
airplane	*avión*
airport	*aeropuerto*
bicycle	*bicicleta*
boat	*barco*
bus	*bus*
bus stop	*parada*
bus terminal	*terminal*
train	*tren*
train crossing	*crucero ferrocarril*
station	*estación*
neighbourhood	*barrio*
collective taxi	*colectivo*
corner	*esquina*
express	*rápido*
safe	*seguro/a*
be careful	*cuidado*
car	*coche, carro*
To rent a car	*alquilar un auto*
gas	*gasolina*

gas station	*gasolinera*
no parking	*no estacionar*
no passing	*no adelantar*
parking	*parqueo*
pedestrian	*peaton*
road closed, no through traffic	*no hay paso*
slow down	*reduzca velocidad*
speed limit	*velocidad permitida*
stop	*alto*
stop! (an order)	*pare*
traffic light	*semáforo*

ACCOMMODATION

cabin, bungalow	*cabaña*
accommodation	*alojamiento*
double, for two people	*doble*
single, for one person	*sencillo*
high season	*temporada alta*
low season	*temporada baja*
bed	*cama*
floor (first, second...)	*piso*
main floor	*planta baja*
manager	*gerente, jefe*
double bed	*cama matrimonial*
cot	*camita*
bathroom	*baños*
with private bathroom	*con baño privado*
hot water	*agua caliente*
breakfast	*desayuno*
elevator	*ascensor*
air conditioning	*aire acondicionado*
fan	*ventilador, abanico*
pool	*piscina, alberca*
room	*habitación*

NUMBERS

1	*uno*	22	*veintidós*
2	*dos*	23	*veintitrés*
3	*tres*	24	*veinticuatro*
4	*cuatro*	25	*veinticinco*
5	*cinco*	26	*veintiséis*
6	*seis*	27	*veintisiete*
7	*siete*	28	*veintiocho*
8	*ocho*	29	*veintinueve*
9	*nueve*	30	*treinta*
10	*diez*	31	*treinta y uno*
11	*once*	32	*treinta y dos*
12	*doce*	40	*cuarenta*
13	*trece*	50	*cincuenta*
14	*catorce*	60	*sesenta*
15	*quince*	70	*setenta*
16	*dieciséis*	80	*ochenta*
17	*diecisiete*	90	*noventa*
18	*dieciocho*	100	*cien*
19	*diecinueve*		
20	*veinte*		
21	*veintiuno*		

Index